KEW: GARDENS FOR SCIENCE & PLEASURE

Royal Botanic Gardens

KEW
Gardens for Science & Pleasure

Edited by F Nigel Hepper

Stemmer House

Publishers, Inc Owings Mills, Maryland

ISBN 0-88045-010-X

Design by HMSO Lynda Sullivan

*Unless otherwise stated,
archival and photographic
material is held at Kew.*

FRONTISPIECE
The Pagoda at Kew in autumn.
Photo: M. Svanderlik

copy 1
4/18 7
STEMMER House
24.95

Foreword

The Royal Botanic Gardens are unique among the botanic gardens of the world and during their long history they have maintained a tradition of excellence in both botany and horticulture.

The Herbarium at Kew contains more than five million preserved plant specimens collected over two centuries from every continent. This vast 'reference library' of the plant kingdom serves not only British scientists but botanists from all over the world.

In the Jodrell Laboratory research on the anatomy, biochemistry, cytogenetics and physiology of plants provides not only a clearer understanding of plant biology, but also basic information which can be applied in the development of new crop plants, the search for new drugs, fungicides and insecticides and in numerous other ways. At Wakehurst Place living seed can be kept for prolonged periods in the cool dry conditions of the 'Seed Bank' and this facility is becoming increasingly important as a living reserve of valuable and sometimes endangered species.

In the Museums, the economic importance of plants is emphasized and the collections provide examples of the many ways in which mankind has used plants. Kew's interest in economic botany is by no means restricted to the past, however, and even now the Gardens are concerned with acquiring and disseminating knowledge on economic plants suitable for cultivation in different regions of the world, particularly the arid tropics. As the world's fossil fuel reserves become depleted, mankind will be forced to turn once more to plants as its primary source of fuel, medicinal compounds and chemical intermediates. Kew will have an important role to play in this transition.

All parts of the Gardens are served by the Library. This is an internationally famous specialist collection of over 750 000 items which has been a significant factor in maintaining Kew as a centre of academic excellence. All the world's important botanical periodicals are available, including *Curtis's Botanical Magazine* and the *Kew Bulletin*, which are amongst those published by the Gardens themselves.

It is, however, the Living Collections which attract most visitors to Kew and Wakehurst Place, and even if many of these visitors know little of botany it is certain that they appreciate the splendid displays of rhododendrons, strelitzias and other species first brought to Europe by collectors from Kew. They also appreciate how much care and skill is required of the Gardens staff and horticultural students who maintain that standard of excellence which has always been associated with 'Kew Gardens'.

In writing this foreword it is my hope that *Kew: Gardens for Science and Pleasure* will provide interest and enjoyment as well as an insight into the many functions and responsibilities of this most beautiful of scientific institutions.

Professor E. Arthur Bell   *Director, Royal Botanic Gardens, Kew*

EDITOR
F. Nigel Hepper

CONTRIBUTORS

J.P.M.B. **Professor J. P. M. Brenan** Lately Director, Royal Botanic Gardens, Kew

C.A.B. **C. A. Brighton** Higher Scientific Officer, Cytogenetics Section, Jodrell Laboratory

R.D. **Ray Desmond** Formerly Chief Librarian and Archivist

L.E.F. **Dr Linda E. Fellows** Principal Scientific Officer, Biochemistry Section, Jodrell Laboratory

I.K.F. **Dr I. K. Ferguson** Principal Scientific Officer, Officer-in-Charge, Palynology Unit, The Herbarium

B.H. **Brian Halliwell** Assistant Curator, Hardy Herbaceous Section

R.B.H. **R. B. Hastings** Assistant Scientific Officer, Kew Museums

F.N.H. **F. Nigel Hepper** Assistant Keeper, The Herbarium

J.L. **John Lonsdale** Gardens Supervisor, Wakehurst Place

B.M. **Brian Mathew** Principal Scientific Officer, The Herbarium

S.J.O. **Dr S. J. Owens** Senior Scientific Officer, Cytogenetics Section, Jodrell Laboratory

P.R. **Dr P. Rudall** Senior Scientific Officer, Anatomy Section, Jodrell Laboratory

A.D.S. **A. D. Schilling** Deputy Curator, Wakehurst Place

J.B.E.S. **John B. E. Simmons** Curator, Living Collections Division

R.D.S. **R. D. Smith** Principal Scientific Officer, Plant Physiology Section, Wakehurst Place

H.S. **Hugh Synge** Research Officer, IUCN Conservation Monitoring Unit based at Kew

OFFICIAL PHOTOGRAPHERS

T. A. Harwood Principal Photographer

M. Svanderlik Senior Photographer

The Editor and Contributors gratefully acknowledge the assistance received from many colleagues in the preparation of this book.

Contents

Introduction

The Royal Botanic Gardens, Kew, situated within the built-up area of Greater London, holds a special place in the hearts of its numerous admirers. Every year more than a million people come to the Gardens, some as regular visitors, others, among them many from overseas, making a botanical pilgrimage for which there may be only one opportunity in a lifetime. The popularity to which all this attests is largely based on the reputation for the exceptional ornamental beauty of Kew as 'gardens for pleasure'. Many have heard of the rural aspect of its bluebell woods, extensive lawns and tranquil lake. For others the principal attractions will be the spectacular rose gardens, the glorious azaleas or the unusual plants in the Rock Garden. Few will fail to be fascinated by the exotic tropical collections in the greenhouses–including orchids, insectivorous plants and giant waterlilies. With close on 50 000 species and varieties of plants in the Gardens, there is little chance of visitors being disappointed by lack of variety.

Moreover, this vast collection of plants from every corner of the world is set in an attractive historic landscape with splendid architectural features. Of these the Pagoda, a ten-storeyed structure that provides a principal focal point in the landscape, is a conspicuous reminder of the Garden's eighteenth-century foundation by Princess Augusta, mother of George III. It was the botanic garden she created there at her home on the banks of the River Thames, a favoured location for royal residences, that formed the nucleus of the great garden that was to come. Development, however, was not straightforward. When, on the death of Princess Augusta in 1772, George III inherited her estate, he joined it to his own lying alongside and brought in Sir Joseph Banks to direct the Gardens in a scientific manner. Nearly fifty years of great activity followed but, on the death of Banks and the King in 1820, the Gardens suffered a serious decline that was not arrested until 1841, with the appointment by the Government of Sir William Jackson Hooker as the first official Director. Under his distinguished leadership, and at a time when the British Empire was expanding, Kew developed its role as a leading botanic garden and scientific institution of truly international stature. The impetus of that first official Directorship has profoundly influenced the subsequent development of Kew, where, to the present day, the international and scientific scope of its work has been maintained and extended.

As a site for a national botanic garden Kew is not without disadvantages. The limitations imposed by its poor soil and location in the Thames Valley led, in the 1960s, to the search for a satellite garden. The choice of the Sussex estate of Wakehurst Place was made largely because of its many features that are complementary to those of Kew. For example, although the two estates are only some 50 kilometres (31 miles) apart, their climates are surprisingly

Princess Augusta, mother of George III, could hardly have realized that her private botanic garden in Surrey, 3.6 hectares (9 acres) in extent, was to form the nucleus of one of the most famous gardens in the world. The present Royal Botanic Gardens cover some 120 hectares (300 acres) and the satellite estate at Wakehurst Place occupies nearly twice that area.

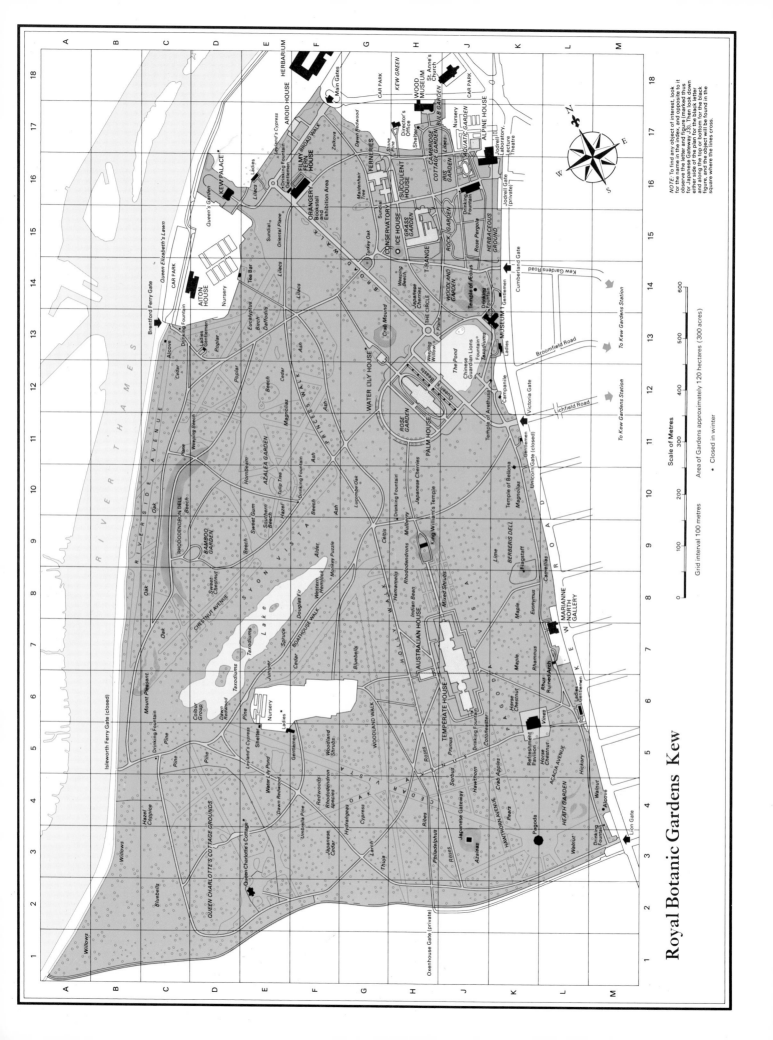

Royal Botanic Gardens Kew

different. The dry summer atmosphere of the Thames Valley, coupled with the sandy soil at Kew, contrasts with the cooler, moister air of the high Sussex Weald, where the delayed start of spring at Wakehurst enables tender species to survive better, since they begin to grow after danger from frosts is largely past. The air is cleaner away from the built-up area, though the situation in London has greatly improved with the virtual elimination of coal fires. The collections of trees and shrubs are also complementary – Kew having mature, historic trees while Wakehurst has newer plantings, including fine collections of rhododendrons and species from the southern hemisphere.

Though Wakehurst Place does provide a location where a number of relatively tender plants can be grown outdoors, really tender plants do require protection in greenhouses. Since the seventeenth and eighteenth centuries Kew has been famous for its conservatories but the nineteenth century saw rapid development in the technology of greenhouse construction. When the Palm House was first opened to the public in 1848, elegant Victorian ladies and top-hatted gentlemen must have gazed in wonder at the exotic plants in this revolutionary glass and cast-iron structure. Some years after the completion of the Palm House an even larger structure was built to house those plants that flourish in cooler climates but still need some protection from frost. The Temperate House, still one of the largest ornamental glasshouses in the world, has recently been brilliantly restored to its pristine condition.

A vast fund of horticultural experience underlies the successful cultivation and display of plants from habitats ranging through arctic tundra, alpine scree, temperate lowland and tropical rain forest to equatorial desert. There are, unseen by the public, extensive supporting facilities for propagating and raising plants for indoor and outdoor display as well as for scientific purposes. Through a specialized aspect of Kew's educational role, selected students benefit from this accumulated knowledge of the Royal Botanic Gardens in the courses offered by the School of Horticulture.

The very popularity Kew and Wakehurst Place have acquired through the beauty and interest of their landscapes and the plants cultivated and displayed in them may obscure what, after all, is their primary role as 'gardens for science'. The discovery of the immense flora of the world, its classification and naming and the publication of literature disseminating information resulting from the scientific investigation of plants have been Kew's basic tasks since the Directorship of Sir William Hooker. That orientation was already fore-shadowed in the time of Banks, as was an awareness of man's dependence on useful plants. The story of quinine and rubber provide only two examples of Kew's long involvement in economic botany. The continuous expansion of Kew's scientific programme has called for the development of other disciplines and lines of research – plant anatomy, physiology, cytogenetics and, in recent years, electronmicroscopy and biochemistry. Most of this work is undertaken at the Jodrell Laboratory, Kew, but work on physiology is also based at Wakehurst, as is an important and relatively new development, the Seed Bank.

Kew's long involvement in the scientific study of plants not only has enlarged the collections of living plants in the Gardens but also has resulted in the accumulation of exceptionally rich archives in the Museums, Herbarium and Library. These provide invaluable reference material for Kew's own scientific staff and for visiting research scholars. Exhibits in the Museums and in the Gardens that draw on this archival material are valuable supplements to the display and labelling of growing plants.

One feature of Kew's activities that continues to grow is its involvement in the conservation movement. Through its international contacts and programmes of research Kew has received early alerts of the rapid deterioration of natural environments in many parts of the world. It has, with other scientific institutions, played its part in publicizing the destruction and threatened destruction of habitats, such as tropical rain forest, and the loss of their component plant and animal species. Through its links with other botanic gardens and with international conservation agencies it is actively engaged in gathering and collating information about plants in danger of extinction. Practical measures are also taken to safeguard some threatened species by propagating and cultivating them. On a more local level, at Kew and Wakehurst Place large areas have been set aside as nature reserves for British and European plants and animals and a nature trail at Wakehurst provides a living lesson in ecology. The scale and rapidity of environmental degradation is such that Kew is doing all it can to ensure the conservation of habitats and plant species for future generations.

To present in one volume a comprehensive history of the Royal Botanic Gardens at Kew and at Wakehurst Place and an exhaustive review of the research and allied activities undertaken by them would hardly be possible. In any event, it would not provide the interested layman with a useful and balanced introduction to these remarkable gardens. The essays that follow, in which words and pictures are complementary, are intended to convey a broad view of Kew's history and the horticultural and scientific work that have given the Gardens their worldwide reputation. Members of staff from many disciplines have written for the non-specialist about work undertaken at Kew and, in doing so, have described not only the aspects of the Gardens that are accessible to the public but also those not generally known or appreciated. The picture that emerges should demonstrate that Kew remains faithful to its historic dual role in being gardens for science and for pleasure.

F. N. H.

Opposite: the exotic plant-life of the Palm House is still, as it was in the nineteenth century, a major attraction at Kew. More than a million visitors a year come to the Gardens and, behind the scenes, numerous scientists, from Britain and abroad, benefit from the rich collections and the excellent facilities for research that are available at both Kew and Wakehurst Place.
From *Illustrated London News* (1852).

At Wakehurst Place, as at Kew, there is ample opportunity to enjoy in a relaxed way the exceptional richness of the plant collections and the beauty of their settings. This curved seat at Wakehurst overlooks the Himalayan Glade.
Photo: T. A. Harwood.

TAB. V.

Fig. 5.

Fig. 6.

Fig. 8.

Fig. 7.

Fig. 9.

Fig. 4.

Fig. 1.

Painted, Engraved, & Published by John Miller according to the Act. 1786.

The Historical Setting
of Kew

A Royal Home

Many people must have wondered why one of the world's greatest botanical gardens is situated where the soil, mainly sand and gravel, is so poor. The location of the Royal Botanic Gardens, Kew – 'Kew Gardens' – is simply one of those accidents of history.

Presumably it was the proximity of Richmond to London, from where it could be reached easily by the Thames, as well as the picturesque sweep of the river that attracted the royal court. Henry I had a manor house there. Edward VI lived in some splendour at Shene, which Henry VII renamed Richmond when he built a palace there. Richmond was for long a fashionable town, so it was not surprising that, about 1721, the Prince and Princess of Wales chose Ormonde Lodge in what is now the Old Deer Park adjoining Kew Gardens as a summer residence.

In the late seventeenth century, William III had enlarged the Lodge and employed George London, the well-known nurseryman at Kensington, to landscape and plant the grounds. After the King's death it was leased to the Duke of Ormonde who, upon being exiled in 1715, was forced to abandon what a contemporary account referred to as 'a most delicious habitation'. When the Prince of Wales succeeded to the throne as George II in 1727, Ormonde Lodge (at this date known as Richmond Lodge) was settled on his spouse, Queen Caroline, as a potential dower house in the event of her surviving her husband. Having an unrestrained enthusiasm for gardening and a reckless disregard for expense, Caroline engaged Charles Bridgeman to transform the grounds. Bridgeman, whose work heralded a departure from the geometric formation of the gardens of the early 1700s, created a sequence of pastoral scenes with cultivated fields and a network of paths that meandered through carefully disposed areas of woodland. A summer-house, a dairy, a small domed temple (complete with an altar) and other garden buildings placed at suitable vantage points gave cohesion to Bridgeman's informal plan.

These buildings were probably all designed by William Kent, who was certainly responsible for the two best known ones, the Hermitage and Merlin's Cave. When Count Kelmansegge saw the Hermitage in the 1760s he dismissed it as 'a grotesque building which seems as if it had stood many hundred years'. Its octagonal interior displayed busts by the sculptor Rysbrack of eminent British scientists and philosophers such as Boyle, Locke, Newton and Wollaston. Merlin's Cave, described by one unimpressed observer as 'an old haystack thatched over', was populated with wax figures of Merlin and his secretary, with Elizabeth, wife of Henry VII, Queen Elizabeth and her nurse, and the goddess Minerva in attendance. 'An unintelligible puppet show', Horace Walpole called it. As Merlin was supposed to have predicted the

Opposite: one of the species having the closest historical association with Kew is the bird-of-paradise flower (*Strelitzia reginae*). Its special connection is through its scientific name given in honour of the Queen of George III, when Kew was a royal residence. Queen Charlotte (1744–1818) was from the family of Mecklenburg-Strelitz.

The plant growing in the Temperate House is reputed to be from the original introduction from South Africa by Sir Joseph Banks in 1773. Its strikingly coloured flowers are pollinated by sunbirds. There are only four species in the genus, which belongs to the banana family, Musaceae.

This splendid water-colour by John Miller (formerly Johann Sebastian Müller) is in his rare *Icones Plantarum* (1780, pl 5). His son, John Frederick Miller (*fl* 1772–94), worked for Banks at Kew as botanical artist.

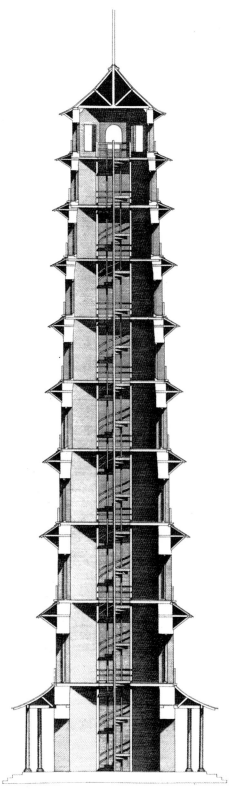

The Pagoda at Kew, a folly built quickly and rather cheaply during 1761–2, reflects the fashion then current for chinoiserie. It is said that the eighty glass dragons that once adorned it were removed to help pay George IV's debts.

From Chambers, *Gardens and Buildings at Kew* (1763).

Hanoverian dynasty this whimsical conceit could be said to have had some symbolic justification. Stephen Duck, a self-educated Wiltshire farm-boy enjoying a minor reputation as a poet, was installed to look after a small library of modern authors. Mrs Duck helped her husband to show round the crowds of curious visitors, when he was not composing verse. George II, who viewed his wife's garden activities as 'childish, silly stuff', thought Merlin's Cave a piece of extravagant nonsense. Despite, however, the ridicule it provoked, imitations of this bizarre folly soon appeared elsewhere and a couple of London taverns adopted its name.

One of the things the first three Georges had in common was a positive dislike of their eldest sons. George II denounced his eldest offspring, Frederick, as 'a monster and the greatest villain that ever was born' while, according to that unreliable gossip Lord Hervey, Queen Caroline once confided to him that, if her prayers could be answered, then Frederick's life would not be a long or happy one. Even his pious sister, Caroline, was said to pray daily and earnestly for his demise.

In view of this hostile relationship it is surprising that in 1730 Frederick should choose to live at the White House, whose estate ran parallel to that of Richmond Lodge. The White House, the site of which is marked by a sundial on the lawn in front of Kew Palace, had been the home of the Capel family. Years earlier Sir Henry Capel's garden, famous for its choice shrubs and orange trees, had been admired by John Evelyn, who was himself an experienced gardener. Capel's timber-constructed house was demolished and replaced by a more substantial dwelling in William Kent's classical style.

Whatever his personal defects, Frederick to some extent redeemed himself through his energetic patronage of the arts. He cultivated the friendship of eminent writers and artists, including Alexander Pope, his neighbour on the other side of the River Thames in Twickenham. He was a keen gardener and devised ambitious plans for the grounds of the White House such as an aqueduct, a mount adorned with statues of philosophers, a long greenhouse and the planting of many exotic trees. His friends, some of whom did not share his enthusiasm, were conscripted into working in the garden. One such reluctant helper was George Bubb Dodington, whose diary contains the disagreeable memory of working 'in the new walk at Kew', the meagre reward for his toil being just 'a cold dinner'.

In the midst of all this horticultural activity Frederick suddenly died in 1751. He left his widow, Princess Augusta, with a large family and enormous debts. She sought some consolation by taking an interest in gardening and Lord Bute. Augusta, whom Lord Waldegrave described as being of moderate intelligence with few ideas of her own, came from Saxe-Gotha in 1736 to marry Frederick. After her husband's death, according to contemporary gossip, she fell completely under the influence of the charming and persuasive Lord Bute.

Lord Bute had lived modestly in the family home in Scotland, passing his time studying botany until 1746, when he came south with the intention of entering London society. Friendship with Frederick led to an appointment in the Prince's household shortly before his death. By the mid-1750s Lord Bute had become one of the most important and most hated men in the country. It was widely believed Princess Augusta was his mistress. The young Prince of Wales, completely infatuated with him, sought his advice on becoming King in 1760 and eagerly welcomed him as Prime Minister in 1762.

Under the guidance of Lord Bute, Princess Augusta continued the

horticultural improvements started by her late husband. According to Horace Walpole, Bute 'raised hillocs to diversify the ground'. In 1757 William Chambers, a young, ambitious architect, who had made two brief visits to China, was appointed architectural drawing-master to the Prince of Wales and commissioned to re-landscape the grounds of the White House.

Architects and Landscapists
Chambers's work at Kew swept away the garden started by Frederick. A small physic or exotic garden was laid out near the house. Nearby was a formal flower garden and a Chinese-style aviary. A short walk led to a menagerie with a delicate Chinese pavilion in the middle of an ornamental pond. A large lake which bisected the grounds lay north of two irregular fields surrounded by a belt of trees. Probably no other garden in the country could compare with the number and diversity of garden buildings in Princess Augusta's garden. Classical, Gothic, Chinese and Islamic styles were all represented. A fashion in

William Andrew Nesfield (1793–1881), an artist who abandoned water-colours to become a very successful garden designer, landscaped the grounds at Kew during the 1840s. A number of the vistas and avenues that have now come to splendid maturity were conceived by him. The most spectacular is probably Pagoda Vista, which is closed at one end by the Pagoda and at the other by the Palm House. Another Kew feature, the Temperate House Lodge, was designed by William Eden Nesfield, the landscapist's eldest son.
Photo: T. A. Harwood.

9

Linnaeus named the American shrub *Stuart-ia malacodendron* after John Stuart (sometimes incorrectly spelt Stewart), 3rd Earl of Bute (1713–42), who was described in his time as 'an ingenious gentleman who knows Dr Linnaeus' methods extremely well'. Lord Bute was influential in the planning and planting of Princess Augusta's garden at Kew. This watercolour is by the German-born G.D. Ehret (1708–70), who worked in England for many years, some of the time at Kew.

Sir Joseph Banks (1743–1820), friend of George III and President of the Royal Society for 42 years, established an international reputation for Kew.

chinoiserie allowed Chambers to exploit his knowledge of Chinese architecture. Kew could boast the first pagoda in Europe. Started in the autumn of 1761, its rapid construction intrigued Horace Walpole living in Twickenham. He informed Lord Strafford that 'we begin to perceive the Tower at Kew from Montpellier Row; in a fortnight you will see it in Yorkshire'. When it was finished the following spring it had reached almost 50 metres (163 ft), its ten roofs bright with plates of varnished iron of different colours and adorned with eighty glistening glass dragons. It was flanked on either side by the dome and minarets of the Turkish Mosque and the arched colonnade and fragile lantern of the Alhambra. The Ruined Arch, conceived by Chambers as a romantic classical ruin with fallen masonry carefully disposed around its base, served as a bridge to take carriages and cattle over one of the principal walks in the grounds. The miniature façade of a Gothic cathedral, designed by Johann Henry Muntz, conformed to the pervasive spirit of architectural extravaganza.

Most of the buildings were erected with remarkable speed and probably not intended to endure–a bridge over the lake was constructed by torchlight during one night in order to be a surprise for Princess Augusta next day. Of the few buildings that now survive, the Orangery is the most pleasing expression of Chambers's skill but even that was altered during the reign of William IV. When the garden was finished in 1763 Chambers recalled that 'originally the ground was one continued dead flat: the soil was in general barren, and without either wood or water. With so many disadvantages it was not easy to produce anything even tolerable in gardening'. Nevertheless he observed with justifiable pride that 'what was once a desert is now an Eden'.

While Chambers was happily engaged in transforming the garden and designing buildings, Princess Augusta and Lord Bute were enlarging the plant collections. In 1759 William Aiton, a Scots gardener who had trained in the Chelsea Physic Garden (a garden founded by London apothecaries in the 1670s), was employed to take charge of a physic garden of about nine acres. Following the death of Lord Bute's uncle, the Duke of Argyll, in 1761, some of the choicest trees from his estate in Twickenham were replanted in Kew. A splendid maidenhair tree (*Ginkgo biloba*) still survives near the ferneries. One of the leading plant introducers of the day, Peter Collinson, writing in 1766 to his friend John Bartram in North America, judged Kew 'the Paradise of our world, where all plants are found, that money or interest can procure.' When Aiton published his *Hortus Kewensis* in 1789 he listed 5600 plants in cultivation.

Soon after his accession in 1760, George III employed Capability Brown to remodel the grounds of Richmond Lodge. With all the thoroughness for which he was renowned, Brown swept away Bridgeman's wildernesses and their serpentine walks together with Kent's Hermitage and Merlin's Cave. They were replaced by undulating lawns dotted with clumps of trees, the lake (not to be confused with the present one) was improved and what is now Rhododendron Dell was excavated as a miniature valley.

Sir Joseph Banks

On the death of Princess Augusta in 1772 her son, George III, inherited her garden at Kew and united the two estates. Lord Bute, no longer the friend of the monarch, was replaced as horticultural adviser at Kew by Joseph Banks. Banks had recently returned to England from a voyage around the world on the *Endeavour* under Captain Cook. He was to become a very influential man in

scientific and horticultural affairs. He encouraged plant exploration (Chapter 14), and it has been calculated that during the reign of George III about 7000 new plant species were introduced into Britain. Banks's entrepreneurial skills were aptly acknowledged in the *Florist's Journal* in 1840, which assessed him as being a man 'having no pretensions to profound knowledge himself, but excellent tact in finding out and great liberality in rewarding those who had.'

While Kew was steadily acquiring an international reputation in horticultural matters, George III and his large family made it their home for brief visits. The Queen's Cottage (Chapter 12), a charming example of the cottage orné style, built about 1772, made a delightful summer-house and a place for tea for the royal family. The last grand tea-party was held there in 1818 on the occasion of the double wedding of the Duke of Clarence and the Duke of Kent at Kew Palace. Near the Queen's Cottage a menagerie housing exotic animals from Africa, Australia and India was a favourite place with the royal children. Before the end of the eighteenth century Love Lane (the present Holly Walk marks part of its route), which had divided the two royal estates, was closed and the two gardens were merged into one.

When the White House was pulled down in 1802 a castellated palace, designed by the Surveyor-General, James Wyatt, was started where the Brentford Gate car park is now situated. Known locally as 'The Bastille', it was never finished and George IV ordered its demolition in 1827.

From time to time the royal gardens were opened to the public and the *beau*

The maidenhair tree (*Ginkgo biloba*) was introduced to Europe about 1730 from Japan. It is, however, indigenous to central China, where it still occurs in part of its original mountainous habitat. It is a 'living fossil', being the only surviving representation of the Ginkgoales—an order placed between the conifers and the cycads—which were widespread in Jurassic and Cretaceous times. It is a deciduous tree, with the male and female separate. The famous male tree at Kew was transferred in 1761 from the Duke of Argyll's estate in Twickenham.
Photo: M. Lear.

The Queen's Cottage, built in the 1770s as a summer house for the royal family, has recently been refurnished and a collection of contemporary engravings that once adorned its walls has been reinstated.
Photo: T. A. Harwood.

The Temple of Aeolus and the mound on which it stands near the Pond were created by Chambers. When the temple was rebuilt by Decimus Burton in 1845 it unfortunately lost its revolving seat. At the beginning of this century, when this photograph was taken, pelicans, storks and a crane graced the lawns of Kew.

monde came by carriage and boat to enjoy the pleasures of Kew. For the last ten years of his life George III was completely deranged, a shrunken old man with long white hair and beard wandering through the rooms of Windsor Castle. Kew Palace was now seldom occupied. Built in 1631 by a prosperous London merchant, Samuel Fortrey, the Palace is also known as the Dutch House because of its style. Fortrey was a merchant of Dutch extraction and his initials and those of his wife, Catherine, appear with the date above the front door. The Palace had been leased by some of George III's sisters. The King used it as a nursery for some of his numerous progeny and moved there after the White House had been demolished. Queen Charlotte, who died there in 1818, was its last royal occupant.

Both George III and Sir Joseph Banks died in 1820 and the destiny of Kew was now in the hands of the son of William Aiton, William Townsend Aiton, who also supervised other royal gardens for George IV. George IV's many other interests and activities kept him away from Kew. His brother, William IV, was responsible for transferring one of the conservatories attached to Buckingham Palace to Kew in 1836 where it now serves as the Aroid House. King William's Temple near the Temperate House was erected in 1837 as a tribute to William IV. It was designed by Sir Jeffry Wyatville and originally contained busts of the royal family.

The Hooker Dynasty at Kew
For some years Kew had been attacked for its illiberal policy in exchanging or giving cuttings and seeds to other gardens and gardeners. Despite this and

other criticisms of its management, William Hooker, Professor of Botany at Glasgow University, was petitioning to be considered for the post of Director there. The Treasury, which had for some time viewed Kew as a financial burden, in 1837 appointed a committee headed by Dr John Lindley and two gardeners, Joseph Paxton and John Wilson, to report on the state of all the royal gardens and in particular Kew. Lindley's report, which was submitted in March 1838, was critical of the management of the garden at Kew and in suggesting improvements strongly recommended that it 'should either be at once taken for public purposes, gradually made worthy of the country, and converted into a powerful means of promoting national science, or it should be abandoned.' The Treasury discreetly shelved the report but continued agitation in scientific circles forced the government in 1840 to accept responsibility for the small botanic garden and pleasure grounds at Kew. The following year Sir William Hooker at last achieved his ambition of becoming Director. Apart from Lindley there was probably no other person better qualified for the post. He had an international reputation as a botanist and experience in developing the botanic garden at Glasgow University.

Sir William's tasks were formidable ones. The small botanic garden formed in 1759 and the adjacent arboretum were desperately overcrowded. Clearly his first priority was more space. By 1845, when W. T. Aiton retired, he had got control of all the pleasure grounds. More greenhouses were built. The Palm House, designed by Decimus Burton, was completed by the engineer Richard Turner in 1848. Twelve years later work was begun on the Temperate House.

The landscape gardener W. A. Nesfield reshaped large areas of the grounds, making the new Palm House the pivot of his layout. He enlarged the pond (all that remained of the eighteenth-century lake) in front of the Palm House, and created a number of the vistas, walks and avenues which are now such distinctive features at Kew. His Broad Walk linked the Palm House with Decimus Burton's Main Gate on Kew Green.

The small building facing the Aquatic Garden had been a fruit store until Sir William converted it into a museum of economic botany in 1848 (Chapter 14). When this became full another museum, designed by Decimus Burton, was opened in 1857 overlooking the Pond. Five years later the Orangery became a wood museum. When the King of Hanover's residence on Kew Green became available on his death in 1851 Sir William turned it into a herbarium and library.

All these improvements were made despite the desire of Sir Benjamin Hall, the First Commissioner of Works, to make Kew a public park and the persistent interference of the Duchess of Cambridge and her daughter, Princess Mary Adelaide, who unfortunately lived close at hand in Cambridge Cottage on Kew Green. An extension of the hours when the gardens were open encouraged the public to flock to Kew. The trickle of 9000 visitors during Sir William's first year as Director reached half a million by 1865.

When Sir William Hooker died he left behind him a well-established botanic garden of approximately 100 hectares (250 acres). His unrivalled private herbarium and library, which, with characteristic generosity, he had made available to botanists during his lifetime, were purchased in 1867 to form the nucleus of the present collections.

His son Joseph, who had been Assistant Director at Kew for ten years, succeeded him. Joseph Hooker was already famous as a botanist and explorer. His voyage with Captain James Clark Ross in 1839–43 to Antarctica produced

William Townsend Aiton (1766–1849) was the son of William Aiton, whom he succeeded as superintendent of the royal gardens at Kew in 1793. Three years later, he also assumed responsibility for the adjacent gardens of the former Richmond Lodge. In addition, he was in charge of all the other royal gardens and supervised work at Windsor, Kensington and Brighton. After the death of Sir Joseph Banks in 1820, he had the undesirable task of having to maintain the gardens at Kew at a time when the Treasury viewed them as a burden. He relinquished his control of the small botanic garden at Kew to Sir William Hooker in 1841 and four years later, when Aiton retired, the pleasure ground also passed to Hooker. On Aiton's death, his vast correspondence was unfortunately burnt by his half-brother. Had it survived, this correspondence would have been an invaluable source of information on Kew's early development.

13

In the late eighteenth and early nineteenth centuries, active exploration in many parts of the world led to a rapid increase in the number of recorded plant species. Sir Joseph Banks and his Kew collectors were responsible for numerous plant introductions to Europe.

Top, left: *Sophora microphylla* was collected in New Zealand by Banks himself in 1772. It was grown at Kew and painted by Margaret Meen. A bush of this species in the Duchess Border flowers profusely in May. Tankerville Collection, Kew Library.

Right: the Australian genus *Banksia* was named after Sir Joseph Banks by Linnaeus the younger. This plant of *Banksia integrifolia* was raised in 1821 from seeds gathered by the Kew collector Allan Cunningham at Port Bowen, Australia, and painted in 1829 by George Bond, a gardener at Kew, who, in 1826, succeeded Thomas Duncanson as botanical artist.

Bottom, left: *Erica abietina*, a heath introduced as a greenhouse plant from South Africa by Francis Masson in 1774, was drawn by Francis Bauer (1758–1840) and published (as *E. coccinea*) in *Delineations of Exotic Plants cultivated at Kew* (1796, pl 25). This artist worked with Banks at Kew from 1790, painting many of the new introductions. He and his equally talented brother Ferdinand rank among the greatest of botanical artists for the beauty of their illustrations and for the accuracy of their delineation of plants, which was based on careful dissection.

Above: of the four species of *Berberis* sent back to Kew by Hooker, the choicest is perhaps *B. concinna* from Sikkim.
From *Curtis's Botanical Magazine* (1853, pl 4744).

Among the spectacular Himalayan plants introduced by Sir Joseph Hooker as a result of his explorations in Nepal and Sikkim, 1848–51, were a number of rhododendrons. These were drawn by Walter Fitch from Hooker's field sketches and published in *The Rhododendrons of Sikkim-Himalaya* (1849).

Top, left: one of Hooker's most important introductions, *Rhododendron thomsonii*, was named after his friend and travelling companion Thomas Thomson, who collaborated with Hooker on their *Flora Indica* (1855). This species is reasonably hardy at Kew.

Bottom, left: the noble, broad-leaved *Rhododendron hodgsonii* was named after another of Hooker's close friends, Brian Hodgson of Darjeeling. It is comparable to *R. falconeri*, which is widely grown in British gardens.

Bottom, right: *Rhododendron dalhousiae* is depicted growing as an epiphyte.

For more than forty years, years that were critically formative for Kew, the Gardens were under the direction of two men, father and son, who were of outstanding abilities. Sir William Jackson Hooker (left) was Director from 1841 to 1865 and Sir Joseph Dalton Hooker (right), Assistant Director from 1855 to 1865, was Director from 1865 to 1885.

his classic floras of Antarctica, New Zealand and Tasmania and established his reputation as a taxonomist and plant geographer. In 1847–51 he collected many new plants in Nepal and Sikkim. Although he continued to develop the gardens his principal contribution was the creation of Kew as a centre of scientific research, especially in the classification of plants and their distribution throughout the world (plant systematics and phytogeography). In 1876 the Jodrell Laboratory, donated by his friend T. J. Phillips Jodrell, was opened near the original museum Sir William had founded nearly thirty years earlier. In 1877 a wing was added to the Herbarium to house the expanding collections.

In 1882 the Marianne North Gallery became the latest addition to the buildings at Kew. Miss North was one of those indefatigable Victorian ladies who had the leisure, money, stamina and determination to indulge her interest, one could say obsession. For almost thirteen years she travelled the world, oblivious of discomfort, painting plants in their natural habitat. Her relentless industry yielded a formidable number of paintings: 848 of them are now on display, locked together in a tight mosaic practically from floor to ceiling.

In the same year as the Marianne North Gallery was opened, the Rock Garden was built to receive a large collection of alpine plants bequeathed by George Joad. Owing to a lack of funds for its construction, any available stone was used including an old ruin in the gardens known as the Stone House, which was supposed to have been built by the small sons of George III as part of their practical education. A pinetum was also planted near the lake and the complex of greenhouses known as the T-range was erected.

Sir Joseph Hooker retired in 1885, although he continued to use the scientific resources of Kew almost up to his death in 1911. For nearly forty-four years the Hooker dynasty had directed the fortunes of Kew. Sir William

16

with his abundant energy, imagination and administrative skills transformed a moribund royal estate into a major botanic garden. His son built on these firm foundations, extending Kew's scientific activities and establishing a standard of excellence through his own researches and reputation.

Into the Twentieth Century

William Thiselton-Dyer, who had married Sir Joseph's eldest daughter, became Kew's next Director, having been Assistant Director for ten years. During his term of office two wings were added to the Temperate House in 1899 and another to the Herbarium in 1902. In 1896, with some reservations, he engaged the first women gardeners at Kew. To ensure that their presence did not distract their male colleagues, they had to wear a knickerbocker suit, thick woollen stockings and a most unbecoming peaked cap. The Diamond Jubilee of Queen Victoria in 1897 was marked by the presentation of the woodlands surrounding Queen's Cottage with the Queen's wish that they be maintained in a semi-wild state. Upon the death of the second Duke of Cambridge in 1904 the last royal property was added to Kew. This was Cambridge Cottage on Kew Green, the home of many distinguished people. Lord Bute's family, Sir John Pringle (George III's physician), and the young princes, Edward and William, had lived there. In 1838 it passed to the first Duke of Cambridge. Sir William Thiselton-Dyer was an able administrator but was handicapped by an autocratic and often unsympathetic manner. An unfortunate confrontation with some of his gardeners led to his resignation.

With Sir David Prain, an eminent authority on Indian botany, as the next Director, Kew entered upon a period of relative tranquillity. The only eventful year was 1910, when Cambridge Cottage was converted into a wood museum and the Japanese Gateway, a replica of the ancient one in Kyoto, was transferred from the Japanese–British exhibition at Shepherd's Bush.

Sir Arthur William Hill, who followed him as Director in 1922, ten years later added yet another wing to the Herbarium. The Australian House was opened in 1952 during the directorship of Sir Edward Salisbury, who was

The Palm House, completed in 1848, is a superb example of early Victorian engineering skills, a perfect combination of functionalism and elegance. Horses were used in the Gardens until the 1950s when they were replaced by lorries and tractors.
Photo: F. N. Hepper.

Near the Pagoda, on a small hillock that was previously the site of the Mosque, an architectural fantasy designed by Sir William Chambers, stands another oriental building, the 'Gateway of the Imperial Messenger' or 'Chokushi-Mon'. The structure is a nearly full-size replica of a sixteenth-century gateway built for the great Buddhist temple of Nishi Hongwangi at Kyoto, Japan. The replica was exhibited at the Japanese-British Exhibition in 1910 and afterwards re-erected in the Gardens.

Japanese Kurume azaleas selected by the great plant collector E. H. Wilson are an attractive feature on the south side of the mound, where an engraved rock was placed in 1979 as a memorial to the Japanese poet Kyoshi Takahama (1874–1959).
Photo: T. A. Harwood.

succeeded by Sir George Taylor in 1956. Sir George's main achievements include another wing to the Herbarium (the pattern seems to be one about every thirty years), the creation of the Queen's Garden behind Kew Palace, the restoration of the Palm House and the acquisition of Wakehurst Place.

After Sir George's retirement in 1971, Professor J. Heslop-Harrison expanded the scientific aspects of Kew by establishing the Conservation Unit and by making a wing of his house on Kew Green into a cell-physiology laboratory – he also obtained official support for expeditions and formed the Micropropagation Unit in the new Aiton House. When he resigned in 1976, Professor J. P. M. Brenan, who was Keeper of the Herbarium and a distinguished taxonomist, succeeded him. In spite of an economic recession he saw the completion of the Administration building and the refurbishing of the splendid Temperate House before his retirement in October 1981. The present director, Professor Arthur Bell lately of Kings College, University of London, is no stranger to Kew having co-operated with staff in the area of plant biochemistry and cytotaxonomy for a number of years.

Kew has gone through numerous metamorphoses since it was the home of the royal family in the eighteenth century. Some of our most distinguished landscape gardeners have shaped and remodelled it. Successive Directors have all contributed to its development. Kew is still changing, yet the past can never be completely obliterated. That is one of its attractions and the source of much of the pleasure it gives to so many people today.

R.D.

Gardens for Pleasure

In keeping with Kew's origins as royal gardens elegantly set in a landscape containing handsome and historic buildings, some of the Gardens' features are maintained specifically for their ornamental and amenity value. There are complementary features, too, at Wakehurst Place, the estate in Sussex that, since 1968, has been 'Kew in the country'.

The Main Gates, Kew, designed by Decimus Burton, 1848

⚜ 2 ⚜
Planting to Please the Eye

On a brilliant day in April or May thousands of visitors make their way to Kew. Probably few of those who pass by the blaze of colourful flowers realize that this is a botanic garden with a collection of living plants primarily grown for scientific study. At Kew, however, ornamental plantings are made to please the general public, who have most interest in the commercially available plants they know and can grow for colour and fragrance in their own gardens.

Bedding

Bedding was a nineteenth-century garden fashion. It was a revolt against the informality and naturalism of the previous century and was, in fact, a return in part to the formality of the seventeenth century. Amongst an influx of new plants were many showy annuals and perennials that provided colour during the summer months, although some were tender. They did not associate well with other kinds of garden plants and looked better when grown on their own. Following the industrial revolution, many rich industrialists bought estates and land on which they built fine mansions. Wishing to ape the established gentry they constructed large and elaborate gardens, which in design and content had to be status symbols. These landowners vied with each other for the highest standard of design, maintenance, excellence of produce and the biggest collection of plants. In these gardens it was the conservatories and their plants which came to be highly prized. What could be more ostentatious than to plant out in the open during the summer months much of the contents of these greenhouses? These greenhouse plants associated well with the new plant introductions and so in combination came to form the basis of bedding.

This new fashion quickly gained favour and expanded greatly, becoming increasingly elaborate in design and content, and reaching the height of florid ornamentation at the end of the last century. In design, beds were formal and near, or on the approach, to the house, much resembling simplified seventeenth-century parterres. A change occurred after the First World War when, following the sale and break-up of many of these estates, those within or near to towns or cities were sold to local authorities. Under new management these gardens became public parks with bedding continuing much as before. A decline set in after the Second World War, when increased costs and a reduced availability of skilled labour put the future of this labour-intensive garden feature in jeopardy. English gardens have their peak of display in spring, and nothing has been yet found to replace bedding in the provision of summer colour. Bedding has still retained a place in post-war gardening, though with an ever-decreasing range of plants. It is interesting also to note that in spite of this reduced selection the commercial plant breeders annually introduce a flood of new ornamental varieties, properly known as cultivars.

Opposite: the Rose Garden near the Palm House has always been popular. The roses originally planted on the Pond side were replaced by ornamental bedding earlier this century, but the rose beds on the south side are still much as they were in Edwardian times, although the terms placed against the holly hedge have since been removed to the Queen's Garden. The tower, designed by Decimus Burton in the style of an Italian campanile, is the disguised flue for the boiler house heating the Palm House.

Some modern bedding suffers from the juxtaposition of many different colours. At Kew, the use of a limited palette – shades of one colour or two or three contrasting colours – is a deliberate choice.

Left: spring bedding near the Main Gate consists of bulbs and hardy herbaceous plants. Photo: F. N. Hepper.

Below: summer bedding is of annuals and tender plants.

Opposite: the herbaceous island beds in the Duke's Garden are permanently planted with perennials, such as poppies, iris and geum. Cambridge Cottage, used as the Wood Museum, lies beyond.
Photos: T. A. Harwood.

The bedding at Kew is situated in two main areas: the important parterre in front of the Palm House, and along the Broad Walk. The present design of the Palm House beds was laid out in the early years of this century. Originally they were planted up with roses, as are the present beds behind the Palm House. The whole area was designed as a formal setting for this handsome Victorian greenhouse. In the planning and planting of the bedding in front of the Palm House, the whole area is treated as two separate but identical halves. Each matching group of beds, corresponding with its twin set, is planted up with the same kind of plants, whilst there is a common colour scheme overall.

The Broad Walk, which leads from the Palm House Pond to the Orangery, has as focal points at each end urns set on plinths in the middle of circular beds. It is not possible from any one position to be able to see all the beds along the Broad Walk, and they are sufficiently far apart to allow each pair to be seen in isolation, with planting identical in each pair.

Since bedding was devised to provide colour during the summer months, the plantings of late May and early June have to provide a spectacle from June to September. The plants are removed as the floral display comes to an end and before early frosts damage tender species. Once cleared, beds are dug over, organic matter added and the beds prepared for re-planting. Gardeners do not like flower beds to be empty for seven months of each year, for nature, taking its course, will fill them with weeds. During this period gardeners use the beds for another kind of bedding. In the English climate, a winter bedding display is not possible, so the aim is for colour in the spring. The main spring flowers in a seventeenth-century parterre were bulbous, especially tulips. With the similarity of these two styles, bulbs are again the dominant plant, also using tulips, the only difference being that in modern bedding there is a mass display of one kind, whereas in the seventeenth century many different kinds were planted in one bed.

Of the various tulips offered for sale by bulb growers, the most popular, colourful and showy are the Darwins. As these tulips flower in May, the emphasis in public parks has been to plan their spring bedding to flower in this month. Yet it is during May that English gardens provide their greatest display and so bedding plants flowering in this month lose much impact. By careful planning, however, tulips and other bulbs can be chosen to flower in April, even March and, following a mild winter, late February. Three of the newest tulip groups (which take their name from the dominant parent species of the group) have been much used at Kew: Kaufmanniana, Fosteriana and Greigii; the first group flowers in March, the second in early April and the last in late April. Whereas the display of summer bedding should last three or four months, the spring bedding is expected to flower for only four weeks. With the exception of daffodils, of which there are tens of thousands naturalized in the grass of the Arboretum, many other bulbs besides tulips have been used at Kew, including grape hyacinths, dwarf bulbous iris, Dutch iris, *Scilla*, *Allium*, *Ornithogalum* and *Camassia*. In spring bedding, bulbs are planted to grow through a ground cover of old favourites such as wallflowers, polyanthus and daisies or the less usual spotted dead-nettle (*Lamium maculatum* cultivars), lungwort (*Pulmonaria* species and cultivars) and purple fennel (*Foeniculum vulgare* 'Purpurea'). Following the removal of spring bedding, beds are prepared for replanting and all planting at Kew has to be finished in three weeks.

While the spring bedding has been growing and flowering, plants for the summer bedding have been raised under glass. Many kinds such as petunia,

Staff and students planting out summer bedding in the Broad Walk beds.
Photo: F. N. Hepper.

French marigold and sweet tobacco are raised from seed, while heliotrope, calceolarias and scarlet *Verbena phlogiflora* are propagated from cuttings. Some of the glasshouse plants that were ostentatious in last century's bedding are still used, for example the orange-flowered *Streptosolon jamesonii*, pale blue *Plumbago auriculata* (*capensis*) and the palm-like *Cordyline australis*. Amongst the unorthodox plants that have been used in some years have been vegetables such as Swiss chard with its brilliant white stems, the French bean 'Royalty' with its purple pods, and a non-hearting lettuce. So often it is thought that only flowers provide colour in a bedding display and few people realize foliage has a whole range of colours besides green and grey. There are plants with white or yellow variegation; red leaves in *Iresine herbstii*, blue in *Ruta graveolens* 'Jackman's Blue', purple in *Tradescantia pallida* 'Purpurea', yellow in golden marjoram (*Origanum vulgare* 'Aurea') and sulphur-yellow in *Helichrysum petiolatum* 'Limelight'.

There will always be many old favourites amongst the bedding plants, but each year will see the use of some not normally considered for bedding, as well as different combinations of more orthodox ones. Kew is ever ready to experiment and its bedding is never conventional, though it remains colourful and exciting.

Herbaceous Island Beds

Herbaceous borders, once the highlight of an English garden, developed in the latter part of the nineteenth century reaching their zenith in Edwardian times. They combined the naturalism of the eighteenth century with the formality of the nineteenth, providing colour during the summer when it was usually in short supply. Seen usually as two straight parallel borders backed by hedges on either side of a central path, herbaceous borders were only effective on the grand scale, being overpowering in a small suburban garden. Careful planning was necessary in placing plants so they were graded in height, adjacent groups of flowers did not clash, flowers were produced in every month from May until October and there were no extensive gaps before or after flowering. Much effort was needed in staking, dead-heading and general maintenance. Following the Second World War, when labour was in short supply and expensive, such borders seemed doomed to disappear owing to the high cost of upkeep. However, as with the best of any garden feature, they have survived, albeit in a modified form. Largely through the influence of a commercial nurseryman, Alan Bloom, island beds have come to replace herbaceous borders as a reasonably economical and attractive way of growing herbaceous plants.

An island bed can be made to any size or shape and is designed for all-round viewing. The same kind of herbaceous plants are used, but by careful selection, staking is largely unnecessary, closer planting helps in the suppression of weeds and more versatile displays become possible as the ideas develop. In a small garden where space is at a premium it is possible to include annuals, biennials, bulbs and even shrubs which no purist would have tolerated in the old herbaceous border. It has also become possible to present plants differently, for while also planning a succession of blooms for six months, all could be had in flower in any chosen month, all plants could have flowers and/or foliage of the same colour, while foliage could replace flowers in providing colour.

Island beds are to be found in the Duke's Garden, which is an enclosed area in front of the Wood Museum in Cambridge Cottage, hence the alternative name of Cambridge Cottage Garden. In addition to six beds planted to provide

The old cottage garden favourite the crown imperial (*Fritillaria imperialis* var. *lutea*), has been grown in British gardens for more than four hundred years since its introduction from the Middle East. There are plantings by the Palm House Pond, in the Bulb Garden and in the Queen's Garden.
Photo: J.B.E. Simmons.

The Aquatic Garden was laid out in 1909 near the Jodrell Laboratory. In the large central tank is a collection of waterlilies, which flower in summer. The four pools at each corner contain various other aquatic plants such as the brandy bottle (*Nuphar lutea*) (below), pickerell weed (*Pontaderia cordata*) and bullrushes or reed-maces (*Typha* species). Between these small tanks and parallel to the long sides of the large tank, are two beds of British marsh plants, where may be seen king cups (*Caltha palustris*), Lodden lily (*Leucojum aestivum*) and water figwort (*Scrophularia aquatica*).
Photo: J. Fielding.

colour from May until October, there is a blue border, another of grey-leaved plants and a third in which are plants with coloured foliage.

Bulbous Plants

The Cambridge Cottage Garden has an inner garden separated from the island beds by a low wall on which are a number of planted urns. In this garden a series of beds are planted up with the more common bulbs, all of which are available from commercial sources. 'Bulb' is used here in its horticultural sense to mean any plant with an underground storage organ. Although the main flowering display is in spring, there is something in flower during every month of the year. Bulbous plants are to be found mainly in Liliaceae, Amaryllidaceae and Iridaceae and these beds have been used as an educational exhibit to explain the floral characteristics of these three families. Some of the irises that were formerly in the Iris Garden have been replanted here. Maintenance of the beds is not easy since some species increase too rapidly, while others die away, so it is necessary to lift and replant from time to time.

In a border at the foot of one of the walls is another educational exhibit of variegated plants. The different causes of variegation are explained and by means of a code letter on each label it is possible to know which kind each plant is exhibiting.

Tender Plants

At the far end of the Cambridge Cottage Garden is an area which is a sun-trap, being enclosed on three sides by walls; it is also protected from wind. A south-facing wall is a favoured place in a garden, for adjacent to its vertical surface is a microclimate in which the temperature of the air is a few degrees higher than in the surrounding atmosphere. The wall receives sunshine throughout the day, some of which is reflected and some absorbed to be released as heat slowly during the night. When rain falls some is shed by the wall so the soil at its foot remains relatively dry. The effect of increased radiant heat in winter also reduces frost penetration. By planting against a south-facing wall it is possible to grow plants normally considered too tender for the district. Protection is provided in spring to precocious growth and flowers. At the other end of the year it benefits late blooms for which early frosts are a hazard. The extra summer warmth and drier soil helps to ripen wood thoroughly, so producing a plant better able to withstand winter cold. This drier and warmer soil is beneficial to bulbs since it not only provides protection to early and late blooms and growth, but encourages thorough ripening of the bulb resulting in regular flowering. While these beneficial conditions are most marked to plants growing by a south-facing wall, one facing west is almost as favourable.

The walls in this garden have been used to provide protection to a wide range of tender plants, as has that outside the Duke's Garden, the bed created there being known as the Duchess Border. In these borders can be seen several kinds of bottlebrush (*Callistemon* spp.) from Australia, olive (*Olea europaea*), pomegranate (*Punica granatum*) from the Middle East, lobster's claw (*Clianthus puniceus*) from New Zealand and the pineapple guava (*Feijoa sellowiana*), in the myrtle family, from Brazil. Some of the less common bulbs to be found in the Duchess Border include species of *Tigridia* and *Rigidella* from Mexico, *Nerine* species from South Africa and *Leucojum nicaeense* from southern France.

B.H.

An attractive bulb that makes a handsome display in late summer and autumn is *Nerine bowdenii* (below). In the Duchess Border, a less hardy relative, *Nerine sarniensis*, forms part of a collection of tender bulbs and woody plants that are generally considered glasshouse subjects in the south-east of England. Photo: T. A. Harwood.

❧ 3 ❧
The Queen's Garden
A Seventeenth-Century
Pleasance

The Creation of a Seventeenth-century Garden

We have already seen (Chapter 1) that Samuel Fortrey built his Dutch House at Kew in 1631. Much later it was occupied by George III's family and it is now known as Kew Palace. Eighteenth- and nineteenth-century paintings and prints show the area to the north of the Palace as a tree-lined meadow where sheep grazed. It is assumed that no garden was created previously because the land was subject to flooding by the Thames, a problem that continued until the tow-path was raised. By 1959, this area had become derelict and Sir George Taylor, then Director, conceived the idea of creating a garden contemporary with the Palace. Its subsequent design developed after extensive reference to books and plans of the period and visits to extant seventeenth-century gardens. This research revealed that estates of the mid-seventeenth century consisted of a number of small gardens, each enclosed, with differences of level frequently used to create a surprise effect on entry. Into an area of less than an acre have been fitted four small gardens, two walks and other garden features. Work on landscaping began in 1963; it was completed six years later when the garden was officially opened by Her Majesty Queen Elizabeth II on 14 May 1969.

Left: the laburnum walk, which lines three sides of the sunken Nosegay Garden, forms a golden tunnel over the path during the month of May. The three-arched loggia on the north side of Kew Palace is a reconstruction that restores the appearance of this front to that shown in old prints.
Photo: T. A. Harwood.

Right: the formal design of a seventeenth-century parterre shows to best effect when viewed from above. The view from an upper window of Kew Palace shows a pattern of clipped box hedges surrounding small beds. Dwarf shrubs have subsequently replaced the floral bedding shown here.
Photo: F. N. Hepper.

The brick-paved entrance to the Queen's Garden is a sheltered area with grape vines, an apricot and a fig tree planted against the surrounding walls. Tubs containing oleander bushes are put out here during the summer months.
Photo: T. A. Harwood.

In the seventeenth century, when the great waves of plant introductions from all over the world had hardly begun, the gardener considered the medicinal as well as culinary and ornamental qualities of the relatively limited range of species and varieties available.

Opposite, top: 'Oil of cammomill', wrote Gerard (*Herbal*, 1636) 'is exceeding good against all manner of ache and paine, bruisings, shrinking of sinues, hardnesse, and cold swellings'. The 'upholstery' of the seat in the Nosegay Garden is a living cushion of sweet-smelling chamomile (*Chamaemelum nobile*, also known as *Anthemis nobilis*). The cultivar used is the non-flowering 'Treneague', which is a modern name for an old cultivar known to Gerard and Parkinson – the normal form is illustrated.
From Kohler, *Medizinal Pflanzen* (1898, 3:210).

Opposite, bottom: the Christmas rose (*Helleborus niger*), a native of central and southern Europe, flowers, as its name implies, during the winter months. Although the flowers are highly regarded for their beauty, Gerard records in his *Herbal* (1597) that 'A purgation of blacke Hellebor is good for mad and furious men, for melancholike, dull and heavie persons, for those that are troubled with the falling sicknesse, for lepers . . .'
From *Curtis's Botanical Magazine* (1787, pl 8).

The main door on the south side is approached by a flagged path between two areas of lawn edged by box. Entrance to the garden to the west of the main door is down steps between raised beds with rosemary in one and old roses in the other. Passing between two brick pillars, the visitor comes into an area paved with and patterned in brick. It was on such areas that potted plants were stood during the summer months. These could be tender, usually evergreen shrubs or, as they were called, 'green(e)s' such as oranges, lemons, oleanders and bays. At the onset of winter these would be moved into the protection of orangeries or green(e) houses. Steps lead up a lavender bank to a raised walk which cuts the main part of the garden in two; immediately behind the Palace it is formal, to the west is a sunken garden, which, though formal in design, is informally planted.

The Nosegay Garden

By the seventeenth century, the monastery herb gardens of the Middle Ages had diversified so that, although the contents of each were not strictly separated, there were vegetable, fruit, herb and nosegay gardens. It was a period when hygiene was still considered of little importance; people rarely washed themselves or their clothes, windows were small and infrequently opened, houses were not very clean and, there being no sanitation, the smells were unpleasant. Ground floors were of stone or stamped earth, and to make these rooms warmer they were covered with straw. In the parlour and dining rooms straw would be replaced with fragrant strewing herbs, either fresh or dried. In bedrooms, mattresses were stuffed with straw and little attention was paid to cleanliness of bed linen, so it is not surprising that beds were often alive with bugs and fleas. To mask body odours and to induce pleasant dreams, the mattresses might instead of straw be stuffed with lady's bedstraw (*Galium verum*), which acquires a pleasant fragrance on drying. To keep infestation of fleas and bed bugs at bay, wormwood (*Artemisia* species) might be used as well.

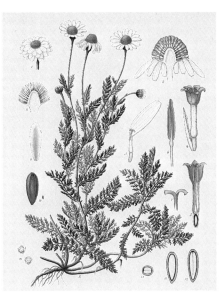

In towns and cities roads were often unpaved and infrequently provided with drains. Transport depended on animals and to their droppings was added rubbish swept from the houses and contents of chamber pots thrown from upstairs windows. Streets therefore were quagmires in winter, full of swirling dust in summer and at all times smelled most foul. When ladies, and gentlemen too, ventured forth, they carried posies or nosegays made of fragrant-leaved plants with some sweet-smelling flowers pressed to their noses, for these not only helped to disguise the stench but were thought to give protection against the plague. Even today nosegays are carried by judges in procession at the beginning of the legal year, continuing a practice of earlier centuries when they were thought to offer protection against gaol fever. Plants grown for strewing, making posies, decorating the home or for garlands were all grown in a nosegay garden and it is as a nosegay garden that the sunken portion of the Queen's Garden has been planted.

The lower parallel perimeter paths are lined with dwarf box and the other side with germander (*Teucrium chamaedrys*). Along the cross paths between clipped pyramidal yews are lines of the small Burgundy rose, *Rosa* 'Parvifolia'. A centrepiece to the garden is a gilded wrought iron pillar of the period which came from Hampton Court and is thought to have been one of a pair of gate piers. Taller plants are confined to the beds on either side whilst low-growing and prostrate plants are to be found on the sloping banks. A mulberry and strawberries have strayed from the fruit garden, cardoon and chives from the vegetable garden and borage and fennel from the herb garden.

Some of the plants growing here that would have been used for strewing are wormwood (*Artemisia* species), sage (*Salvia officinalis*), and bergamot (*Monarda fistulosa*), while pinks, thrift, French and African marigolds, bluebells and Christmas roses were used for posies. At the northern end of the Nosegay Garden is a seat. Wooden and iron seats did not appear in gardens until the latter part of the eighteenth century and before that time these were either of stone or living plants. This one has a back and arm rests of clipped box and is cushioned with chamomile.

The raised walk is in the open on one side of the rectangular sunken garden, with the path on the other three sides passing under a shady bower. Here laburnums have been trained over a framework and pleached. Pleaching is a method of pruning where all branches are cut hard back annually to a trained framework which results here in freedom of flowering without an excess of foliage to hide the flowers. In May, when the laburnum is in flower, this bower becomes a golden tunnel.

The raised path leads to a gazebo – an early garden building of which a summer-house is a modern counterpart. It was here that anyone could rest, take shelter from the weather, inspect the garden and savour its perfumes. This gazebo is based on one at Packwood, a garden in Gloucestershire. In the tail of the modern weather vane that surmounts the gazebo can be seen the initials of some of the people who were concerned in the design and construction of the garden. At the side of the gazebo is a small collection of trees and shrubs. In the early years of the seventeenth century, trees did not feature greatly in gardens except in avenues or when planted for shade; it was only in the closing years of

the century that they came to be grown for ornament. The tulip tree (*Liriodendron tulipifera*) which can be seen here was a new arrival in English gardens and probably introduced by John Tradescant from Virginia in about 1654. Garden shrubs were mainly evergreen and those with fragrant flowers or aromatic or coloured foliage were most prized. Planted near to the gazebo where visitors resting can appreciate the scents of flowers are myrtle (*Myrtus communis*), mezereon (*Daphne mezereum*) and mock orange (*Philadelphus coronarius*).

The Parterre Garden

Descending the steps in front of the gazebo, the visitor enters a parterre enclosed by yew hedges. The parterre had evolved from the Tudor knot garden to become a geometric and symmetrical pattern of beds each edged with box. While these beds might contain coloured earths or grass, it was more usual for them to be planted with low-growing shrubs or flowering plants.

Continental Europe favoured clipped evergreen shrubs such as lavender, thyme, rosemary or lavender cotton, while England tended more towards flowering plants. It was in France that parterres became most elaborate; beds resembling living tapestries, which the French referred to as '*parterre broderie*', had the lines of their elaborate designs kept sharp by constant clipping. Such gardens were not intended to be walked in but were for viewing at a distance: from a raised walk, balcony or a second-story window. In England, whilst this type did occur, it was more usual to follow a less regimented system where only

the box edging was trimmed and within each bed was grown an assortment of plants that were allowed to flower. Formerly at Kew these were planted up twice a year to provide spring and summer displays as for bedding, which was a nineteenth-century modification of a seventeenth-century parterre. In bedding, planting would be of a few flowering plants for mass effect; in *parterre anglais* there would be very many different plants. In the Queen's Garden the replacement planting includes: rosemary, gilded sage and curry plant, one kind to a bed, each of which is clipped with the box.

In gardens of the period, much use was made of statuary and architectural features, which were often incorporated into the geometric designs of a parterre. The centrepiece in the parterre is a Venetian well-head, which came from Bulstrode Park and was presented to Kew by Sir John Ramsden. The design of the garden also incorporates a rectangular pond, to which water is supplied by a fountain. This is a cast of Verrocchio's Boy with Dolphin and, like the original in the Palazzo Vecchio at Florence, it is mounted on a stone ball with lion masks. Behind the pond is a curved stone seat, which is parallel to the pair of beds behind and to the yew hedge at the northern end of the garden. Arranged against this hedge are five terms – carved heads of mythical figures, each on its own pedestal; they were commissioned in 1734 by Frederick, Prince of Wales, from Peter Scheermaker. The beds of the parterre are set in pebbles, although the pond surrounds have been paved with York stone. This type of paving has been used also against the face of the Palace, whence steps lead up to a restored three-bayed loggia; potted bay trees stand here during the summer.

Crossing the front of the Palace one enters another shaded walk passing under an avenue of hornbeams. The trees have been allowed to develop a trunk and a trained framework of branches; the twigs are then clipped annually so as to produce a 'hedge on stilts' or boscage. A path leads from the end of this avenue up a mount. The mount had long been a feature of English gardens; for example, there was one at Hampton Court as early as 1533. Either natural or artificial, mounts were raised places in a garden where the owner could admire his own estate, view the surrounding countryside or ascertain what his neighbour was doing!

This one is artificial, having been fashioned from an enormous heap of cinders and ashes which came from Kew glasshouse boilers in the days when these were coal-fired. During landscaping the heap was rounded, covered with soil and planted up with box. Between the clipped box, a path winds up to a gilded wrought-iron rotunda. Although this is a fine example of modern wrought-iron work, it is seventeenth century in design. Amongst the scrollwork are four royal cyphers (E II R) and between each is the floral emblem of the four countries comprising the British Isles: for England the rose, for Scotland the thistle, for Wales the leek and for Ireland the shamrock. Standing under the rotunda there is a good view of the entire Queen's Garden, and, if one turns round, it is possible to see the River Thames over the boundary wall. The path continues over the mount along the edge of a woodland being developed into a wilderness garden.

Seventeenth-century Garden Plants

Although there are a number of other period gardens throughout Great Britain that have been preserved, restored or planted, only a few others have restricted their planting solely to what was in cultivation prior to the year 1700. In the search for authentic plants, the species have presented no problems for these

Above: the Virginian dragon's head (*Physostegia virginiana*), first cultivated in 1683 by James Sutherland in the Edinburgh Botanic Garden, was one of the many plants brought to Europe from North America during the seventeenth century. John Tradescant the younger and later John Banister, a missionary, enriched British gardens with herbaceous and woody species, especially from Virginia.
From *Curtis's Botanical Magazine* (1800, pl 467).

Opposite, top: the common sage (*Salvia officinalis*) 'is singular good for the head and braine, quickneth the scences and memorie, strengtheth the sinewes, restoreth health to those that have the palsie' according to Gerard's *Herbal* (1597). It was, and still is, used in cooking as a seasoning agent. This is an illustration of the cultivar 'Grandiflora', which has dark purple flowers. Other old-fashioned cultivars planted in the Nosegay Garden include the red sage 'Purpurascens' (which was considered more efficacious than the others) and the lesser sage 'Minor' (which was valued most of all); the gilded sage 'Icterina' is massed in the parterre.
From Bentley and Trimen, *Medicinal Plants* (1880, pl 206).

Opposite, bottom: the sunken area that forms the Nosegay Garden includes plants that would have been used for decoration of the home, for chaplets, posies, nosegays and as strewing herbs. There are also medicinal and culinary herbs, vegetables and fruits that have strayed from other sections of the garden.
Photo: T. A. Harwood.

could always be raised from seed. To find cultivars has provided many more problems since few of those grown in the seventeenth century are still in cultivation; an extensive search of nurseries and old gardens has gone on and still continues. Before anything is planted, it will be necessary to check through old books to ensure that it was being grown in English gardens three hundred years ago. This can be a long and exhausting task for the system of nomenclature was different from that used today, and common names, too, have changed.

The seventeenth century saw gardening take its place alongside hunting, shooting and fishing as a leisure pursuit for the gentry. Nurseries were springing up to provide plants for these gardens. Gardens were becoming status symbols and when nurseries had been ransacked for their rarities, the wealthy were sending out the first collectors to bring back plants from other countries. The first books on gardening were appearing at that time and it is from these that it has been possible to find out what was then grown. Those most frequently consulted are: John Gerard's *Herbal*, first published in 1597 with further editions in 1633 and 1636, and *Paradisi in Sole* and *Theatrum Botanicum* by John Parkinson, the former printed in 1629 and the latter in 1640. In addition there were lists of plants grown in gardens, two by John Gerard of 1596 and 1599 and two by the John Tradescants, father and son, of 1634 and 1683. The first British botanic gardens were founded during the century, that at Oxford in 1621 and the other at Edinburgh in 1670; John Sutherland who had charge of the latter garden published a list of plants in cultivation there in 1678. It is clear from the early literature on cultivation that plants were grown for some utilitarian purpose, especially for food, flavouring or for medicine, and if they had beautiful flowers or attractive foliage this was of secondary importance. The books by Gerard and Parkinson were illustrated with woodcuts. There was a description of each plant with names in several languages, including English, and a 'Virtue' under which heading was recorded the plant's use. On the plant labels prepared for the garden extracts have been taken from these virtues. At that time spelling was not very accurate and it was by no means uncommon to find the same word spelled in several different ways on one page. These extracts are spelled exactly as they appear in the books. On the label in addition to the virtue is the present botanical name, the common name that was in use in the seventeenth century, the author's name and the date of the publication whence the information has been taken.

The plant which today we call double bulbous buttercup (*Ranunculus bulbosus* 'Flore pleno') was called 'the great double Crowfoote' by John Gerard in his *Herbal* (1597, p 810). The virtue for this plant was 'if it be hanged in a linnen cloth about the necke of him that is a lunatike in the waine of the moone . . . he shall foorthwith be cured'. The annual sunflower (*Helianthus annuus*) was called by Gerard (1597, p 614) 'the Indian sun flower', 'the golden flower of Peru' and 'the flower of the Sunne'. Under virtues we read 'the buddes before they be flowred, boiled and eaten with butter, vinegar, and pepper, after the maner of Artichokes, are exceedingly pleasant meate, surpassing the Artichoke farre in procuring bodilie lust.' (Perhaps this is why the flower buds disappear at Kew before they have a chance to open!)

At the beginning of the seventeenth century, very few plants were grown just for ornament, although numbers increased as the century progressed. Of the herbs which were grown, sage was valued for flavouring and medicine, but there were also forms with ornamental foliage and others with flowers of improved size or colour. One group of plants grown solely for ornament, though, were the spring-flowering bulbs, of which the tulip was most popular. This was a relative newcomer to English gardens, having arrived towards the end of the sixteenth century from Turkey, but had quickly become widely grown. Already there were many types, of which those with broken colours (which today we call Rembrandts after the Dutch painter) were the most highly prized.

The Garden of pleasant Flowers.

307

Left: 'carnations or July flowers as they are properly called from the month in which they bring forth their beautiful flowers, are indeed the pride of summer as tulips are the glories of spring', according to John Rea in *Flora, Ceres and Pomona* (1676). In this book he lists 361 different carnations, including 'The Red or Clove Gilloflower', which is grown at Kew.

Carnation flowers steeped in vinegar were used as a pickle, according to John Evelyn in *Acetaria: A Discourse on Sallats* (1699). From Parkinson, *Paradisi in Sole* (1629, p 307).

Many of the plants in the Queen's Garden bear labels with dated quotations from herbals of the late sixteenth and seventeenth centuries. If no virtue can be found, a date is included when the plant is known to have been in cultivation in Britain.

Opposite, top: most of these herbals were illustrated with woodcuts, such as this of the sunflower (*Helianthus annuus*). The quality and accuracy of herbal illustrations was very variable.
From Gerard, *Herbal* (1597, p 612).

Opposite, bottom: the small French marigold (*Tagetes patula*) was an early introduction for the flower garden from Central America. Gerard considered that 'the whole plant is of a most ranke and unwholesome smell, and perisheth at the first frost'.
From Gerard, *Herbal* (1633, p 750).

Tulips, which had been introduced into England from Turkey about 1576, quickly became the most popular of spring bulbs; long lists of varieties appeared in books of the seventeenth century by Gerard, Parkinson, Rea, Hanmer and Tradescant. Some of the groups which appear in today's bulb catalogues–for example, Earlies, Doubles and Parrots–were known to these writers. The most popular were those with broken flower colours that today are collectively referred to as Rembrandts, after the painter of the Dutch School.

Simon Verelst (1644–1721), who painted these Rembrandt tulips, was a highly accomplished Dutch artist who lived in England, where his works were in great demand. From the Sir Arthur Church Collection, Kew Library, presented by Lady Church in 1916.

Among the tulips to be found in this garden are a few species as well as some authentic old varieties (or cultivars) which can be seen in various borders. Almost as highly prized as tulips were the spring-flowering auriculas, which have retained their popularity as garden plants to the present day. Of summer favourites were carnations and pinks and there is a collection of some period cultivars of the latter to be seen on the banks around the Nosegay Garden. At the present time roses are the most widely grown of summer flowers; these, too, were featured in seventeenth-century gardens, although three hundred years had to pass before our hybrid teas and floribundas were to appear. At that time, the kinds of roses in gardens were either species or what today we would call shrub roses. A collection of these can be seen at the entrance to the garden or at the foot of the mount.

B.H.

✣ 4 ✣
The Sir Henry Price Garden
Wakehurst Place

The Origins of the Garden

The last private owner of the Wakehurst Place mansion and garden was Sir Henry Price. He was a successful businessman and a very keen gardener—his name and that of Wakehurst Place appeared on exhibitors' cards at the Royal Horticultural Society's shows for over twenty-five years. When he died in 1963, the estate was bequeathed to the National Trust with a substantial endowment, and on 1 January 1965 it was leased for a peppercorn rent to the Ministry of Agriculture, Fisheries and Food for use as an additional garden to the Royal Botanic Gardens, Kew.

It is fitting, therefore, that a portion of the estate should specifically bear the name of Sir Henry Price, and formal dedication by the Duke of Gloucester took place in June 1975. Visitors now greatly enjoy this floral tribute, which takes the form of a garden of herbaceous summer flowers. It lies beside the mansion which is a fine stone building erected by Edward Culpeper during the reign of Elizabeth I in the second half of the sixteenth century. The Culpeper family were owners of the estate for over two centuries, from 1468 to 1694, when Sir William Culpeper sold it to pay off his gambling debts. But the present house replaced an earlier one and there is evidence that the area had been inhabited since prehistoric times. A flint arrowhead was retrieved from Bethlehem Woods and a Roman road actually ran through what is now the site of the car park.

A gardener at work in the early morning mist preparing the Sir Henry Price Garden in 1974. This walled garden, which formerly provided herbaceous cut flowers for the house, has been carefully converted into a summer garden for the enjoyment of visitors. Photo: A.D. Schilling.

After the Culpepers, the estate successively passed into the hands of the Lydells, Clarkes and Peytons, who were all related. In 1869 it was bought by Lady Downshire, who carried out many alterations to the fabric of the mansion. These were continued by Thomas Boord until 1903, when Gerald Loder, later Lord Wakehurst, bought the estate and began to create his great garden.

Loder had a passion for plants. Although he was a member of Parliament and he eventually became chairman of the Southern Railway, his great interest was woody plants, especially of the southern hemisphere (see Chapter 11). But it was Sir Henry Price (who bought it in 1930) who maintained Loder's garden, eventually leaving it to the nation. The potential of the estate was carefully assessed by the then Director of Kew, Sir George Taylor. He realized the opportunities it could give for expanding and developing the work of the Royal Botanic Gardens in a richly diverse terrain, complementary in so many ways to Kew itself.

The site chosen, which previously formed part of the estate's kitchen garden, contained numerous small beds for the culture of cut-flowers for the house. It took the form of two terraces and also possessed a dilapidated pergola and a lean-to greenhouse for peaches and nectarines. It was obvious

that this area would be ideal for development along the lines of a traditional cottage garden but the problem was in deciding upon the details of layout and colour scheme. There are already several famous British 'colour gardens', especially those at Sissinghurst and Hidcote which have had great influence elsewhere. Blue gardens, white and silver, silver and pink, they are all most effective but regularly seen, and the desire was to make an original display rather than copy one of them. While planning a scheme for the new garden it was suddenly realized that, instead of trying to decide what to put in, it was better to agree what to leave out. If all the 'hard' colours of the gardener's palette were to be discarded – the yellows, true blues, orange and scarlet – an amazing wealth of subtle harmonious colours would then be left. They would blend together if set against soft textures and silver foliage. Pink, lilac, mauve, purple, maroon and all the intermediate tones give a pool of infinite depth from which to draw. By careful planning they would give continuous enjoyment from early summer right through to autumn.

Work on the garden began in 1972 with the removal of the pergola and greenhouse, the terraces were converted into one gentle slope, the numerous vegetable beds were altered and merged into a few larger ones, and the paths were re-surfaced.

In the spring of 1973, following completion of the landscaping and planting, several garden ornaments were added. An elegantly decorated seventeenth-century lead cistern was placed at the western end as the focal point. Its date (1659) is marked on the front, together with the initials 'PL' and other decorations including *fleur-de-lis*, suns and faces. The ornamental seat against the southern wall was presented by Lady Price, as was the Cumbrian slate plaque on the wall above, which bears the coat of arms of the Price family and a commemorative inscription.

The Planting

The majority of the plants within the garden are of a perennial, herbaceous or sub-shrubby habit, but in addition annuals and also some woody shrubs have been planted to add substance and widen the interest while maintaining the

Above, left: a detail of the seventeenth century lead cistern now used as a feature in this garden.
Photo: J. Dickie.

Above, right: adjacent to the Sir Henry Price Garden lies the Pleasaunce, a garden of totally different character. Within its walls a clipped yew hedge, with four arches, encloses a cruciform layout of flower beds in grass. At its centre is a small pool with a stone fountain in the form of a boy.
Photo: J. Dickie.

Opposite: a late summer view of the matured garden showing the layout of formal beds with their blend of harmonizing coloured foliage and flowers, set against the mellow sandstone of the walls and Mansion. Beyond are tall giant redwoods planted over a century ago, soon after their discovery in the mountains of California.
Photo: J. Dickie.

Walls with their different aspects create special microclimates for plants. The tender Chinese *Clematis armandii* is an evergreen and flowers in profusion on the south-facing wall of the Sir Henry Price Garden.
Photo: A.D. Schilling.

A north-facing wall in the Pleasaunce provides shelter as well as moist conditions for the spectacular Chilean shrub *Crinodendron hookerianum*. It is a member of the family Eleocarpaceae, other representatives of which are seldom cultivated in Britain. The Pleasaunce is well suited to a number of other unusual species, such as the rare coral plant (*Berberidopsis corallina*), and a collection of British ferns.
Photo: J.B.E. Simmons.

colour theme. The annuals here include old cottage garden favourites such as love-in-the-mist (*Nigella damascena*), delicately patterned painted-tongue (*Salpiglossis sinuata*) and, perhaps the most telling feature in the whole garden, large plantings of the beautiful sage *Salvia horminum* in adjacent groups of its purple-blue and pink forms.

The woody shrubs and sub-shrubs cover a wide range of habit and colour. *Hydrangea aspera*, a good form of *Microglossa albescens*, a purple-leaved clone of Venetian sumach (*Cotinus coggygria*) and *Weigela florida* 'Foliis Purpureis' on the eastern borders add variety and depth to the predominantly grey textures of the planting, while opposite the rich crimson-purple flowers of *Rosa rugosa* 'Roseraie de l'Hay' add further height to the scene. Other shrubs such as *Clerodendrum bungei*, *Ceanothus* 'Gloire de Versailles' and *Spiraea japonica* 'Fortunei' grow nearer the centre of the garden. Many of the dwarf shrubs are native to the Mediterranean region, and as well as being of horticultural value several have herbal or medicinal properties which make them of economic importance. The purple-leaved form of common sage (*Salvia officinalis*) is here, as also is hyssop (*Hyssopus officinalis*), various forms of rosemary (*Rosmarinus officinalis*) and rue (*Ruta graveolens* 'Jackmans Blue'). A wide variety of lavenders is also represented, and as well as old favourites such as *Lavandula* 'Hidcote' and *L.* 'Munstead', there are less often seen hybrids, such as the pink-flowered 'Jean Davies'. The French lavender (*L. stoechas*), the rare and tender *L. latifolia*, *L. involucrata*, and the very tender *L. dentata*, which is native to Spain, also can be seen scattered through the garden.

Other grey-leaved sub-shrubs have been used in quantity as well as variety to accentuate the overall effect of soft and mellow textures within the garden. *Artemisia* species grow in flowing drifts intermingling with the greys of the Patagonian *Senecio leucostachys*, the Mediterranean *Ballota acetabulosa*, *Senecio cineraria*, *Phlomis italica* and *P. purpurea*, the delicately cut-leaved *Chrysanthemum haradjanii*, and the Himalayan *Anaphalis triplinervis*. But *Stachys* 'Silver Carpet', which was strategically sited around the centrepiece of the garden, proved a disaster as it fell prey to mildew. Rather than fight the problem the planting was changed to that of *Helichrysum petiolatum*, which, although tender, more than made up for the extra work of its annual propagation by its delightfully elegant habit and rapid rate of growth.

The advantages of walls and fences, with the latitude afforded by their various aspects, have naturally been exploited. Growing on the cooler and shadier north-facing sandstone walls is the deliciously fragrant deep maroon-crimson and recurrent-flowering climber *Rosa* 'Guinée'. Even darker in its colour of flower is *Clematis viticella* 'Royal Velours'. From a distance accentuated by the shady situation, these deep maroon flowers appear to be almost black.

Several different Asian species of the genus *Indigofera* are planted on the south- and west-facing fences. By contrast, the dwarf *I. kirilowii* with bright pink flowers may be seen at the edge of the eastern border. This is native to north China, Korea and South Japan; although sometimes killed to ground level by winter frosts, new growth is produced the following year. A relative of the genus *Indigofera* is the Himalayan shrub *Desmodium tiliifolium*, which may be seen growing against the south-facing fence.

Although this area has been planned as a summer garden, several earlier-flowering plants have been included in order to spread the season of interest as widely as possible. The late winter-flowering *Daphne bholua* is here, as also is

the early spring-flowering *Clematis armandii*, the fragrant and delightful *Primula* 'Lilacina Plena', the almost perpetually blooming wallflower *Erysimum linifolium* 'Bowles's Mauve', various species and cultivars of *Bergenia*, and the noble-leaved *Podophyllum hexandrum*. It is very tempting to list and describe many more examples of variety within this garden but that would result in these paragraphs reading like a catalogue. What should be added, however, is an example or two of botanical interest within the collections. Those who hunt around will discover *Geranium yunnanense* (which was collected by Kingdon Ward as No. 5897) and *Bergenia purpurascens* (No. 13549 collected by Yu) growing here, as well as such gems as the seldom seen violet-mauve Russian annual *Dianthus amurensis*, the strange and rare liver-purple flowered black salvia of the Himalayas (*S. castanea*) and that now scarce, old and delightfully-scented garden hybrid *Dianthus* 'Charles Musgrave'.

Eryngium species and hybrids are also here in variety from 'Miss Willmott's Ghost' (*E. giganteum*), the European *E. planum*, to the strangely beautiful Mexican *E. proteiflorum*.

Not everyone likes the pseudo-blue of *Rosa* 'Blue Moon' but when coupled to other plants of subtle hue and planted to float above a sea of grey of *Senecio cineraria* and *Artemisia canescens* the effect can be very striking. It is such juxtapositions that give this garden its particular character.

In keeping with the Wakehurst tradition of representing a wide range of Australasian species, several plants from this region of the world have been incorporated into the scheme. Some of them were collected by Harold Comber, who was born in Sussex in 1897, and later worked for some time at Wakehurst. Notable examples of his introductions are the Australian *Ozothamnus rosmarinifolius* and the more tender mauve-blue and pink forms of *Olearia phlogopappa*. Also in the plantings are the New Zealand *Cassinia vauvilliersii* billowing elegantly with white flowers in one of the central beds, *Leptospermum* species to give height, and the Tasmanian shrub *Ozothamnus antennaria*, also with white flowerheads.

Wakehurst Place is probably best known as an example of woodland gardening on a grand scale. Yet it is this secluded walled garden, so richly planted with unusual and beautiful flowers, that guarantees for Sir Henry Price an enduring and fitting memorial with a secure place in the future of the estate.

A.D.S.

The pedestal urn in the centre of the garden was presented by Lady Price, the wife of the previous owner. In the foreground is a mass planting of the annual sage *Salvia horminum* in its various colour forms.
Photo: T. A. Harwood.

Living Botanical Collections

The plants grown at Kew and at Wakehurst Place, totalling nearly 50 000 species and varieties, constitute one of the world's most comprehensive collections of living specimens maintained for scientific study. There are representatives from almost every habitat, including arctic tundra, alpine scree, temperate lowland, tropical rain forest and equatorial desert.

The maidenhair tree *(Ginkgo biloba)* drawn by Joanna A. Langhorne

❧ 5 ❧
The Rock Garden and Alpine House

The Rock Garden

Every year thousands of enthusiastic plantsmen enjoy the wide range of interesting plants in the Rock Garden. Its design differs from any of the various 'rockeries' constructed at Kew during the nineteenth century, most of which were simple arrangements of stones, sometimes in the form of grottoes. There was, however, one constructed on the mound over the Ice House but in later years the alpines planted here were largely replaced by hardy ferns.

In 1882 a rock garden was built on the present site to provide a setting for a collection of alpine plants which had been bequeathed to Kew from the estate of George Joad. Although there was a Treasury grant of £500, money must have been short in that year for, apart from a private donation of Cheddar limestone, other stones came from dismantled rockeries and demolished buildings, supplemented with logs and tree trunks. This rock garden was constructed to represent a Pyrenean mountain valley in miniature, with suitable niches for the plants.

Over the following fifty years the rock garden was constantly changing as extensions were made or new features incorporated. During this period the dressed stone and tree stumps were replaced with water-worn limestone from Somerset, Gloucestershire, Derbyshire, Yorkshire and Westmorland. This was very hard and in summer absorbed heat, so aggravating the drying out of the light Kew soil. In 1929, during the construction of the 'island' at the northern end, Sussex sandstone was used for the first time. Sandstone, which is acidic, is relatively cool in summer and some of the moisture it absorbs is released to the surrounding pockets of soil. The decision to replace all the limestone was being put into effect when the Second World War broke out. Work was abandoned but began again in 1949, continuing on a regular basis for the next twenty years, during which time the entire Rock Garden was rebuilt.

As early as 1906, Sir William Thiselton-Dyer, the then Director, had said that the Rock Garden should not be hidden away but ought to be fully exposed to view. Even so, for over sixty years it was isolated by mature trees already on site and by banks of shrubs. These informal hedge-like screens were gradually removed during the 1950s, as were many of the trees, so that today only four are left standing.

The present Rock Garden is almost half a hectare (over an acre) in extent, having been constructed on a level site. It is made up of a series of perimetrical banks to east, west and north around a central island. These banks, which are approximately 3 metres (8 ft) high and reach a maximum height of 4 metres (12 ft), have been built up with soil excavated from making paths. Into these banks have been built large rectangular pieces of Sussex sandstone to represent outcrops.

Opposite: The Rock Garden covers about half a hectare (more than an acre) and provides habitats for a wide range of species. The high banks on either side and the central 'island' have been built up from soil excavated from the paths. They are capped by conifers which, being well away from the paths, provide a background for the plants. Several thousand species, many seldom seen elsewhere in cultivation, are accommodated in pockets of soil, crevices and screes.
Photo: T. A. Harwood.

Gentians are popularly associated with mountains and rock gardens. Many species are difficult to grow in the Thames valley, but *Gentiana septemfida* (below) is one of the easiest and does well in the Rock Garden.
Photo: F. N. Hepper.

43

Some weather-worn natural limestone was used for the Rock Garden when it was built in 1882, in an attempt to imitate a Pyrenean valley. Limestone was found to be less suitable than sandstone, which retains more moisture and was eventually used to replace it.

The size of the Rock Garden allows for bold plantings. On top of banks farthest from paths much use has been made of conifers. Those chosen have been either naturally small or low-growing or are sports of normally large forest trees. The sombre mountain pine (*Pinus mugo*) is a small, multi-stemmed European tree rarely exceeding 2 metres (6 ft), while *Juniperus conferta* from Japan is prostrate and bright green. There is a number of small cultivars of Lawson's cypress (*Chamaecyparis lawsoniana*) and a prostrate form of Weymouth pine (*Pinus strobus* 'Prostrata') which is a propagant from one on the original rock garden of 1882. In addition to conifers there are many flowering shrubs, but instead of being used to fill up space they frame rocks or provide focal points. *Jasminum parkeri* from northern India makes a small dome-shaped bush perhaps 60 cm (2 ft) in height, of rather wiry shoots with small evergreen pinnate leaves and tiny yellow flowers produced in summer. The plant on the island has been placed at the top of a rock face and has come to form a curtain of shoots which largely cover it. Similarly *Cotoneaster conspicuus* has formed a screen of branches which hug the rock. This provides two displays: the first with the masses of fleeting white flowers and a second from the long-lasting red berries.

Several locations have been created to allow for the cultivation of plants with special requirements. Streams which flow away from three waterfalls provide permanently moist soils at their edges. Along the banks have been planted moisture-loving primulas and iris and there is the beautiful double kingcup (*Caltha palustris* 'Flore plena') with golden-yellow flowers in April, while in August white-bracted flower-spikes rise above reddish heart-shaped leaves of the rarer and interesting *Houttuynia cordata*. This interesting species, in the lizard's-tail family (Saururaceae), occurs from the Himalayas to Japan and Java. Seeds of it were sent by Nathaniel Wallich from Nepal to Kew, where it first flowered in 1826.

In complete contrast are plants which require perfect drainage and a total absence of surface moisture. For these plants screes have been constructed, which in older books are referred to as moraines. Both are geological terms for accumulations of rocks on high mountains. Screes have resulted from the disintegration of exposed rocks by alternate freezing and thawing; a moraine is rocky debris left behind as glaciers retreat. When such a jumble of rocks, however formed, becomes stable and the spaces between filled with soil, certain plants will colonize them. In rock gardens, screes are constructed by filling a trench or gulley with graded rocks to provide perfect drainage. On top of this is an organic-rich soil well supplied with broken rock and the whole is topped off with a layer of coarse gravel or stone chips. Garden screes constructed in this way are ideal for carpeting and cushion plants that require a hard régime so as to grow tight, hairy, grey-leaved plants, and those with large rosettes that are adversely affected by winter damp. At Kew there are three areas of scree, one of which provides a means of access via stepping stones between the Rock Garden and Grass Garden. Nearby are a number of raised beds which have been constructed in the same way as for a scree but have been built up above ground, materials being retained by dry stone walls 45 cm (30 in) high. Raised or scree beds have been gaining in popularity in recent years for they provide a place to grow alpines in a small garden, being easier to construct than a rock garden and are well suited to older people who have difficulty in bending. Some of the plants grown on the screes are the white-flowered shrubby crucifer *Ptilotrichum spinosum*, from south-west Europe; an emerald-green carpeter,

44

Azorella trifurcata, from Ecuador; and a speedwell, *Veronica cinerea*, with grey leaves and bluish flowers from Turkey.

The remaining specialized areas of the Rock Garden have been modified to grow peat-loving plants. On the west side under one of the remaining pines, where branches provide light shade, copious quantities of peat have been added to the soil to retain summer moisture. Some choice plants are to be found here: *Kalmiopis leachiana*, a North American small ericaceous evergreen shrub with pink flowers; a miniature Solomon's seal, *Polygonatum hookeri* from the Himalaya; and from New Zealand, *Cyathodes colensoi*, a low-growing evergreen shrub with overlapping small pointed leaves that are brownish.

Throughout the rest of the Rock Garden there is a large collection of plants that provide good cover of rocks or fill pockets of soil. Kew's climate, in which the summers are relatively warm and dry and the winters are wet with erratic fluctuations in temperature, makes the cultivation of high alpines difficult. The plants grown have been carefully selected for their tolerance of these climatic conditions. Like so many rock gardens, that at Kew is at its most colourful in spring, reaching a peak in May, but there is something in flower or of interest in any month of the year. It has become the policy in recent years to grow only plants that have come either direct from the wild, or have been raised from seed collected there. Originally plants had come from nurseries or other gardens but now these are being gradually replaced.

In the reconstruction of the Rock Garden, which was not completed until the end of the 1960s, blocks of Sussex sandstone weighing as much as two tons were used to create the appearance of natural outcrops broken up with gulleys and small waterfalls.
Photo: R. I. Beyer.

Woodland Garden

In nature alpine plants occur on mountains above the natural tree line. Trees do not stop abruptly but thin out, become smaller and are replaced by alpine scrub. This change of vegetation has been reproduced at the southern end of the Rock Garden where, instead of another rock bank, there is a border of shrubs which gives on to a woodland garden. Woodlands have three layers: tree canopy, deciduous or evergreen shrubs and a ground cover of mainly herbaceous plants.

In the woodland the tree layer is deciduous, consisting mainly of oaks and birches, which provides natural shade and in summer raises the atmospheric humidity. In addition trees provide support for climbers. One of the attractive climbers in this woodland is the evergreen coral plant (*Berberidopsis corallina*) which comes from Chile and has bunches of pendant red flowers. The shrub layer is mostly evergreen, with rhododendrons predominating. Flowering of the ground-cover plants begins in January with hellebores (*Helleborus*), building up through the spring to the main display in May. This is when the rhododendrons are in flower, as are many woodland primulas and a few species of *Meconopsis*, including the blue poppy (*M. betonicifolia*).

To the west of the main woodland garden a new portion has been planted on the other side of the boundary road. The reason for this extension is to soften the harsh line of the road and provide additional planting space for new plant acquisitions. In this area is an uncommon hardy heath, *Erica maderensis*, and the Asiatic representative of the British primrose, *Primula heterochroma*, from Iran. The mature part of the woodland was planted on one side of the base of a mound formed from silt dredged out of the area that was to become the Palm House Pond. On its top is the classical Temple of Aeolus, which was designed by Sir William Chambers and rebuilt here to the original design in 1845. In the grass which covers the slopes are many spring-flowering bulbs: snowdrops, daffodils and narcissus. The first cutting of the grass does not take place until

45

the foliage of these has died down so that for a period in summer these slopes can look untidy. Amongst the trees on the mound are several interesting magnolias, which flower in spring, and beside the grass path that meanders through the woodland garden there is a large black walnut (*Juglans nigra*). Growing parasitically on its roots is the toothwort *Lathraea clandestina*, which in April produces masses of bluish-mauve flowers immediately above the soil surface.

Tufa and Troughs

At the northern end of the Herbaceous Ground, near the former Alpine House and the Museum Store, is a paved area with a number of tiny sand beds in each of which is set a block of tufa. Tufa is a form of water-deposited lime; its hardness may vary but it is soft enough to be drilled easily. The holes so formed can take a small quantity of soil into which can be inserted seedlings, rooted cuttings or small plants. Once the soil has been colonized, plant roots begin to penetrate the tufa so as to obtain further nourishment. Tufa is porous and in periods of rain will absorb moisture. The sand beds in which the tufa is set are watered regularly during the summer months and from it the tufa can absorb this moisture. Although lime-loving plants are best suited to cultivation on tufa, many others that normally dislike alkaline conditions seem to grow well. The kinds of plant best suited to growing on tufa are those which grow slowly or are naturally small growers. One example is *Saxifraga grisebachii*, which is cultivated for the scarlet bracts it produces in April, and of which the Wisley form is considered to be the best. When planted on tufa both this cultivar and the species develop even more brightly coloured bracts.

A centrepiece on this paving is a large limestone horse-trough which has been filled with the same materials that are used for making a scree. A few pieces of tufa embedded in the scree material create a landscape in miniature. Into and between the tufa have been planted a number of tiny choice plants. One of these is the delightful *Paraquilegia anemonoides* from Kashmir, which has tiny bluish pendant lantern-like flowers that are produced in April above finely divided grey foliage.

Along two sides of this paved area and at the foot of the brick walls are narrow borders which provide growing space for climbers and a number of 'bulbous' plants. *Cyclamen africanum* and *C. graecum* flourish here, though usually considered unsuitable for growing out of doors as they are rather tender and flower poorly if they do not receive a thorough baking. From Mexico is *Zephyranthes grandiflora* which produces quite large, pink, trumpet-shaped flowers in summer. *Massonia pustulata*, a rare bulb from South Africa, is dormant in summer. It begins growth in early October, producing a pair of short, broad, strap-like blistered leaves. These lie flat on the ground and from between them develops a stemless spherical head of tiny white flowers, which may be pink in bud. This bulb, which flowers in November and December, seems hardy in this position for it has flowered regularly for a number of years. The genus *Massonia*, incidentally, was named after Francis Masson, who spent many years in South Africa collecting plants for Kew, having been landed there by Captain Cook in 1772.

To balance the first paved area there is a second one at the western end of the Museum Store, to the north-east of the Rock Garden, on which are two troughs made of hypertufa (cement in which peat is incorporated). In the larger trough is a collection of British mountain plants and the smaller contains a few New

46

The Rock Garden contains a very wide range of plants requiring well-drained conditions.

Opposite, top to bottom: in the screes, *Papaver rhaeticum*, better known as *P. alpinum*, freely seeds itself in colour forms from bright yellow to pale orange.

    Androsace foliosa, a stoloniferous plant from the Himalayas, is a distant relative of the primrose.

    The St John's Wort *Hypericum olympicum*, which is native to parts of Greece, has a dwarf form, shown here, that is often grown under the name *H. polyphyllum*.
Photos: T. A. Harwood, G. E. Nicholson, D. M. Joyce.

Above: damp soil beside the streams at the front of the rock outcrops is ideal for moisture-loving plants, which may include primulas, irises, monkey flowers and double king cups.
Photo: T. A. Harwood.

Right: wide gulleys simulating stony moraines and screes provide good conditions for deep-rooted plants of open habitats. In May the screes are gay with magenta *Geranium cinereum* var. *subcaulescens*, rose *Erodium guicciardii*, yellow *Genista sagittalis* and *Papaver rhaeticum*, and whitish *Aethionema pulchellum* and thyme.
Photo: T. A. Harwood.

47

The genus *Primula* has a large number of species, some of which are difficult to cultivate in the relatively dry conditions at Kew. None the less, there are representatives in the Rock Garden, the Alpine House and the Woodland Garden.

Seed of *Primula sikkimensis* was sent to Kew in 1850 by Joseph Hooker during his Himalayan expedition. (Today the plants in the Rock Garden and elsewhere at Kew are mainly of known provenance, many of the seeds having been gathered in the wild by members of the horticultural staff.) Plants of the species shown grow in the moist, semi-shaded beds at the foot of the Mound.
From *Curtis's Botanical Magazine* (1851, pl 4597), illustration by W. H. Fitch.

Zealand mountain daisies (*Celmisia* species), which have beautifully felted leaves. More tufa blocks are set into the brickwork for a further rich selection.

The Alpine House

A glasshouse to protect high mountain plants may seem a paradox. However, in nature plants from these high elevations are dormant and dry during winter under a permanent snow cover that provides protection against extreme cold and desiccating winds. Growth of these plants does not resume until most of the snow has melted in late spring, by which time night frosts, if they still occur, are light. In southern Britain it is rare in winter to have a snow cover and temperatures can fluctuate from many degrees of frost to well above freezing. Plants beginning to grow in mild spells may be damaged or even killed when severe frosts return. Plants have a greater tolerance of dry cold than wet cold. It is the damp in winter, a lot of rain, in association with cold that causes most plant damage. An alpine house, therefore, is intended to keep plants dry in winter. Mediterranean species and many bulbs also benefit from being kept dry in summer, and both these groups of plants need extra warmth at this season to flower well. An alpine house is unheated and ventilators are kept wide open at all times, being closed only during the severest weather or when foggy. Even without heat the glass can keep out 4.5°C of frost and so offer protection to precocious growth or flowers.

For many years at Kew there was a traditional alpine house towards the northern end of the Herbaceous Ground. The first house was built on this site in 1887, only five years after the Rock Garden was laid out, enlarged in 1891 and rebuilt with further extensions in 1936. It was a low structure with a ridge, side ventilation and an internal central path between parallel benches about one metre (3 ft) high and of the same width.

The new alpine house opened in 1981 is a complete contrast with the more traditional kind. It is situated beyond the Duchess Border to the west of the Jodrell Laboratory. As we see in Chapter 7, it resembles a cube with a pyramid on top and it is surrounded by a water-filled moat. Whereas the conventional way has been to grow and stage plants in pots or pans on glasshouse benches, within this house they are planted directly into the ground. The whole area has been landscaped so as to produce a rock garden built of Sussex sandstone under a glass cover where visitors can walk protected from adverse weather conditions, especially in winter and early spring. There is a waterfall which takes water by means of a short stream into a pond. Around its edge the soil is permanently moist and has been planted up with those plants that revel in a soil that never dries out. Members of the family Restionaceae need such conditions – species of the genus *Restio* tend to replace grasses, which they resemble, at high elevations in Tasmania; from that island can be seen the graceful *R. tetraphyllus*. Another monocotyledon, also from Tasmania, is *Xyris muelleri*, which has twisted iris-like leaves and in June produces yellow flowers with three fringed petals opening in succession at ten each morning but fading to white and shrivelling by four in the afternoon. Growing between the rocks that form the waterfall are ferns and a Japanese gesneriad *Conandron ramondioides*, which produces masses of bluish-purple flowers for a long period in summer.

There are other areas in the house to cater for plants with special requirements. A contrast to the first is one for dry-loving plants: here are a few high-latitude cacti from North America, such as *Escobaria vivipara*. Somewhat

The new Alpine House, opened in 1981, incorporates unusual features in its design. Numerous automatically operated ventilators are included in its pyramidal roof and it is surrounded by a water-filled moat. Photo: J.B.E. Simmons.

similar are two for scree plants, on one *Cotula atrata* from New Zealand can be seen. A small gulley has been modified for the growing of peat-loving plants and among the species growing here is *Primula modesta* var. *fauriei* from Japan. Another scree provides for lime-lovers (calcicoles) such as the spectacular *Saxifraga longifolia* of southern Europe.

The dominant feature of this house is a large rectangular bench which has high sides. During construction coolant pipes were attached to the base and covered with about 30 cm (12 in) of sand into which potted plants are plunged. There are two sections: one maintained at 0–9°C and the other at 5–21°C.

The former and smaller section is used for the cultivation of Arctic alpines, a difficult group of plants to grow successfully. For six months of the year plants in arctic regions are dormant under a snow cover. When the snow melts, growth has to be rapid so that flowering and seed ripening is complete before plants die down again. Pioneering work with this group of plants took place at the Botanic Garden in Copenhagen in an insulated glasshouse with a refrigerated basement in which plants were stored during the winter. At Kew plants are transferred to a cold store in late October and brought back into the house in May. Above the bench is a bank of lights connected to a time control so that it is possible to increase day length and produce a night of no more than one hour of darkness. Trials are still being carried out with plants from Iceland, Greenland and the Antarctic fringes. Success has been achieved in bringing to flowering *Primula scandinavica*, which is somewhat similar in appearance to the Scottish primrose, *P. scotica*, which is also grown here.

The larger section of the bench was intended for the cultivation of another difficult group of plants, those from mountains along the equator. From Mount Elgon, Kenya, at 3300 metres (11 000 ft) comes *Lobelia lindblomii* which is prostrate and has tiny blue flowers, and from Mount Kenya is the giant species *L. sattimae*, which can reach 3 metres (10 ft) in height. *Calceolaria darwinii* comes from mountains far from the equator in Chile and Patagonia. This tiny plant, which has large pouched flowers and bizarre colouring, can, with care and patience, be cultivated outside in the rock or peat garden – on this refrigerated bench, however, it flowers more profusely. The Iranian *Dionysia curviflora*, although one of the easiest and longest cultivated species in this specialist group of plants, has often proved to be difficult to flower in cultivation. On this bench, with its controlled soil temperatures, there has been a profusion of pink flowers on these cushion plants. It has long been suggested

49

Opposite, top and bottom left: the interior of the Alpine House is landscaped to include a small waterfall, pool and bog. A choice collection of unusual species is planted in the screes inside the Alpine House. There are acid and alkaline screes, and an area for xerophytic mountain plants.
Photos: F.N.Hepper.

Right, top: the Mexican *Phlox mesoleuca* has a range of colour forms, including one which is a brilliant red. It is one of the species planted in the bank at the southern entrance to the Alpine House.
Photo: F.N.Hepper.

Right, bottom: a feature of the Alpine House is the refrigerated bench, which has two sections providing controlled soil temperatures. One section is for arctic alpines, while the other accommodates plants from mountains in the tropics such as *Espeletia schultesii*, a giant member of the Compositae with felted leaves, which comes from Venezuela.
Photo: F.N.Hepper.

Opposite, bottom right: in front of the Jodrell Laboratory are two high standing frames in which are planted groups of *Iris* requiring warmth and dryness during their dormant season. One frame is planted up with section Juno, including *Iris aucheri*, and the other with Oncocyclus, Regelia and their hybrids.
Photo: M.Svanderlik.

A changing selection of interesting plants, generally in flower, is shown in a special display shelf in the Alpine House.
Photo: T. A. Harwood.

that the reason why this plant so often failed to flower in cultivation is that the cushion is not subject to complete dormancy in the winter. The common factor which has produced success in such widely differing plants is a soil temperature in which there is a reduced fluctuation between day or night or at different seasons of the year.

The Surrounds of the Alpine House

Landscaping extends outside the house. Rock banks have been built up against the sides of the moat. In soil pockets there have been numerous plantings of recent introductions from many parts of the world. Extremely brilliant are some of the colour forms of *Phlox mesoleuca* from Mexico: one is a rather ordinary pink, another is a bright yellow and yet another is tomato red. *Campanula lasiocarpa* comes from North America and Japan but the plant here from the latter country is much neater and produces rather larger bluish flowers than the usual form seen in cultivation. Another species which is confined to the Olympic Mountains of Washington State just south of the Canadian border is *C. piperi*. In nature this is a crevice plant and here it has been planted to grow between rocks.

Around three sides of the Alpine House are high brick walls, which isolate it from the older glasshouses in the area not open to the public. At the base of these walls have been constructed a number of beds and borders. Planted here are climbers, which will break the harshness of the walls and absorb some of the reflected heat. There are two species of *Hydrangea* – the deciduous *H. petiolaris* from Japan, and, from Mexico, *H. seemannii*, which is evergreen. In addition, there is *Acacia pataczekii*, a recently discovered Tasmanian species. It is a non-climber planted against the wall, which it is hoped will provide sufficient protection to allow for successful cultivation out of doors.

The shaded north and west banks have been planted almost entirely with plants requiring moist summer soil conditions. Such conditions are difficult to produce at Kew because of low summer rainfall and a light sandy soil. Terraced banks of peat blocks have been constructed with controlled overhead misting, which allows cultivation of a wide range of smaller woodland species and peat lovers. Popular families, such as Liliaceae, Gentianaceae, Primulaceae and Ericaceae, are well represented.

To accommodate an increasing collection of Japanese woodland and mountain plants, a new peat garden has been built in front of the Alpine House in the shade provided by the Jodrell Laboratory. Whereas the stepped beds behind the house are formal, the lay-out in front is more interesting as it is more informal.

On the paved area to the east of the Alpine House and sheltered on two sides by the brick walls are several stone sinks and troughs in which miniature landscapes have been created with tufa and sandstone. Here are grown some tiny plants that would otherwise be swamped by stronger species if grown together.

The new Alpine House and the plantings associated with it have required considerable specialist attention and enormous propagation and nursery support facilities. The happy result has been the cultivation and display of an exceptional range of unusual, fascinating and beautiful plants, which have attracted many enthusiasts to Kew.

B.H.

✤6✤
The Herbaceous Ground
A Plantsman's Garden

The Herbaceous Ground is a part of Kew that reminds us of a teaching physic garden of previous centuries. This garden, of particular interest to the botanist, student and plant enthusiast, lies in the north-east corner tucked between the Rock Garden and Kew Road.

In the sixteenth century the then new botanic gardens were founded especially for teaching medical students the appearance of the plants used as medicine – hence the name physic garden or *hortus medicus*. Numerous small beds with narrow paths between them facilitated demonstration of the herbs. It is still possible to see this type of layout in its original form in some European gardens, such as at Padua in Italy and in Linnaeus's Swedish garden at Uppsala. Nowadays most botanical gardens possess an area where the plants are grouped together as collections, although usually to demonstrate the relationships between plants and not to show their medicinal properties.

The Herbaceous Ground at Kew was formerly used as a royal vegetable and fruit garden, but in 1847 a number of cross walls were swept away and the area was incorporated into the Royal Botanic Gardens. At that time there seem to have been various ideas as to how the area should be developed. In the Kew Archives there is a plan prepared by Decimus Burton, dated 1847, showing a design for a parterre. Instead, a number of collections of herbaceous plants were brought together and arranged there in beds. Between 1866 and 1870, while the Cumberland Gate and its approach roads were under construction, some rearrangement of the ground took place. During this time the rectangular beds were laid out as they are at present on either side of a central path and planted up according to the nineteenth-century Bentham and Hooker system of classification, devised by George Bentham, an eminent botanist who worked in the Herbarium, and Joseph Hooker, the second Director of Kew; this system was also used for the arrangement of the Herbarium. The system has undergone certain modifications as the concept of the relationships in some plant families has changed. For example, Geraniaceae is now split into three separate families, Geraniaceae, Oxalidaceae and Balsaminaceae. In the nineteenth century plant families were known as natural orders, which explains an alternative name, Order Beds, still sometimes used for the Herbaceous Ground.

Generally there is one family to a bed, although the largest, Compositae, takes up thirty beds, while small families – such as Violaceae, Capparaceae and Resedaceae – share a single bed. With the possible exception of the Rock Garden, there is a greater concentration of plants here than anywhere else out-of-doors at Kew. Although there is always something of interest, these beds are at their most colourful in summer.

The representation of monocotyledonous families is minimal, with only the

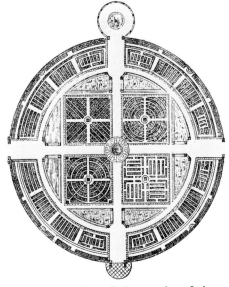

The physic garden at Padua, northern Italy, which dates from 1545, vies with that at Piza as the earliest of all botanic gardens. The plan shows a concentric arrangement of narrow beds, in which were planted medicinal herbs used by physicians of the day. Student physicians were instructed in the medicinal properties of plants and the differences between them.

Several thousand species are grown in the Herbaceous Ground, where the arrangement of plant families follows the Bentham and Hooker sequence. In June a scarlet oriental poppy (*Papaver bracteatum*) and large plants of the white-flowered sea-kale (*Crambe cordifolia*) are conspicuous (right). The Rose Pergola bisects the Ground and the Jodrell Laboratory lies at the furthest end.
Photo: F.N.Hepper.

In the Herbaceous Ground, the legume family (Leguminosae) is well represented by species in many genera. *Lathyrus grandiflorus* (bottom, left) an annual climber from southern Europe, is related to the sweet pea. A dwarf lupin, *Lupinus nanus* (bottom, right), is a native of California.
Photos: G.Lewis

sedges and rushes at the southern end of the ground. This is because there are extensive collections of grasses and bulbs in other parts of Kew, as we shall see. But in the borders on either side of the western boundary wall, between the Herbaceous Ground and the Rock Garden, there are onions, day-lilies, narcissi and other representatives of these families.

The central path which leads right through the Herbaceous Ground from the Woodland Garden to the Jodrell Laboratory passes under a pergola. The uprights and cross-members of this structure support a collection of vigorous climbing roses such as 'Easlea's Golden Rambler', 'Albertine', 'Chaplin's Pink' and 'Meg'. To extend the flowering season and to give some variety, a number of strong-growing species of *Clematis* have been introduced. One which catches the eye in late summer is *Clematis tangutica*, which has pendant, lantern-shaped, yellow flowers; when these fade they are gradually replaced with fluffy seed heads, which carry the display into winter.

The walls around three sides of the ground also provide support for climbing plants, while south- and west-facing walls give protection for some tender plants. On the shady eastern boundary wall is a collection of ivies, mainly cultivars of *Hedera helix*, which were planted during the decade between 1920 and 1930. One of the plants which can be seen on the western wall is the well known sweetly scented white-flowered common jasmine (*Jasminum officinale*). A climber which is grown for its colourful foliage is *Actinidia kolomikta*; the leaves are heart-shaped, half white and half green, the whole being suffused with pink. In one of the borders a viciously spiny Chinese quince (*Cydonia cathayensis*) has been trained against the wall. It produces very large greenish fruits that change to yellow as they ripen, perfuming the air with a delicious fragrance. A rather tender variety is the vigorous climber *Isotrema griffithii* from Nepal – in late May, as its new leaves are unfurling, it produces a few, very large, dark-brown, velvety flowers reminiscent of those of the warm glasshouse climber *Aristolochia elegans*, sometimes popularly known as Dutchman's pipe.

The maintenance of the Herbaceous Ground is labour intensive. Every year during the winter the beds are dug, compost and manure being incorporated to help maintain fertility and moisture in the poor soil inherited at Kew. With the onset of spring the sowing of tender annuals takes place under glass, although many of the hardier ones are sown outside in April. As the annuals and perennials begin to grow support is provided by brushwood which is inserted amongst the developing stems and by flowering time will scarcely be seen.

Springtime warmth sees not only the growth of the desired species but of those unwanted ones commonly called 'weeds'. In a garden such as this of cultivated wild plants, the horticultural staff must know the differences between those that are wanted and those that are not, and this takes specialist knowledge and experience.

Seed-collecting takes place from early summer to late autumn and demands keen observation to ensure correct timing of each species in order to gather adequate quantities of well-ripened seeds. This is particularly difficult given the vagaries of the British weather and the intricate dispersal mechanisms of many species (see Chapter 9). Naming and correct labelling of the collection are other matters which demand special attention and present particular problems in order that the Herbaceous Ground may be of the greatest use to visiting plantsmen.

Among other members of the legume family grown in the Herbaceous Ground are *Vicia villosa* var. *varia* (top), which is widespread in continental Europe, and *Hedysarum coronarium* (bottom). The latter has been in cultivation as an ornamental in Britain, where it is known as Italian sainfoin, for at least 300 years. In its native region, the Mediterranean, it is grown for fodder, making fields conspicuously red when in flower.
Photos: G. Lewis and F. N. Hepper.

Massive clumps and graceful inflorescences of pampas grass (*Cortaderia selloana*) are seen at their best at Kew where they have ample space. The plant was introduced into Europe from South America, where it is sometimes cultivated for the manufacture of paper. Although there is a difference in the spelling of the epithet, this species was named after Friderich Sellow (1789–1831), a German who collected plants in Brazil and Uruguay. Photo: F. N. Hepper.

The Grass Garden

The Grass Garden, which is an extension of the Herbaceous Ground, is to be found to the north of the Rock Garden on the site of the former Iris Garden. The layout is formal, with a statue of The Sower sculpted by Sir Hamo Thorneycroft RA in 1886, as a focal point, and planted up only with representatives of the grass family (Gramineae). The intention of this garden is to display scientific, educational and decorative grasses important to agriculture and horticulture. The beds contain an extensive collection of wild grasses from the five continents—at one extreme of size there is the giant *Miscanthus japonicus*, which can reach two metres (80 in), while the sand bent (*Mibora minima*), a native British species, may be only a few centimentres (*c.* 1 in) high.

Two long beds are used to exhibit cereals. In one are those from cool temperate regions—such as wheat, barley, rye and oats—while in the other are the sub-tropical cereals—maize, millet and sorghum. Included with the temperate cereals are some of the primitive forms of wheat, such as emmer, with a collection of cultivars ranging from those of the last century to those of the present day. Both winter and spring wheats are grown and there is a season of about eight weeks in late summer and early autumn when the ripening ears can be appreciated. At this season the beds have to be netted to protect the grain from birds, which would otherwise wreak havoc among the cereals.

Nearby is a series of small brick-lined beds to display lawn grasses. These are of two sizes. In the larger are commercial lawn grass mixtures for special purposes, such as cricket pitches, tennis courts, bowling greens and private gardens. In the smaller are some of the individual grasses that these mixtures contain.

Another bed containing an educational display is composed of British grasses from various habitats: heaths, moorland, chalk downs, coast, woodland and cultivation. Since the grass family is very large, it is divided up for convenience into a number of sub-families and tribes, with some representatives of each being grown.

56

Although mention has been made of the botanical and educational aspects of the Grass Garden, nothing has been said about the ornamental value of grasses. Apart from pampas grass, usually *Cortaderia selloana*, grasses are rarely considered as having beauty in their own right. Whereas pampas and other strongly growing grasses, such as *Stipa gigantea*, need plenty of space and are best on their own as specimen plants, others can be used in the same way as more conventional foliage or flowering plants. The blue-leaved fescue (*Festuca glauca*) looks well when used in bedding with a pink-flowered form of *Begonia cucullata* (*semperflorens*), while maize (*Zea mays*), either green or variegated, can be used as a dot plant. Interest can be introduced into a mixed border by using grasses with coloured foliage. Red switch grass (*Panicum virgatum* 'Rubrum') has reddish foliage, while in Bowles' golden grass (*Millium effusum* 'Aureum') the gold colour of spring fades during the summer. Several have variegated foliage. *Phalaris arundinacea* 'Picta', gardener's garters, has white margins and reaches at least a metre in height (40 in) and is suited to the back of a border. In striped sweet meadow grass (*Glyceria maxima* 'Variegata') the variegation is cream and, when young, the leaves are suffused with purple. Although in nature this is a grass of wet places, it is equally at home where the soil is dry, and in such conditions is less rampant. For the front of a border a suitable one is *Hakonechloa macra* 'Aureola', which is small and has beautiful golden variegation.

Amongst those with attractive flowers is the silky, silvery haresfoot grass (*Lagurus ovatus*), which can reach knee height. Squirrel-tail grass (*Hordeum jubatum*), which is not so tall, produces barley-like heads. *Pennisetum orientale* is a smaller grass, in which the flowers are a mauve-pink and fluffy.

Probably the best known of grasses grown for its ornamental seeds is the greater quaking grass (*Briza maxima*). This is often gathered from the garden for use in dried-flower arrangements. The most unusual grass must be Job's tears (*Coix lachryma-jobi*), which has blue-brown bead-like fruits, often threaded for necklaces. *Zea mays*, besides providing the grain maize or sweet corn, has ornamental foliaged cultivars and others in which there is a whole range of coloured cobs.

We can see that grasses can be ornamental and have many uses in the garden. Whilst all the grasses mentioned are displayed in the Grass Garden, some of the uses to which they can be put can be seen in the bedding or amongst herbaceous plants in the Duke's Garden.

Special attention must be paid to the maintenance of the Grass Garden. In autumn, after the cereals have been harvested, the beds are cleared and dug over, copious quantities of organic matter being incorporated. Afterwards, the soil is trodden firm, raked and sowings made of winter wheats and barley. The remaining cereals, as well as spring wheats and barley, are sown in March. The sub-tropical cereals are raised under glass and planted out in May, when danger of frost is past.

A serious problem among the species and ornamental grasses is the large number of self-sown seedlings. It is a difficult job to distinguish the seedlings of accidental germination from those of desired species. The effort, however, is necessary for the Grass Garden demonstrates to the public something of the vital importance of grasses to mankind as fodder and human food, as well as the botanical diversity of this large and interesting family.

B.H.

57

The greater quaking grass (*Briza maxima*), well known to dried-flower arrangers, is an annual from the Mediterranean region and naturalized in some parts of Britain. It is easily cultivated in open, warm situations and, once established, seeds itself. This grass is recorded as grown in London gardens in 1633.

The illustration is taken from a hand-coloured engraving in *Curtis's Botanical Magazine* (1796, pl 357), which is the oldest surviving coloured illustrated journal. The first volume appeared in 1787. The publication illustrates plants of botanical interest and horticultural merit as a means of introducing them to gardeners. It was founded and edited by William Curtis and has long been associated with Kew. Sir William Hooker was its editor for nearly forty years and an illustration of the Palm House decorates the cover. It is published by the Bentham-Moxom Trust and is still prepared at Kew.

❖7❖
The Development of Greenhouses at Kew

The tender collections at Kew include plants introduced from most regions of the warm temperate, subtropical and tropical parts of the world. The great diversity of plant life discovered on the early voyages of exploration gave a huge stimulus to the development of exotic collections in Europe. Hence Kew's greenhouse collections, formed over the past two centuries, have evolved largely under the twin spurs of plant introduction and the technical development of the plant house.

The greenhouses at Kew provide a wide range of environments for their floral inhabitants. Plants from the tropics to the arctic, from rain forest to desert and from salt flat to mountain top—all have a place at Kew. To provide for this diversity of requirements the collections are broadly divided into two main groups, herbaceous and woody, with the latter occupying the larger structures. The further subdivision, by natural relationships, geographic affinity, or environmental need, is detailed in Chapter 8.

The First Greenhouses

In the late seventeenth century there were greenhouses in the area of the present Gardens at Kew in the once famous gardens of Sir Henry Capel (later Lord Capel of Tewkesbury) and Sir William Temple (the latter located at West Shene in what is now the Old Deer Park). Although nothing now remains of these structures there are some contemporary accounts that help us return over three centuries to the time when 'noblemen and gentlemen of taste' saw the orangery and greenhouse as important additions to their houses.

According to his *Diary*, John Evelyn visited Kew on 24 March 1688 and wrote, 'From whence we went to Kew to visit Sir Henry Capel's whose orangery and myrtetum are most beautiful and perfectly well kept. He was contriving very high palisades of reeds to shade his oranges during the summer and painting those reeds in oil.'

John Gibson in his descriptively titled paper *A short Account of several Gardens near London, with remarks on some particulars wherein they excel or are deficient, upon a View of them in December 1691*, describes several aspects of Sir Henry Capel's garden and notes: 'His two lentiscus trees (for which he paid forty pounds to Versprit) are said to be the best in England, not only of their kind, but of greens.' These trees were the mastic tree (*Pistacia lentiscus*).

Gibson also comments on Sir William Temple's garden nearby (then in decline) and of his greenhouse says 'but his greens that are remaining (being as good a stock as most greenhouses have) are very fresh and thriving, the room they stand in suiting well with them and being well contrived, if it be no defect in it that the floor is a foot at least within the ground'.

Since the engagement of William Aiton in 1759 to found the botanic Garden

Opposite: although nearly a century and a half has elapsed since the giant waterlily (*Victoria amazonica*) first flowered at Kew, it is still a major attraction for visitors. Ever since 1850, plants have been raised annually from seed, which are kept from one season to the next in tubes of water to prevent drying out. Seeds of wild plants were originally brought from Guyana by Robert Schomburgk in 1837 but the first successful introduction came a decade later. For many years the plant was known as *Victoria regia*, after Queen Victoria, but according to the rules of priority in naming it should be called *V. amazonica*.

Walter Hood Fitch (1817–92) was the only botanical artist at Kew for over forty years. He worked for a meagre salary and no guaranteed pension but his output was prodigious and his accuracy unerring. His magnificent hand-coloured lithographs of the giant waterlily, published in a folio entitled *Victoria Regia* (1851), helped earn him the award of an annual pension of £100.

Popular interest in Kew as a botanic garden with strange plants started soon after its foundation. Of special interest were the greenhouse plants, as shown by the engraving in the *Illustrated London News* of 17 October 1846. The outsize cactus *Echinocactus platyacanthus* (*ingens*) was then known as *E. visnaga* – the epithet being Mexican for toothpick. The cactus weighed a ton, yet it had been hauled across rough desert country from San Luis Potosi to the Mexican coast for presentation to Kew by Frederick Staines.

Opposite: taken in 1846, when photography was still in its infancy, this picture of the interior of the Palm House under construction (bottom) includes, it is thought, the figures of Decimus Burton, the designer, and Richard Turner, the engineer.

A detail of the Palm House (top) shows the delicacy of its structure and glazing.
Photo: M. Svanderlik.

at Kew which was laid out in 1760, many plant houses of historic importance have been erected and preserved. The oldest remaining of these is the Orangery. Orangeries were very much a seventeenth-century concept, as already indicated, in which prized 'foreign greens' such as bay, myrtle, rosemary, and citrus (oranges and lemons) could be overwintered. Plants which retained their leaves during the winter when all else in the garden was withered or dead had long been regarded as symbols of undying life, and thus foreign evergreens of economic use became particularly important. Incidentally, the words 'greenhouse' and 'conservatory' appear to be of seventeenth-century origin and are both credited to the writer John Evelyn. The greenhouse was where greens could be kept during the winter, and the conservatory where they were 'conserved' from frost. To that extent they were synonymous, as they are today, although their usage has changed with the changed purpose of plant houses – the greenhouse generally being the structure in which plants are raised for the home and garden, and the conservatory the one in which they are displayed. This, of course, is further confused by use of the word glasshouse as usually applied to the structure operated by commercial growers – but what now, as plastic replaces glass?

The present Orangery at Kew was not constructed until 1761, making it a rather late example. It is however a splendid building whose neo-classical façade lends distinction to the surrounding grounds. It was designed by Sir William Chambers for Princess Augusta, the Dowager Princess of Wales, and consists of a large main south-facing room measuring approximately 43 by 9 metres and 7.6 metres high (142 by 30 by 25 ft) with a run of narrow lean-to service rooms at the rear. Originally it was heated by means of hot-air flues built into the floor and rear wall but this was later replaced by a conventional hot-water system. Unfortunately oranges and lemons cannot now be maintained in this building since the moisture required for their well-being is not compatible with the preservation of the building – the citrus plants were removed in 1972 after a partial collapse of the ceiling.

Nowadays the word 'stove' is little used, except perhaps by gardeners trained before the Second World War. Originally it was a greenhouse heated by a stove, as opposed to unheated, 'for such foreign greens that need continuous warmth'. The Great Stove at Kew, in its day the largest hot-house in Britain, also designed by Chambers in 1761 for Princess Augusta, is, alas, no longer with us. The site of this lean-to greenhouse, 34.7 metres (114 ft) long, is marked by the Wisteria Cage which can be seen across the lawn from the Orangery, near the Colour Clump. The aged specimen of *Encephalartos longifolius*, which was collected in South Africa by Masson and now inhabits the south wing of the Palm House, is thought to have been housed in the Great Stove from 1777 until its later transference to its present home.

The architectural conservatory was very much an early-nineteenth-century development. The oldest of such structures at Kew is House No. 1 (The Aroid House) designed in 1825 by John Nash for the reconstructed Buckingham Palace. The whole conservatory was actually moved piecemeal from the Palace to its present site in 1836 on the instruction of William IV and modified by Sir Jeffry Wyatville. Curiously, its solid masonry north wall was retained – a heat-saving, but light-reducing feature of earlier south-facing greenhouses and orangeries.

This house, though first used for tropical plants, was given over after the construction of the Palm House (1848) to the cultivation of sub-tropical and temperate trees and shrubs. Then again after the construction of the first part of the Temperate House (1862) it reverted to tropical plants – though this time, and since, to shade-loving rain forest plants, predominantly of the family *Araceae*. This rather heavily structured house has proved well suited to this purpose and the huge leaved anthuriums and philodendrons create a very tropical effect.

The Palm House

The beautifully proportioned Palm House, with its curvilinear structure of iron and glass, is a classic of its time. Designed by the architect Decimus Burton, in conjunction with and strongly influenced by the engineer Richard Turner, and constructed between 1844 and 1848, it has scarcely, in function, been surpassed by any modern conservatory. Standing on a raised terrace, formed of sand and gravel taken from the lake site at Kew, it appears much larger than its actual dimensions. It covers a ground area of 2248 square metres (24 200 square ft), larger than the once famous but now demolished palm house at Chatsworth but, surprisingly perhaps, only approximately half the area of the Temperate House.

It was constructed at a time when technology was advancing rapidly. Hot-water heating systems and hinged high-level ventilators gave much improved temperature control; new construction methods in the use of iron and also the availability of good quality sheet glass (from 1833), from which also a previously prohibitive tax was removed in 1845, collectively stimulated the development of the conservatory.

Unfortunately, the fear of sun-scorch on leaves resulted in the Palm House

Evening light behind the Palm House makes it appear like a gigantic glass bubble in which are silhouetted palms and other tropical plants. Photo: M. Lear.

The cross bars of the wings of the Palm House were designed to give structural rigidity and an ornamental pattern. The wing illustrated contains the cycad collection. Photo: L. Sullivan.

being glazed with a yellowish-green glass, tinted by the inclusion of copper oxide. The main part of the Temperate House was also similarly glazed and the use of this material was not abandoned until the end of the nineteenth century with a resultant improvement in growth of the plants, and even then a few green panes remained in the Palm House until it underwent major repair in 1956–8.

The main disadvantage of an iron and glass construction is the different rates of expansion of these two materials, which leads the putty holding the glass to crack and fall away with consequent corrosion. The ironwork itself is also susceptible to rusting in the humid conditions created for the plants. In practice it proved difficult to hold a minimum temperature of 16°C during winter in the centre section, which restricted slightly the range of plants that could be grown, particularly tropical palms. However, since the construction of the new boiler house with oil-fired (now gas) burners in the early 1960s the range has increased and even quite common plants not previously grown, such as the coconut and African baobab tree (*Adansonia*), can now be seen luxuriating within.

The new boiler house is situated near the Italian Campanile, designed by Burton, and the hot-water heating mains are carried in the underground tunnel, between the Campanile and Palm House, that was once used to carry trucks of coke to the boilers situated under the house. The Campanile was intended both as a water tower and flue for the boilers. Flue pipes, running above the walk-through tunnel, were intended to draw off the waste gases from the boilers. Not surprisingly, the scheme was unsuccessful and was replaced by

The Waterlily House (No. 15) was originally designed by Richard Turner to accommodate the *Victoria* waterlily, which was later transferred to another house. Today tropical *Nymphaea* species and cultivars are grown in it, together with the sacred lotus (*Nelumbo nucifera*), papyrus (*Cyperus papyrus*) and many tropical plants of economic importance. Horticultural diploma students in training gain experience by working in each section. Photo: T. A. Harwood.

two chimneys, one for each boiler house, exhausting through the ridge of each wing. These were removed after the construction of the new remote boiler house. The old subterranean boiler houses, when originally constructed, were subject to quite serious and frequent flooding, since they were below the level of the Pond.

Despite its problems this structure has provided excellent conditions for a wide range of plants, most notably the priceless collection of cycads – the plant world's equivalent of dinosaurs. Other collections include the true palms (Palmae) (p 78), the screw pines (*Pandanus*), the ginger family (Zingiberaceae), economic plants such as banana, coffee and cocoa (p 133) and many other tropical trees, shrubs and climbers (p 82).

The Waterlily House (No. 15), situated at the north end of the Palm House, was designed by Richard Turner and constructed in 1852. The roof glazing pattern and ventilators have subsequently been altered (1965), but it still remains a delightful house and it is interesting to compare it with the Australian House built a century later. The iron frame members are original, and worthy of note is the inclusion of light ornate reinforcing rings in the trusses. Originally intended for the giant Amazon waterlily (*Victoria amazonica*), the pool is now used for a collection of *Nymphaea* species and hybrids, some other aquatics such as the sacred lotus (*Nelumbo nucifera*), the original stock of which was introduced to Kew by Sir Joseph Banks in 1784, papyrus (*Cyperus papyrus*) and a collection of climbing cucurbits – this family, Cucurbitaceae, includes several important economics such as the melon, cucumber, bottle gourd and luffa.

63

The Temperate House

Although the largest greenhouse at Kew, covering 5209 square metres (48 392 square ft), the Temperate House has always had a Cinderella-like role – lost, as it were, to many visitors because it is sited in the depths of the Arboretum. Sir William Hooker reasoned that since its contents would be of the same character as those of the Arboretum then that is where it should be located. Perhaps it is of such personal idiosyncrasies that great gardens are made.

It was intended to house plants of borderline hardiness whose blossoms could be damaged by spring frosts – the 'winter garden' concept – and for a wide range of warm-temperate trees and shrubs from southern Africa, Australia, Asia, Chile, southern Europe and New Zealand that had been gathered together at Kew. Later its use was extended, in the South Wing, to include subtropical trees and shrubs. Since its reconstruction (official re-opening in May 1982), it can, for the first time, be seen more nearly as its architect intended, and perhaps it will also now become more widely appreciated.

In his original specification Sir William Hooker asked for a house providing maximum ventilation by means of wooden sashes which could be repaired easily by the Gardens staff. The design was undertaken by Decimus Burton, who styled the continuous ornamental masonry façade with stuccoed piers topped with urns, and featured a roof of straight rafts 'necessarily adapted' to allow the roof to be uncovered during the summer. An 'ingenious apparatus' of a wheel and screw power was designed by the contractor's engineer to allow the three upper tiers of sliding roof sashes to pass over one another to stack on the lowest (fourth) tier. Unfortunately this latter did not prove very effective;

The Temperate House was designed by Decimus Burton. This illustration from *The Builder* of 12 January 1861 proved to be a somewhat optimistic projection as construction, described there as 'now in progress', continued with several hiccups due to financial constraints until the end of the century.

presumably the wooden sashes swelled and stuck within the iron frame. Eventually, between 1936 and 1939, during necessary re-roofing repairs, three runs of continuous hinged ventilators were added to the lower roof, leaving the main roof virtually unventilated above the gallery until its reconstruction in 1980.

Commenced in 1860, the first phase consisted of the Octagons (completed in 1861) and the Main Block (1862). The foundations of the two Wings were also laid out, but money for their completion was not forthcoming and it was not until the end of the century that the Wings (South 1897, North 1898) were completed, during the directorship of Sir William Thiselton-Dyer. The whole building thus opened to the public in 1899, some thirty-nine years after the scheme was initiated.

Not only did the house suffer from an unusually protracted period of construction, it also had a number of functional problems, other than ventilation. The heavy structure of the Main Block, orientated as it is approximately north/south, allowed very little light to penetrate in winter, severely limiting the range of plants that could be grown. The Octagons, with boilers beneath, became too hot and dry at times, since the four chimneys in each Octagon were built into the supporting piers. The chimneys were very low and allowed the waste products of fuel combustion to be deposited back on the glass, which became blackened. This further loss of transmitted light meant that little else but conifers could be grown in the North Octagon, with some conservatory pot plants brought in when in flower. Such bringing in of a regular supply of replacement plants in flower even extended to the Main Block and South Octagon. The rain water supply also proved insufficient for dry periods, and was made worse by many of the down collection pipes becoming blocked. A new ring main was installed in 1966 to link together the six large eighteen thousand gallon underground storage tanks, so as to make better use of the supply.

Most of these problems have been resolved in the recent reconstruction. One seeming reverse is the return to a narrow glazing-bar spacing (the pattern having been altered during both the phases of construction and re-roofing) but by the use of a new specifically designed aluminium alloy bar, of which 16km (10 miles) was required, light obstruction has been reduced and maintenance minimized. New ventilators have been formed which operate automatically. A new boiler house, in the nearby Stable Yard, with three large efficient boilers, has replaced the eight Octagon basement boilers making it possible to use the Octagons above for collections as originally intended. Spiral stairs have made the two basements accessible from inside the house, the south basement having been converted for equipment storage and staff use, replacing the internal and external sheds, and the north to a display area for public use.

During dry spells the rain-water tanks can be topped up by a small deionization plant which treats the chlorinated alkaline mains water since it would otherwise be lethal to many of the plants in the collection. Other new features, such as the removal of the unsightly banks of heating pipes, fitting a high-level heating coil in the Main Block, bird proofing, providing high-level (cat-walk) access, gallery renovation, the replacement of the side benches with beds, recontouring the Terrace and laying a paved path, all make their contribution to both the economy of operating the house and the enjoyment of visitors.

Completed now in one style, with all the façade urns added as originally

The Kashmir cypress (*Cupressus cashmeriana*) is cultivated in the Temperate House, as are other tender conifers, including *Araucaria* and species of the Southern Hemisphere genera *Callitris*, *Dacrydium*, *Podocarpus* and *Widdringtonia*.

Above: the magnificently refurbished Temperate House, photographed here from the top of the flagstaff, glistens in the sun. The north-south alignment and the sooty deposits on the glass reduced illumination to an extent that limited the range of plants that could thrive there. The rebuilding, including the re-siting of the boilers, has greatly improved the growing conditions.
Photo: R. Howard and T. A. Harwood.

Left: since the reconstruction of the Temperate House, the interior landscaping and path layout have been reorganized and new plantings made.
Photo: T. A. Harwood.

Above: the Canary Island House displays many plants endemic to those islands, including the dragon tree (*Dracaena draco*), and species of *Echium* and *Aeonium*.
Photo: F. N. Hepper.

Above, right: the Australian House, built of aluminium in 1952, becomes yellow with flowering wattles (*Acacia*) in early spring.
Photo: T. A. Harwood.

Right: the Sherman Hoyt diorama represents the Californian Mojave Desert and contains succulent plants from the southern part of the United States and Mexico, such as prickly pears (*Opuntia*), mammillarias, agaves and *Yucca aloifolia*.
Photo: J. B. E. Simmons.

The Chilean wine palm (*Jubaea chilensis*) was raised in 1846 from seed collected in Chile by Thomas Bridges and transferred from the Palm House to the Temperate House in 1860. Photo: S. W. Rawlings.

intended, the building, as already suggested, approaches more closely than ever its designer's original architectural concept and with improved growing conditions the collections will now also achieve Kew's original aim. Within the house the plants have been arranged phytogeographically, making use of the natural variations in microclimate now produced by the structure, with the addition of traditional features, such as some sub-tropical crop plants.

Prior to reconstruction the collection held in the Australian and Temperate Houses amounted to nearly 3000 species and varieties. Very few could be retained *in situ*, for example, the giant Chilean wine palm (*Jubaea chilensis*). This plant and a few large companions were shrouded in polythene to survive without heat – or a roof – the severe winter of 1978–9. Most of the collection was repropagated and the progeny are now well on the way to re-establishing the splendour of this house, in its time the largest in the world and one of the marvels of the Victorian age of gardening.

The Small Collection Houses

Returning to the site of the Great Stove, there were, by the time the Palm House was constructed, a number of small greenhouses which had been erected after 1761 to house the Botanic Garden's expanding collections, and especially the exciting plant discoveries from the newly developing settlements in Australia and South Africa. Having little to recommend them architecturally, these houses have been regularly replaced and extended. Their contents, however, comprise some of the richest and most interesting collections at Kew.

Dr Lindley's Report undertaken in 1838 lists the greenhouses on this site, which then consisted of some 'stoves', two of which, one 18.3 metres (60 ft) long, the other 15.2 metres (50 ft), on the site of the later Tropical Fernery (No. 2), contained mainly tropical stove plants with ornamental foliage and aquatics. A small span greenhouse (constructed in 1803, demolished in 1892) on the site of the later Temperate Fern House (No. 3) held part of the overflowing collection from New Holland (Australia) and the Cape of Good Hope (South Africa).

Adjacent to this was a 12.2 metres (40 ft) long, 'dry stove', with two compartments, for succulent plants. In 1854 the collection housed here was transferred to a new succulent house (No. 5). This particular house was ventilated by use of hinged ventilators on a lantern formed at the ridge; the previous structures, as can be seen from illustrations in Gosse's *Wanderings through the conservatories at Kew* (1856), were ventilated by sliding roof sashes. Constructed in 1955, its replacement structure of similar dimensions and on the same site featured continuous hinged ridge ventilators, which in turn, technically, have been superseded in the glasshouse industry by wider opening angle (70°) ventilators as now seen on Kew's propagation greenhouses. In his *Records* (p 177) John Smith comments wryly on the 1854 structure as being 'not without its faults, for its direction being north and south and the angle of the roof being low, the unnecessarily massive iron girders prevent the rays of the sun from freely reaching the plants'. Such is the way in which gardeners over the ages have tended to view the aspirations of their fellow architects in respect to greenhouses.

On the site of the present House No. 4 there was originally a lean-to greenhouse, 18.3 metres (60 ft) in length, built in 1792 to house more of the New Holland and Cape of Good Hope plants, including 'some noble Banksias'.

68

It was doubled in size in 1844 and extended further in 1845 with additions by Decimus Burton, reconstructed in 1892/3 and again in 1963, when it acquired rather monstrous internal ferro-concrete frame members.

In 1838, according to the Lindley Report, there was a further small greenhouse, 9.2 metres (30 ft) long, also containing New Holland and Cape of Good Hope plants. Even more important was the famous 'Botany Bay House' (1788–1856) which was some 33.5 metres long, 5.2 metres wide and 4.3 metres high (110 by 17 by 14 ft) and crowded with many plants, mostly from New Holland. This evocatively named greenhouse conjures pictures from history of that bay, near modern Sydney in Australia, where Captain Cook landed in 1770 during his epic voyage with Joseph Banks and bestowed upon it the name of Botany Bay in recognition of the many new discoveries Banks made there.

A new range of greenhouses, called the New Range and later the T-Range, was built nearby in 1868–9, again on the site of previous greenhouses, one of which, in 1862, had held begonias, while others held stove and economic plants. In 1897 the Nepenthes House (No. 9A) was added and in 1899 part of the Range was rebuilt to a new plan. In 1928 the cool houses for carnivorous plants and pelargoniums were added and in 1931 the Sherman Hoyt houses for succulent plants were also appended, the latter thanks to a large donation by an American citizen of that name. The year 1931 again saw the need for some reconstruction of parts of the Range, continuing the seeming pattern of a thirty to forty year replacement cycle for tropical greenhouses constructed of timber. By the 1970s these houses showed significant deterioration despite being constructed of teak and regularly maintained (the houses with cooler, drier environments generally have a longer life span) and plans are under way for their replacement with a more energy- and cost-effective structure.

The collections in this complex of greenhouses have for the last century consisted primarily of tender herbaceous plants, these specialist collections expanding into quarters vacated by the construction of the larger conservatories, and then developing in their own right in association with Kew's scientific programmes. The more important of the collections thus housed are the orchids (p 77), ferns (p 76), succulent plants—including bulbs and cacti (p 73), bromeliads, gesneriads, begonias, peperomias, balsams, aquatics and carnivorous plants.

Aluminium Structures

In the second half of this century aluminium emerged as a new and effective material for use as greenhouse glazing bars, galvanized steel being favoured for the framework. The advantages of aluminium are that it needs no painting and does not corrode easily, is of light weight and good strength, allowing a narrow glazing bar, and its expansion is similar to that of glass, thereby reducing breakage; factors which have significantly advanced glasshouse design.

The Australian House This house, which was completed in 1952, reflects the initial heavy use (by current standards) of aluminium with closely spaced glazing bars. Orientated east–west, the structure, which is 28.3 metres (93 ft) long, is designed to provide improved winter light conditions for its occupants—representatives of the Australian flora which were previously grown in the Temperate House. The roof is of a Mansard design giving clear span 15.9 metres (53 ft) wide and 9.8 metres (32 ft) high, with no supporting columns.

Sydney Parkinson was the botanical artist with Sir Joseph Banks on board Captain Cook's voyage of the *Endeavour*. While in Australia he drew this plant that was later to be named *Banksia serrata*. The British Museum received Banks' effects after his death. Later, the objects of biological interest, including Parkinson's work, were separated for the Natural History Museum at South Kensington.

B. serrata was first raised at the nursery of Lee and Kennedy at Fulham and the species is still in cultivation at Kew.

Filmy ferns require a saturated atmosphere without draughts. The specially designed greenhouse for them at the rear of the Orangery fulfils these requirements yet allows visitors to see them by having 'a house within a house'. Since the Filmy Fern House was opened in 1965, an increasingly important collection has been built up of these delicate, slow-growing plants.
Photo: T. A. Harwood.

The structure to date has proved very efficient and virtually maintenance-free with glass breakage a very rare event.

The Filmy Fern House This lean-to style north-facing structure situated to the rear of the Orangery was completed in 1965, replacing a small house adjacent to the Tropical Fern House. The delicate-leaved plants it contains, some with leaves only one cell thick, need humid and shady conditions, and cannot withstand draughts. For this latter reason the previous house could not be opened to the public and its replacement overcomes this by being a house within a house; the public walk within a greenhouse looking in at another sealed house within.

The plants are landscaped into a tufa rock-work wall, which also features a waterfall and pool. Humidity in the house was originally provided by overhead spray lines but because these were not very efficient, and tended to drip, they have been replaced by a large humidifier which distributes a cloud of atomized water into the atmosphere. Most of the filmy ferns are very slow growing and thus initially they have been supported by other ferns, but with time this collection is becoming more and more representative. Some of the largest specimens are of the New Zealand *Leptopteris hymenophylloides*, the Prince of Wales's plumes, and these plants are at least seventy to eighty years old.

The Filmy Fern House, the outer house of which is glazed with diffusing glass and is fitted with retractable blinds, was very much the conception of the late Lewis Stenning (1902–65), who was for many years an Assistant Curator in charge of the Tropical Section before becoming Curator and made a lifetime's contribution to the greenhouse collections at Kew.

The Alpine House The first Alpine House at Kew, located by the Herbaceous Ground, was constructed in 1887, enlarged in 1891 and reconstructed and slightly enlarged again in 1938. It was used as a display house for the flowering of slightly tender or out-of-season montane and other small herbaceous plants and bulbs. Proving very popular with the public, this once seasonal feature had its opening season extended in the 1960s to provide a year-round display. The present new house, opened in 1981, is much larger (14 metres square) with a pyramidal roof 7 metres high. The resulting crystalline design using the minimum of materials allows maximum admission of light, and also gives a feeling of the mountain association of its plants. Excellent ventilation is provided by three flights of ventilators on each roof-face. The house cantilevers over a raised moated concrete base which acts as a gutter, a rain-water tank and a foundation wall all in one, as well as concealing an additional level of louvered ventilation above the water tank.

The interior layout of sandstone rock-work, pool and refrigerated display bench are described in Chapter 5, together with the magnificent plantings both inside and around this splendid modern structure.

The continuity provided for more than two centuries by the evolution of the famous Royal Gardens into an internationally renowned botanic garden has allowed the preservation of a cavalcade of garden history in plantings, landscape and buildings. And it is a particular good fortune that the great interest of the rich botanical collections can be rivalled by the unique historic sequence of greenhouses in which they are contained.

J. B. E. S.

❧ 8 ❧
Exotic Greenhouse Collections

Of the world's estimated quarter of a million species of flowering plants, nearly two-thirds exist in the tropics. With a further 40 000 species occurring in the southern hemisphere temperate lands of Australasia, South America and southern Africa, and a high proportion of the remaining 45 000 northern hemisphere temperate zone plants coming from warm lands such as Mexico, the Mediterranean region and Asia, it will be appreciated that the two hectares of greenhouses at Kew is a small area in which to display so many species.

Yet the greenhouse collections have a surprisingly extensive representation of those species that can both be maintained and contained in these 'glass cages'. Some actually try to escape these confines – the bananas and palms push through the glass of the Palm House roof and the agave flowering poles do the same to the Succulent House. The glasshouse plants at Kew depend for their survival on the continued maintenance of a considerable variety of artificial environments, ranging from humid tropical rain forest at one extreme to dry desert climate at the other.

These greenhouse collections fall into several main groups such as those based on the plants' natural relationships, that is, by family or genus – these are the systematic collections. Although this arrangement is satisfactory when the plant members of the family or genus need similar environmental conditions, it does not suit those that require different habitats. Thus succulent plants derived from many families need dry conditions, while aquatics obviously require water, and both these are accommodated in environmental groupings. Thirdly, geographic groupings have been used historically to organize the otherwise random holdings of woody plants – Australian, Himalayan, Canary Islands and so on. Finally, there are less easily defined groups, such as climbers and economic plants (Chapter 14).

Many compromises have to be made since each environment represents a separate cost, and there is always an economic pressure to restrict the range because of the expense of maintaining the houses. Fortunately most plants possess some degree of environmental flexibility. The following selection of groupings indicates the range of plant life under glass at Kew.

The Main Systematic Groupings

The Aroids (Araceae) This family is most abundant in the tropics, especially in the rain forests of South America and South-East Asia, where many of them climb up the trunks of trees. Their leaves are often very large and leathery, sometimes being perforated or lobed, such as the popular house-plant *Monstera deliciosa*. This plant produces edible fruits that can, however, irritate the mouth if sampled at the immature stage.

The tropical African bulb *Scadoxus multiflorus*, better known as *Haemanthus multiflorus*, was grown in Europe as long ago as the early seventeenth century. It was subsequently lost to cultivation but re-introduced as a greenhouse plant in the late eighteenth century, when contacts with Africa increased.

This brilliant illustration on vellum is unsigned but dated 1787. It is kept in the Kew Library Tankerville Collection, which contains 648 original colour drawings bought by the Bentham-Moxon Trust in 1932 for £775 from a Newcastle dealer after the Earl of Tankerville's auction at Chillingham Castle, Northumberland. Most of the drawings were made at Kew by G.D. Ehret, Simon Taylor and especially by Margaret Meen. In addition, there are twenty coloured engravings or lithographs from drawings by Ehret, Meen, James Sowerby and Francis Bauer.

71

Many species of Araceae make popular house-plants because they tolerate low light intensity, an adaptation necessary to survival on the floor of tropical forests. The ornate foliage of *Dieffenbachia picta* is much more attractive than the inflorescence. Unfortunately, its sap is quite toxic and its effect on the human mouth, if ingested, is described by the plant's common name of dumb cane, a name tragically obtained through the former use of *D. seguine* in the West Indies to torture slaves, whom it would render speechless.

At Kew the tropical aroids grow very successfully, even in the shadiest conservatory. The philodendrons, with their huge leaves and long aerial roots which trail to the ground to absorb nutrients, seem a far cry from their diminutive temperate relatives – such as the familiar cuckoo-pint (*Arum maculatum*) of English hedgerows.

Many species of the large South American genus *Anthurium* are epiphytes, growing with bromeliads and orchids on trees in the forest. Some form huge rosettes; the individual leaves of *A. salviniae*, for example, can be over 1.5 metres (5 ft) in length. Two species, *A. andreanum* and *A. scherzerianum*, are grown commercially for their ornamental inflorescences, though it is actually the brightly coloured spathe below the flower head, as with most aroids, that is the main attraction. Similarly, some *Spathiphyllum* species, streamside aroids mainly from tropical South America, and *Zantedeschia aethiopica*, the arum lily from Africa, are also popular cut flowers.

A number of aroids are adapted to a bog or aquatic existence. *Pistia stratiotes*, the descriptively named water lettuce, is a floating aquatic; some *Cryptocoryne* species grow submerged in water, while others, such as *Lagenandra ovata* from Sri Lanka and the giant *Typhonodorum lindleyanum* from East Africa and Madagascar, are bog plants. The seeds of the latter are adapted to water dispersal and will germinate while still floating in warm water.

The Bromeliads (Bromeliaceae) This large and distinctive family of primarily South American distribution has provided conservatories with a wide selection of attractive and easily grown plants. The best-known member of the family is the pineapple (*Ananas comosus*), which is now widely grown and extensively cultivated in Hawaii, Queensland and elsewhere.

Most bromeliads form rosettes of thick leaves around a short stem. They are well adapted to conserve water and in many species the leaf bases can also absorb water. To assist in this their leaves form a wide funnel to capture rainwater and direct it to the leaf base. In nature plants of such genera as *Abromeitiella*, *Dyckia* and *Hechtia* may be found growing as xerophytes in desert areas, while others, such as the Venezuelan *Bromelia humilis*, even tolerate coastal salty soils. Giant forms of *Puya* occur in the high Andes, but the majority are found in tropical forests, as terrestrials, and more commonly as epiphytes. They are highly efficient as epiphytes, colonizing every suitable perch and even, in the case of *Tillandsia*, telegraph wires.

Kew's collection contains over one-third of the known 2000 species. They form a major display and attract attention throughout the year. In many the flowers are enhanced by brightly coloured bracts or, as in some species of *Neoregelia*, the base of the leaves in the rosette colour to an intense red when flowering occurs. Flowering marks the termination of the rosette, which is usually replaced by one or more new rosettes formed from axillary buds on the stem beneath; each rosette takes two or three years or more to flower.

The Cacti (Cactaceae) Like the bromeliads, this family is predominantly of New World distribution and with its efficient xerophytic form has diversified and colonized a wide range of habitats. Though popularly known as desert plants, they are also widely found in dry tropical forest, as high montane plants and as epiphytes in rain forest. Their resilience to environmental stress, architectural succulent form and colourful flowers have led to their popularity in cultivation. Unfortunately many, such as the golden barrel cactus

(*Echinocactus grusonii*), which can be seen in the Sherman Hoyt collection, are now over-collected to the point of endangering their survival in the wild.

The majority of cacti have reduced their transpiration surface by eliminating leaves in favour of stem succulence, with the further adaptations to a dry climate of possessing a mucilaginous sap and water-storage tissue. The genus *Pereskia*, however, makes use of leaves. It has a woody, conventional tree form but when viewed closely shows the characteristic areoles (small felted cushions) of spines that mark this family. *Pereskia grandifolia*, which is grown in the Succulent House, produces an abundance of flowers each summer. These tree cacti often grow in dry, tropical woodland along with the stem succulent candelabra-like forms as seen in *Cereus* and its relatives.

Some prickly pears (*Opuntia*) shed their leaves and use their often flattened pad-like stems to maintain photosynthesis. These pads readily detach and root where they fall. Some species proved their efficiency as introduced weeds by colonizing large areas of Queensland and New South Wales, where, by 1925, they covered more than 24 million hectares (60 million acres) and were still spreading, until stopped by biological control – in this case using the introduced Argentinian moth-borer (*Cactoblastis cactorum*), whose caterpillars feed on the cactus.

Some prickly pears produce edible fruit, as does the saguaho or sahuaro (*Carnegiea gigantea*), the giant columnar cactus of cowboy films, which can grow to a height of 21 metres (69 ft). When in season the heavy crop of fruit once provided welcome sustenance to the local Amerindian tribes. Other cactus-like succulent plants are mentioned on page 81.

The Cycads (Cycadales) The living cycad collection in the Palm House is one of the most comprehensive in existence. The cycads are sometimes described as living fossils because in evolutionary terms, as the most primitive surviving type of seed-producing plants, they pre-date flowering plants and are found abundantly as fossils in rocks of the late Triassic and early Jurassic periods – when dinosaurs walked the earth. The male and female reproductive organs are borne on separate plants, the seeds developing in a woody cone (except for *Cycas*) which can, in some *Encephalartos*, be very large – up to 60 cm (2 ft) long. In cultivation the large mealy seeds can be formed without pollination, in which case no embryo is present. If fertilized, fresh seed germinates without difficulty, although it is a slow process.

The ten genera have a wide distribution throughout the tropics and sub-tropics. The *Encephalartos* species from Africa can make large plants and they dominate the Kew collections. *E. ferox* is notable for its fiercely spiny leaves and large cones with bright red paired seeds. *E. lehmannii* from South Africa has attractive glaucous blue foliage – in 1947 one specimen was presented to Kew by the then Princess Elizabeth before she became Queen. The fine plant of *E. woodii* from Zululand, which became extinct in the wild in 1918, came to Kew in 1905 as an offset from the only plant ever found, which was a male.

Some of the more delicate and rare cycads, such as *Bowenia* from northern Australia and *Microcycas* from Cuba, are not always put on display as they need to be retained in the nursery houses for protection. However, the vast majority are kept in the Palm House, including many recently acquired New World *Zamia* and *Ceratozamia* species. Noteworthy are large *Dioon spinulosum* from Mexico, with delicate fronds (the seeds of *Dioon* are sometimes ground to provide an edible meal but most cycad seeds are poisonous); *Cycas* from Asia,

The cycads are well represented in the south wing of the Palm House. These plants of ancient ancestry are tolerant of a wide range of conditions in cultivation and live to a great age. A specimen of *Encephalartos longifolius*, collected by Francis Masson in South Africa in 1775, is probably the oldest living greenhouse plant at Kew. A similar species, *E. hildebrandtii* (above), also in the Palm House, came from the coastal belt of East Africa in 1901.
Photo: T. A. Harwood.

73

Left: in recent years Kew's cactus collection has increased owing to field work and scientific exchange with contacts in the New World, and the conservation programme for their reproduction by micropropagation techniques. As with many other sought-after groups, they are over-collected and their habitats are too often threatened.

Trichocereus chiloensis is one of several cacti depicted by Marianne North during her travels in Chile over a century ago.

Bottom, left: the epiphytic orchid *Dendrobium dekochii*, which belongs to the section *Oxyglossum*, is widespread in montane New Guinea. Although it occurs at high elevations and is frost tolerant it is difficult to cultivate since it requires good air circulation, excellent drainage, high light intensity and humidity and low temperatures. The illustration shows a wild plant in Papua New Guinea.
Photo: J. Wood.

Bottom, right: the genus *Paphiopedilum* is one that has been much hybridized by orchid breeders. *Paphiopedilum hirsutissimum* was first sent to England about 1857 from an unknown locality and it was described by Sir William Hooker as *Cypripedium hirsutissimum*. It is an epiphyte and is now known to be a native of Assam, Burma and Thailand.

Opposite: a large plant of the Mexican *Agave hookeri* grew in the Succulent House for thirty-five years before it flowered in 1965. Since agaves are monocarpic it died soon afterwards but its progeny continue alive. Sisal hemp for string is prepared from the leaf fibres of *A. sisalana*.

This coloured drawing by Mary Grierson, who was Kew's official artist from 1960 to 1972, was one of many she executed to provide a valuable record of interesting plants grown.

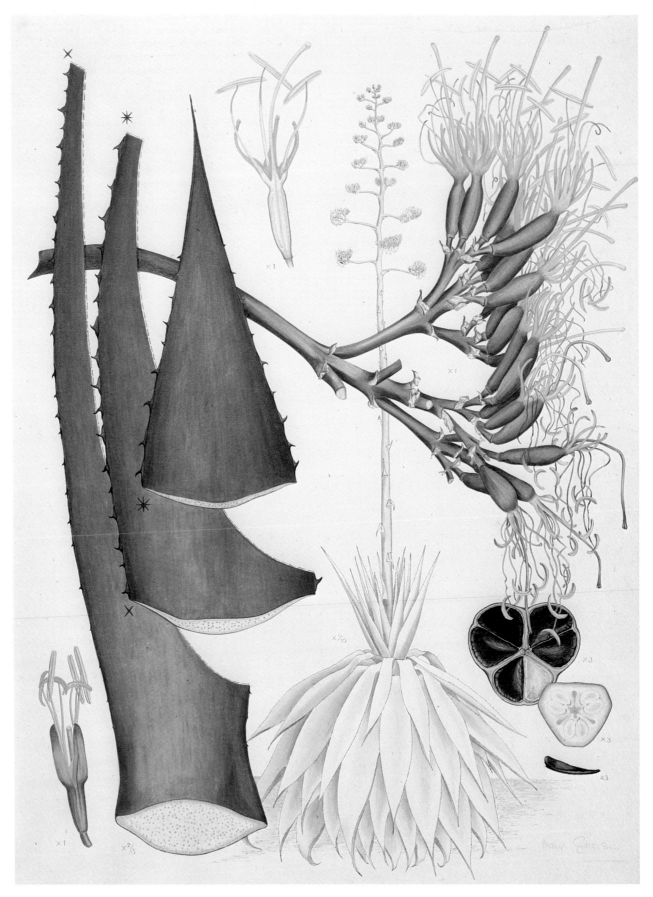

Stag's-horn ferns (*Platycerium*) are some of the most conspicuous plants in the Ferneries, where they are suspended on boards and in baskets. In nature they cling to trees by specially adapted leaves which form a clasping mantle that in some species collects humus behind it. The spores are borne on the undersurface of the divided, pendulous fertile leaves.

The tropical Asian *P. wallichii* (above) was described by Sir William Hooker and figured by Walter Fitch in Hooker's *Filices Exoticae* (1857–9, pl 97). It is seldom in cultivation and not easy but this plant was grown by John Smith (1798–1888), who was Kew's first official curator and an authority on the taxonomy of ferns, as well as being a historian of Kew. He and both the Hookers are buried in St Anne's churchyard on Kew Green and John Smith's tombstone was recently restored by an association of past and present 'Kewites'–the Kew Guild.

with dark green crowns of fronds; *Macrozamia* and *Lepidozamia* from Australia; and the fern-like *Stangeria eriopus* (when first discovered it was mistaken for a fern) from south-east Africa.

The survival of this group of plants over so many millions of years is due, no doubt, to their environmental tolerance, coping equally with tropical forest or seasonally dry climates; to their wound-healing capacity and to their resistance to pests and diseases, as their survival in cultivation attests. Sadly, however, their continued survival in the wild is now seriously threatened by human activity.

The Ferns and Fern Allies (Pteridophyta) The fern collection at Kew developed significantly during the latter half of the nineteenth century under the curatorship of John Smith and has subsequently been maintained and enlarged as one of the major greenhouse collections at Kew. Numerically it now contains over 2000 species, the majority having been collected in the wild, particularly from the tropics. The specimens are heavily used for scientific study, and, as a feature for visitors, both educationally and aesthetically this collection stimulates great interest.

Amongst the tropical ferns it is perhaps the 'giants' that first attract attention. The huge *Angiopteris* species with fronds having bases as thick as a human arm and 4–5 metres (13–16 ft) in length are impressive denizens of wet areas in humid Asian forests. The epiphytic stag's-horn ferns (*Platycerium* species) are more obliging and readily raised from the spores that are borne on the under-surface of the pendulous leaves. Other sterile leaves form a clasping mantle, which in some species also traps detritus behind it. The largest species is the spectacular *P. grande* from the Philippines, which when fully grown may measure more than a metre from top of mantle to tip of leaf.

Many tree ferns are cultivated, particularly of the genera *Cyathea*, *Cibotium* and *Dicksonia*. There is, however, insufficient space to grow more than a few of these magnificent plants, which are perhaps also best seen from above – or with shafts of sunlight glinting through as in nature where they grow along streamsides in mountain forests.

Most ferns are to be found in moist, shady places, especially the filmy ferns (see p 70), which often inhabit the darkest parts of stream gullies in tropical forests. Some, however, are sun-lovers. The gleichenias, for example, colonize cleared areas, usually in poor soils, and they are surprisingly difficult to cultivate; even the use of inorganic fertilizers can cause their demise.

The 'fern allies' *Selaginella*, *Lycopodium* and *Equisetum* may also be seen in the display houses. Of these the selaginellas have a large area set aside for them, some forming scandent climbers on the house columns. The tropical lycopodiums are more difficult to cultivate and need both constant moisture and mossy composts. In the Carboniferous period the horsetails formed tree-sized specimens, but their modern derivatives are much smaller and herbaceous, though their durable deep-set rhizomes enable them to become effective colonizing weeds. One of the largest modern species, *Equisetum giganteum*, comes from South America and produces stems 2–3 metres (7–10 ft) high.

Of the many attractive foliage plants amongst the ferns, the finely divided foliage of the *Davallia* species is of value in corsage work, while maidenhair ferns (*Adiantum*), Boston ferns (*Nephrolepis*) and *Pteris* species and cultivars are well-known as house-plants. There is a great variety of habit amongst the ferns. The rhizomatous *Elaphoglossum crinitum* has simple entire leaves hence the common name elephant's-ear fern; *Jamesonia* species have narrow felted leaves well adapted to growing at 5000 metres (18 000 ft) in the Andes; epiphytes such as the bird's-nest fern (*Asplenium nidus*) perch on trees in the Asian tropics.

The Orchids (Orchidaceae) With some 20 000 species of world-wide distribution, and a vast array of hybrids produced in cultivation, this large family of perennial herbs is very much the province of the specialist grower – sufficient to ensure their own regular World Congress. The greater proportion of Kew's collection consists of tropical epiphytes, though many terrestrials are grown as well.

The first tropical orchid to flower at Kew, in the 1780s, was *Encyclia cochleata*, which was then known as *Epidendrum cochleatum*. At that time the collection consisted of thirteen exotics, several being of West Indies origin. Since then tropical orchids have been in continuous cultivation at Kew, making it probably the oldest collection in Europe. Therefore Kew has been a botanical centre for the study of orchids by specialists such as Lindley, Joseph Hooker, Reichenbach, Schlechter, Rolfe (who founded in 1893 the first orchid journal, the *Orchid Review*) and Summerhayes (who preserved many in alcohol, thereby starting the now vast spirit collection in the Herbarium).

The display of epiphytic orchids in the show houses includes many growing apparently naturally on trees. The trees are, however, artificial, being formed from an outer layer of cork bark over a steel rod frame filled with polyurethane foam – natural cut branches of wood decompose too rapidly in a tropical greenhouse and decay long before the epiphytes become well established. As the plants mature and increase in size, so flowering increases. And though there are now many large specimens from genera such as *Brassavola*, *Bulbophyllum*, *Coelogyne*, *Epidendrum* and *Oncidium*, unless they are particularly gaudy, their flowers are not noticed by visitors. To counter this problem a small case, with a matt black background, is used to enhance a changing display of orchids drawn from the considerable resources of the collection houses, which are not open to the public.

The main terrestrial plantings include a collection of *Cymbidium* species from tropical Asia and some sobralias from tropical South America. Some fine examples of the *Cymbidium* hybrids, now so popular as a florists' flower, are shown in season. In the warmer section of the orchid greenhouses, a number of *Angraecum* species are planted out. Their large long-spurred flowers are pollinated by long-tongued moths and one of them on display, *A. sesquipedale* from Madagascar, has spurs up to a quarter of a metre (10 in) in length. The *Vanilla* species are climbing orchids, trained up on wires to grow in the eaves of the houses, and it is from the seed pods of these plants that the vanilla essence of commerce is derived.

The reserve collection of orchids, used mainly for taxonomic study, comprises some 1700 species. Among them are those such as the jewel orchids, *Anoectochilus*, *Goodyera* and others, which have finely marked leaves but which, as dwellers of humid tropical forest floors, cannot withstand the rigours of a display house. Many, as indicated, are brought into the display house when in flower. The slipper orchids (*Paphiopedilum*) and the beautiful moth orchids (*Phalaenopsis*), with their delicate arching flower stems, also need conditions of high humidity.

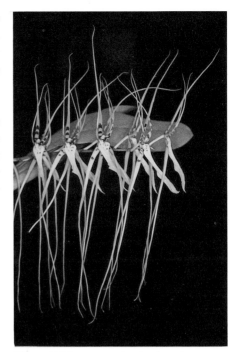

The orchid *Brassia caudata* has been known since the eighteenth century. It is widespread in the humid forests of Florida, Central America and the West Indies, and is represented in Kew's rich collection of this remarkable group of plants.

The first comprehensive classification of the orchids was published between 1830 and 1840 by Dr John Lindley. His valuable collection of about 3000 specimens, many of them types, forms part of the unrivalled Kew orchid herbarium, which now contains some 150 000 sheets. Current taxonomic research is diverse and includes work on tropical East Africa, Papua New Guinea, Borneo and Belize orchids. Revisions of horticulturally important genera such as *Cymbidium* and *Paphiopedilum* are being given priority, and cytological studies on the chromosomes of *Dendrobium* and *Pleione* are in progress at the Jodrell Laboratory. Photo: D. Menzies.

The fan palm *Livistona rotundifolia* is a tall, elegant tree native of the Philippines and Celebes. It grows gregariously, providing abundant leaf material for thatching. The young leaves are used for wrapping food and the split trunks are used for flooring.

A tree has been grown in the Palm House for many years, where it fruits regularly in November and December. The scarlet fruits are eaten by the blackbirds and sparrows that inhabit this greenhouse.
Photo: J. Fielding.

The Palms (Palmae) No family of plants more epitomizes the tropics than the palms – hence the name Palm House for tropical plants, although only one-third is occupied by palms. They also form one of the most useful families from an economic point of view, being second only to the grasses. There are about 2800 species; the great bulk of the family is found in the tropical rain forests of South-East Asia, the West Pacific and the Americas. Surprisingly few species occur in Africa. There are three basic leaf shapes: fan (palmate), feather (pinnate) and bipinnate (two-times pinnate), the latter is only known in *Caryota*. Palm fruits range in size from tiny drupes to the enormous double coconut (*Lodoicea maldivica*) of the Seychelles (see pp 86–7).

With the exception of the south European *Chamaerops humilis* and the Chusan palm (*Trachycarpus fortunei*) from China (of which the original specimens introduced by Robert Fortune in 1846 still stand by the Main Gate), the mature palms at Kew are to be found in the Palm and Temperate Houses.

Many of the species of economic importance occur in the Palm House – the coconut (*Cocos nucifera*) having the greatest value. It supplies not only commercial vegetable oil from copra (dried endosperm), but fibres, timber, food and drink wherever it is grown. The date palm (*Phoenix dactylifera*) yields the familiar sweet fruits, mainly in the Middle East, where it probably originated. The oil palm (*Elaeis guineensis*) originated in the rain forest areas of tropical Africa but is now cultivated throughout the humid tropics on a large scale. It is in fact the highest yielder of oil per unit area of any cultivated plant. Two conspicuous rattan palms (*Daemonorops jenkinsiana* and *Calamus longipinna*) are also grown in the Palm House. Rattans, which provide the popular rattan cane, occur mainly in South-East Asia; they are viciously spiny and they climb by means of barbed whips. Alcoholic drink is prepared from the sap of many palms, including *Caryota*, *Raphia* and *Arenga*. A vegetable is occasionally prepared from the growing point of the cabbage palm *Roystonea oleracea*, a delicacy sometimes called millionaire's salad which tastes to me not unlike asparagus. This removal of the terminal bud kills the tree.

It is to the Temperate House we turn to find the 'kentias' of past palm court days. Seeds of these palms from Lord Howe Island in the South Pacific were once imported in quantity to be raised to grace conservatories. Of the four species endemic to the island it was mostly *Howea belmoreana* and *H. forsteriana*, and to a lesser extent *Hedyscepe canterburyana* that were grown.

The two species of *Rhopalostylis* from New Zealand and Norfolk Island (*R. sapida* and *R. baueri* respectively) form large specimens, but the largest palm at Kew is the Chilean wine palm, *Jubaea chilensis* (*spectabilis*), which was raised in 1846 from seed collected in Chile by Bridges, and transferred from the Palm House to the Temperate House in 1860 when its fronds were some 2 metres (6 ft) in length. It was then transplanted sideways to its present site in 1938, a major task because the leaves were already touching the roof! Since then it has continued in good health despite the removal of the greenhouse roof during the 1970s and lack of heating during reconstruction. It is hoped that it will survive until it is at least 150 years old.

The Geographical Groupings

Australian Plants Horticulture and botany at Kew have been firmly linked with Australia since the earliest times of European contact with that continent. Sir Joseph Banks's Kew collectors sent home much plant material, and subsequent generations of Australians generously provided Kew with seeds of native plants from which a wide range of species have been raised for study and display. The main flowering takes place during late winter and early spring, when the yellow wattles (*Acacia* species) are in full bloom, making the Australian House (p 69) a popular venue at that time of year while the cold winds of winter are still sweeping the Gardens. However, not all the Australian plants at Kew are held in the Australian House – some are hardy and others are included in specialist collections, such as the alpine plants, the cycads, ferns, orchids and palms.

Since the flora of Australia contains over 20 000 species and the climate of this continent ranges from cool temperate in Tasmania, through desert to the tropics in north Queensland the relatively small Australian House with its single environment (winter minimum *c.* 5–10 °C) can hold only a small representation of these fascinating plants, many of which are highly adapted to the harsh Australian environment. Those that are grown, however, create great interest. The *Protea* family (Proteaceae), which has a reputation for being difficult in cultivation, is represented by some free-flowering specimens of *Banksia*, *Dryandra*, *Grevillea* and *Hakea* and the myrtle family (Myrtaceae) by many genera including *Callistemon*, *Eucalyptus*, *Leptospermum* and *Melaleuca*. The acacias or wattles give a fine flowering display in spring and other free-flowering trees and shrubs include species of *Correa*, *Epacris*, *Hymenosporum* and *Prostanthera*. The shadier side of the House also provides a site for *Rhododendron lochae* with its red tubular flowers, the only Australian *Rhododendron*, which has its nearest relatives in New Guinea.

Plants of the Canary Islands For over a century the main representation of this unique island flora, with its many rare endemics, was limited to the Temperate House. While the evergreen forest trees, such as the laurel *Apollonias barbujana*, grew well in this house, the herbs, particularly the sun-loving ones, grew poorly. A new display, constructed in a smaller and lighter house in the T-Range, has, however, proved markedly successful and an attraction throughout the year.

While most of the woody plants remain in the Temperate House, the dragon

The glory pea or Sturt's desert pea (*Clianthus formosus*) is one of many plants painted by Marianne North. This detail shows the semi-prostrate habit. The species is from the Australian desert and was introduced to Europe in 1855. It is sometimes grown in the Australian House, where it flowers for many months. Unfortunately, it is short lived in cultivation unless grafted as a young seedling on to *Colutea arborescens*.

The family Asclepiadaceae has numerous succulent genera – including *Huernia*, *Caralluma* and *Stapelia* – which are popular with collectors. These are interesting botanically because of their specialized pollination mechanism.

Huernia barbata var. *tubata* from South Africa was sent to Kew in 1825 by Thomas Hitchin of Norwich, who was a noted collector of succulents, and drawn by Thomas Duncanson. Duncanson was at that time the botanical artist at Kew, having formerly been a gardener on the staff. Little of his work has been reproduced, although his drawings are accurate and of particular interest since he recorded plants newly received and others, such as succulents, that did not preserve well when dried. N. E. Brown was a noted specialist of this group of Stapeliads in Kew Herbarium.

tree (*Dracaena draco*) and some others have been transferred together with the herbaceous ones. There is of course also a special place for the beautiful red-flowered trailing legume *Lotus berthelotii*, now almost extinct in the wild but used in summer as an ornamental plant outside at Kew.

The giant monocarpic buglosses, such as the pink-flowered *Echium wildpretii* and the blue-flowered *E. pininana*, grow very well in their new situation, as do the endemic species of *Argyranthemum*. Particularly notable are the large succulent-leaved rosettes of the *Aeonium* species and the succulent-stemmed *Caralluma* and *Euphorbia* species.

South African Plants Kew's historic botanical links with South Africa, as with Australia, have over the last two centuries, led to a rich exchange of material. The Cape collections, as they were known in the eighteenth century, have always been well represented and include the spectacular *Strelitzia reginae* (see pages 6, 7).

For the most part the South African collections are dispersed in the systematic, and particularly the succulent plant, collections. However, the Temperate House is home to many South African trees and shrubs, including the Cape heaths (a high proportion of the world's *Erica* species occurs in South Africa). Also some Proteaceae are grown, including the silver-tree (*Leucadendron argenteum*) and a few *Protea* species, though these plants have proved consistently difficult to maintain in a greenhouse. *Plumbago auriculata* (*capensis*) and *Tecomaria capensis* are well-known popular greenhouse plants and others on display include *Alberta* (*Ernestimeyera*) *magna*, *Coleonema* species, *Cussonia spicata*, *Dermatobotrys saundersii*, *Greyia sutherlandii* and *Sparmannia africana*.

When in flower many of the South African bulbs are often displayed in the Succulent House. The blossoms of *Cyrtanthus* are welcome in winter, as are the species of *Gladiolus*, *Moraea* and many others, and in the warmed borders outside other greenhouses *Agapanthus*, *Amaryllis belladonna*, *Eucomis*, *Kniphofia* and *Nerine* provide a fine display in their season.

Environmental and Other Groups in the Greenhouses

Aquatic Plant Collections The giant Amazon waterlily (*Victoria amazonica*) whose huge leaves can expand at a rate of over $6\frac{1}{2}$ square centimetres (one square in) per minute is one of the Gardens' star attractions, and has been ever since it was first successfully introduced in 1849.

There are, of course, many other aquatics of interest, such as the tropical waterlilies of the genus *Nymphaea*, including the blue African waterlily, *N. caerulea*, the Indian red *N. rubra*, and the yellow *N. mexicana* from Central America, which have all, with others, contributed to the many attractive hybrids that can be seen each summer in the Waterlily House.

The sacred bean or lotus (*Nelumbo nucifera*) is also a great attraction, and not surprisingly with its waxy parasol-like leaves on which water runs like mercury, huge pink flowers and large ornamental seed pods. The seeds have a very hard shell and curiously the embryo inside is green; more surprising is their longevity – seeds from a Manchurian peatbog, said to be over 1000 years old, having germinated to form plants that are now cultivated in the East.

Amongst tropical or bog plants are various mangrove species with stilt roots; the floating swollen stems of a mimosa-like plant *Neptunia oleracea*; the fruiting heads of rice (*Oryza sativa*); sagittarias with their arrow-headed leaves; *Echinodorus* with sprays of white blossoms – these and many others add variety in season with other submerged and floating aquatics.

Succulent Plants Adaptation to drought has created many interesting plant forms. Some have underground perennating organs, such as bulbs or rhizomes, others have leaves which are succulent and are modified by the addition of waxes or silvery hairs. The loss of leaves in favour of stem succulence seems to predominate but there are many other adaptations such as may be seen in the Succulent House.

The succulent habit has been evolved by many different plant families, such as the Didiereaceae from Madagascar with *Alluaudia* and *Didierea* being of unusual appearance; the mulberry family (Moraceae) including the notable stem-succulent *Dorstenia gigas* from Socotra, and the Apocynaceae with the appropriately named *Adenium obesum*. The vine family has produced the succulent-stemmed *Cyphostemma* (*Cissus*) *juttae* from south-west Africa, of which one venerable specimen, now nearly a metre high with a girth of just over a metre at its base, came to Kew in 1947. One of the most free-flowering of the stem-succulents in this house is the large *Uncarina grandidieri*, from Madagascar in the family Pedaliaceae – to which sesame belongs. For several weeks in early summer the bare stems of this plant bear a mass of bright yellow flowers – sufficient for it to gain an Award of Merit from the Royal Horticultural Society.

While the cacti are undoubtedly the best known of the stem-succulents, others, such as the *Euphorbia* and *Caralluma*, can take on a very similar form. This similarity of form from unrelated plants is known as parallelism, and is no more than a similar design solution to a particular environment.

The lily family contains stem- as well as leaf-succulents and bulbs. Many members of this family are cultivated, including a collection of African aloes. The large woody-stemmed specimen of *Aloe bainesii* in the Succulent House was a gift to Kew from the present Queen in 1947.

The stonecrop family (Crassulaceae) contains many ornamental leaf succulents, which makes them popular with visitors as a large number are displayed, including the curious, pendulous *Sedum morganianum*, called donkey's tail, from Mexico. A small area in the display house is also set aside for the many bulbs from the *Amaryllis*, *Iris* and lily families, which are brought in when in flower.

The nearby Sherman Hoyt diorama cleverly represents the Californian Mojave desert and contains plants from that region, such as the ocotillo (*Fouquieria splendens*) and other succulents. Adjacent is a benched display of small succulents including the southern African stone plants, *Lithops* and also *Cheiridopsis* species, and several others from the family Aizoaceae and a collection of *Haworthia* species.

General Collections As well as the main groups there are, of course, a host of other plants in the greenhouses representing different families and genera. Among obvious foliage plants are the crotons (*Codiaeum variegatum* cultivars) and the variegated *Polyscias* cultivars. Another fine foliage plant is *Miconia magnifica*, which has huge purple tri-nerved leaves; many similar Melastomataceae such as *Medinilla*, *Osbeckia*, *Sonerila* and *Tibouchina*, are widely grown for their foliage and flowers. Another free-flowering family, Acanthaceae, has

Top: the pattern of ribs that support the huge leaves of the giant waterlily (*Victoria amazonica*) is said to have inspired Paxton's design of the Crystal Palace built for the Great Exhibition of 1851.
Photo: M. Svanderlik.

Bottom: this photograph gives a deceptive impression of the strength of the giant waterlily's leaves. The student gardener was carefully placed on the surface and the leaf was supported underneath.
Photo: S. W. Rawlings.

many representatives – orange *Jacobinia*, the curious red and black flowers of *Ruttya fruticosa* and the well-known *Aphelandra* (which has many other ornamental species that are rarely seen) and *Justicia* species, to name but a few.

Amongst trees and shrubs the figs (*Ficus*) in the Palm House are notable for their foliage, many with leaves having the characteristically wet tropical forest 'drip tip'. Other individual specimens in the Palm House that stand out include *Coccoloba pubescens* which forms a column of huge circular leaves about half a metre (20 in) in diameter. Near it in summer hang the pendant flower chains of the bat-pollinated sausage-tree (*Kigelia africana*), to be outdone in winter by the huge balls of red flowers on the large *Brownea × crawfordii*. *Brownea* belongs to the pea family (Leguminosae) and two other interesting large free-flowering leguminous trees in the Palm House are *Amherstia nobilis* from Burma and known as the pride of India, and the sorrowless tree (*Saraca indica*) with flowers that are scented at night and used in Eastern temples as offerings. All three rapidly produce their young leafy shoots in flushes and at first the young speckled leaves hang down flaccidly before later turning green, stiffening and becoming upright. Not all tropical and subtropical trees flower as expected in cultivation – the *Jacaranda*, for example, misses its dry season, as do the Australian brachychitons.

Throughout the greenhouses at Kew, climbers trail around house columns or up wires under the eaves and roof spaces. Adaptation to the climbing habit involves modification of a surprising range of organs such as stems, leaves and even inflorescences.

The jade vine (*Strongylodon macrobotrys*), a climber from the forests of the Philippines that has pendant chains of jade-green flowers, is a fairly new attraction, whereas the primrose-yellow trumpets of the South American *Allamanda* which flower all summer long, have been popular features in Kew's greenhouses since Victorian times.

Curiosities such as the strangely beautiful black and brown, evil-smelling aristolochias attract attention. The pouched, bird-like *Aristolochia brasiliensis* flowers throughout the year, but the larger-flowered *A. grandiflora* displays its huge flowers much less frequently.

The morning glories provide a free-flowering display. The blue dawn-flower (*Ipomoea acuminata*) gives a long season of flower but the purply-red flowers of *I. horsfalliae* 'Briggsii' appear only in late winter. Seasonal too are the jewel-like pendant racemes of the brown and yellow flowers of *Thunbergia mysorensis*, whereas the larger-flowered *T. grandiflora* from India, of which both the blue and white forms are grown, flowers throughout the summer.

Trailing curtains of the cucumber relatives in the Waterlily House give a feeling of the tropics. For example, the balsam pear (*Momordica charantia*), splitting its orange fruits to reveal red fleshy-coated seeds which are sweet to the taste, hangs alongside large marrow-like wax gourds (*Benincasa hispida*) useful in curries. The cucumber-like luffas (*Luffa cylindrica*), also present, are better known in the bathroom from the dried fibrous skeleton of the fruit after the flesh has dried away, the seeds dispersed and the outer dried skin peeled off.

In the cool houses may be seen the waxy splendour of *Lapageria rosea* from Chile; massed pink flowers of the lobster claw (*Clianthus puniceus*) from New Zealand; the curious passion-flowers (*Passiflora*); and throughout many of the greenhouses there are numerous spectacular climbers having characteristic cat's-claw tendrils belonging to the family Bignoniaceae.

J.B.E.S.

Of the many tropical climbers, one of the most spectacular and regular to flower is *Clerodendrum thomsonae* var. *balfouri*. The species was named, by Professor J. H. Balfour of Edinburgh in 1836, after the wife of a missionary, the Rev. W. C. Thomson. He had sent it in a Wardian case from the banks of the River Calabar, West Africa.

Most of the other climbers in the Waterlily House, where this species grows, are gourds of both economic and scientific interest. Photo: F. N. Hepper.

ᛦ 9 ᛦ

New Plants from Old

In botanic gardens there is a constant need to regenerate plants which have reached the end of their life-cycle, so that they may continue in cultivation. Also, stock has to be increased for distribution and wider use. Many plants are raised from seed, but some do not set seed for a variety of reasons, including climate and lack of natural pollinators, and in such cases vegetative means have to be employed.

The Nursery Areas at Kew

Few of the visitors who see the extensive public exhibition houses at Kew can realize that there are nearly half as many greenhouses again out of sight in the nursery areas, where they are used for the propagation and housing of support and research collections. In this they are further supplemented by outdoor areas for producing hardy herbaceous and woody plants. These nursery houses are not all in one site, for historical reasons, but comprise several small units, each associated with specialist needs; for example, there is a separate Arboretum nursery, and another one for alpine plants.

All of the once separate tropical units have now been merged into one main area near Kew Palace, so as to economize on common services and buildings. The responsibilities for the various collections, however, remain separate, so that, for example, the specialist supervisor in charge of ferns attends to all stages of their regeneration, production and display. This not only increases the depth of skills but ensures that only necessary propagation is undertaken. Without such controls there is a natural tendency to over-produce easily grown plants at the expense of rarities.

There is also a specialized unit, with up-to-date laboratory facilities which cultures plants aseptically in glass vessels providing seed culture, micropropagation and virus-freeing services for the living collections. This is the botanical equivalent of test-tube babies. Raising seeds and spores involves species which are difficult or sometimes impossible to germinate under conventional conditions of propagation. Many rare ferns have been raised from spores for the first time in cultivation using 'test-tube' (*in vitro*) techniques and virtually all of the orchid seedlings at Kew are raised in this way, as are many of the carnivorous plants, such as *Drosophyllum* and *Drosera*, which require great care and attention when raised conventionally. Small samples of rare seeds, after their viability has been checked by dissection or chemical tests, may be subjected to the removal of their seed-coat or even the excision of their embryo for culture under controlled conditions.

The skill of vegetative propagation lies in both the selection of the right material and the ability to keep it alive while it regenerates its missing parts. Our understanding of the processes involved is, as yet, rather imperfect but

Test-tube (*in vitro*) cultivation techniques are of increasing importance in the specialized horticulture of botanical gardens and in the commercial field. This cutting of *Kalanchoe obtusa* has started to flower.
Photo: T. A. Harwood.

Aseptic culture techniques are proving very valuable for raising rare ferns and orchids.

Top: growing a stag's-horn fern (*Platycerium wandae*) from spores can be a slow process. After nearly two years from sowing, the sexually produced sporophytes are beginning to emerge from their prothalli. At a later stage they will be separated but grown on in aseptic culture until ready for pots.

Bottom: this orchid seedling (*Coelogyne ovalis*), from the Himalayan region, has been chemically induced to produce multiple shoots, each of which can be separated off with a scalpel and grown on individually in culture.
Photos: T. A. Harwood.

modern advances in tissue culture have extended the range of possibilities. Micropropagation, as it is called, allows the use of more juvenile material (which is easier to regenerate, but would not be self-supporting in conventional propagation) in a controlled environment which is free of disease and in which plant hormones are used to direct growth.

Micropropagation involves equipment that one associates with a laboratory. Very accurate measurements of the constituents of the growing medium are necessary, while plant containers must be sterilized and airflow cabinets used. These are open-fronted work boxes which place the operator in a stream of constantly flowing, microbially filtered air. Within them, using aseptic procedures, tiny plant components are introduced into the sterilized glass containers. Once placed they are cultured on shelves with the required temperature and light conditions.

Vegetative propagation *in vitro* involves a wide range of plants, sometimes pieces from 'hospital cases' returned from the collections, sometimes rare plants for multiplication or perhaps difficult-to-propagate plants, such as the beautiful tree *Cotinus obovatus*. Success has been achieved with many bulbs and succulents and also with several woody plants, which generally prove the more difficult examples for micropropagation. Virus-freeing has also been required, using techniques involving the minute growing point of the shoot (meristem culture), for research on Commelinaceae. Plants of this family are much subject to virus attacks, weakening growth, and reducing the value of the specimens for scientific study.

The Propagation Environment

In nature, for every thousand seeds produced by a plant only a few are expected to survive to maturity. At Kew, gardeners try to provide conditions that increase the chances of survival – ideally all competition is removed, while soil and other environmental factors are held at the best condition for growth. Although many seeds can be raised out-of-doors, the greenhouse is preferred because of the increased control if offers, and independence of season and weather. This also applies to vegetative propagation where, for many plants, a favourable environment is one that can be shaded and kept warm and moist.

Providing specific environments for the vast range of plants propagated at Kew requires an understanding of the complex relationships involved. For example, humidity is related to temperature, therefore heat generated by the sun shining through the glass has to be restricted by shading, not by opening ventilators which detrimentally increases humidity loss. Humid conditions reduce water loss by the cuttings; similarly the compost must be kept moist, but not so wet as to cause rotting. Cuttings of succulent plants are, as may be expected, better adapted to slightly drier conditions under propagation. For seeds the moisture content of the soil is even more important.

Temperature of itself is an important factor; for stem cuttings the rooting medium is kept warm so as to stimulate the production of roots. For a great many tropical and subtropical plants the optimum seems to be around 24 °C. Air temperature is less significant, cooler conditions being preferred provided they are roughly within 4–5 °C of the normal growing temperature of the plant concerned.

Light is important for cuttings and seedlings, but both are usually sensitive to strong light, for while light is required for photosynthesis, excessive exposure causes desiccation. The day length, or more accurately night length, has a control effect on the growth of many plants, particularly those that experience a seasonal rhythm. The changing night length triggering the internal biological clock that governs, for example, the onset of flowering. Many seeds, particularly those of epiphytes such as the rain forest cacti, are light-sensitive, needing light as well as warmth and moisture to initiate germination.

Synthetic growth regulators, or plant hormones, are used in propagation. Mostly these are auxins, such as IBA (indolebutyric acid), which assist with the development of roots in cuttings of woody plants. Such auxins can inhibit shoot growth (or for that matter, root growth in easily rooted subjects, such as *Jacobinia*). In tissue culture, where a much greater control of tissue differentiation is required, other plant hormones are used—the cytokinins, for example, which stimulate shoot growth while depressing rooting.

The composts used for propagation vary not only according to the needs of the many different groups of plants, but also according to availability and cost. Thus, osmunda fibre and sphagnum moss, once so popular for the cultivation of epiphytes such as orchids, are now restricted in use for both economic and conservation reasons. The pH (the measure of acidity/alkalinity) of the composts is also carefully controlled. The vast majority of tropical plants in cultivation require slightly acidic conditions and for watering a rain or de-ionized water supply is used.

Greenhouse Equipment

Because of the need to maintain high humidity, greenhouses intended for propagation have, traditionally, a relatively small volume, and an east to west orientation to gain the maximum winter light. Changing economics and technology have brought about the development at Kew of unit glasshouses serving a variety of purposes where propagation, growing-on, recuperation (of specimens damaged in the display houses) and the holding of reserve stocks can all occur together under automated environmental control—with micro-climates provided as required within the main environment.

One almost universally used device for the propagation of Kew's trees and shrubs is the mist-propagation unit—a heated cutting bed with an overhead misting line controlled by an 'electronic leaf' (humidistat) that operates intermittently to provide an almost continuously moist surface on the leaves of inserted cuttings.

Closed cases too (small glazed frames) still have a place for establishing imported plant introductions and freshly potted seedlings of delicate subjects, or rooting cuttings. There is also an automated version, called a Dewpoint Cabinet, which maintains a constant high humidity with controlled lighting, and this is particularly useful for establishing imported plant material.

The supplementary controls over the environment used within greenhouses to aid propagation include lighting. High pressure lamps provide additional light to help root cuttings or maintain seedlings over winter, but lower intensity lighting can control the length of darkness and light (the photo-period) which is vital for keeping cuttings active during their first winter, particularly the difficult to establish deciduous azaleas and elms.

Other equipment controls atmospheric humidity (by spraylines or humidifiers) and shading. Some of the newer combined ventilation and heating controls include sensors that modify the basic environment according to the amount of sunlight received.

Proteas, such as *Protea aristata* (above) from southern Africa, represent a real challenge, their requirements for propagation being difficult to reproduce in a greenhouse. Their seed coats contain a germination inhibitor, which has to be removed by soaking and they require cool conditions for germination—the propagation greenhouses are usually too warm. Above all, they are very sensitive to many inorganic fertilizers and to soil alkalinity, dislike being potted or disturbed, can be killed by over-watering, and suffer from fungal decay if kept too warm and humid, especially in winter. This accumulation of difficulties conspires to make their successful cultivation all the more desirable.
Photo: M. Svanderlik.

85

The squirting cucumber, *Ecballium elaterium*, an unusual cucumber relative, is grown each year in the Herbaceous Ground as a summer annual. Many plants have evolved 'explosive' means of distributing their seed, but the force of the squirt with which these seeds are distributed usually surprises the unwary who trigger the process by touching the ripe fruits. Photo: M. Svanderlik.

New Plants from Seeds and Spores

Seeds or spores provide the natural means of multiplication for most plants. However, for a variety of biological reasons, not all plants flower in cultivation and even fewer, particularly greenhouse plants lacking pollinators and being encased in an artificial environment, set seed. Also, seed that is set in cultivated plants may be the result of hybridization, and the seedlings thus not true to their species. The horticultural forms and hybrids that are used in the bedding schemes have been selected over generations for their ease of cultivation so that by the use of standard techniques they can be mass-produced. But for the main botanical collections natural variation is sought with plants raised from seed of wild origin so as to achieve a wide genetic base, despite, of course, the horticultural problems inherent in such an approach. Desirable selections may then be subsequently maintained by vegetative means.

For the great range of seeds and spores that need to be raised at Kew, various techniques are used to ensure germination. For example, small adapted refrigerators can provide specific temperature patterns for sensitive seeds. Seeds of plants from arid lands and mountains often require a daily rhythm of temperature variation between day and night, sometimes as much as 5°C to 25°C, to maximize germination. Refrigeration is also used to extend the storage life of seeds (see Chapter 19) and for the cultivation of arctic plants at Kew (see Chapter 5).

Since ferns produce their spores asexually, most species produce viable spores in cultivation. Also the spores are genetically true but because they are so small, dust-like and readily airborne, samples taken from the collection can be contaminated by the spores of other species. Care is taken when removing fertile fronds to first wash them with clean water before packaging, and then to dry them in order to induce liberation of the spores into a packet. Sowing may be on to a sterilized peat-based compost or on an agar-based medium *in vitro*. All of this requires skilled attention by the propagator and certainly the benefit of having controlled culture has led to an increase of species reproduced in cultivation from spores, some, such as *Angiopteris boivinii*, for the very first time.

Collecting seeds at Kew is an attractive yet demanding task. Collecting at the right moment when the seed is ripe, and before it is lost, requires frequent observation, since the timing varies from season to season. There are amusements too: the capsules of balsam (*Impatiens*), which grows in the Herbaceous Ground, coil instantly when gently squeezed, challenging the collector to catch the seeds as they are explosively ejected.

After cleaning, most seed is stored under refrigeration until required for use. There are exceptions, of course, like the giant waterlily (*Victoria amazonica*), the seed of which is stored in water. Many of the large tree seeds, such as horse chestnuts (*Aesculus*) and oaks (*Quercus*), have a limited life and are stored at a temperature just above freezing, but sub-zero temperatures with a reduction in the seeds' moisture content are used for the long-term storage of suitable seeds.

Seeds vary greatly in size from the minute ones of begonias and orchids (in some orchids a seed pod can contain about three million seeds) to the double coconut (*Lodoicea maldivica*) from the Seychelles Islands, which is the largest, weighing at least 13·5 kg (30 lb) each. Of the thousands of seeds sown each year at Kew the majority are raised conventionally. Many, however, require special treatment of which the smallest and largest seed, as indicated, are examples.

Since orchids in cultivation lack their natural pollinators, they require an artificial means of transferring the pollinia to the stigma to ensure pollination and seed set. The capsule forms slowly and ripens over months. The minute seeds have to be raised by *in vitro* techniques, a nutrient medium taking the place of the fungus (mycorrhiza) which is normally associated with orchid roots and in nature provides essential nutrients. The mature pod is removed from the plant and placed in a desiccator until it begins to split. The seed is then collected and stored (until required for sowing) in glass vials in a cold store at 5°C to prolong its viability. At each sowing a small sample of the tiny seeds is enclosed in a filter paper envelope and sterilized. The paper is then cut open under aseptic conditions and the two innermost pieces with the seed adhering to them are sown entire on to the medium in a sealed and sterilized test-tube. The tubes are kept on growth shelves (providing controlled warmth 19°–21°C and lighting, 16 hours per day) for the long wait for germination, which can take many months. Before the seedlings become overcrowded they are transferred and spaced out into new tubes. Eventually, when large enough, which can be from one to three years from sowing depending on the species, they are removed from their aseptic conditions, the agar carefully washed from their roots, and then potted into a compost based on sphagnum moss. They are kept very humid until established enough to go into the collections.

In complete contrast, the double coconut requires considerable space and a container measuring at least one metre (40 in) on a diagonal from the top corner to the opposite bottom corner.

Thus, it can be seen that the range of requirements for raising plants from seed at Kew is indeed considerable. With cold temperate plants dormancy is an important factor; many, such as the woody Rosaceae, require a period of cold treatment prior to germination, while others, such as holly (*Ilex*), benefit additionally from a warm post-harvest treatment for their seed. Plants which grow in seasonally dry zones usually produce seed that tends to store well at room temperature. Some, like the Australian acacias, are protected by hard coats that need scarifying to improve their chances of germination. Others, such as some cacti, may have chemical inhibitors in their seed-coat which have to be leached away by soaking in water. Many tropical seeds cannot withstand drying; the seeds of cocoa and rubber are notably short-lived and these, with cinnamon, if brought by air from the tropics have to be sown immediately on receipt.

The double coconut palm, *Lodoicea maldivica*, shown growing in its native environment on Mahé, Seychelles, produces the largest known seed of any plant. The giant seeds take up to ten years to ripen and the germination process is also slow. If all goes well, about one leaf a year is produced but for several years the seedling continues to depend upon its connection with the nut.
Photo: F. N. Hepper.

New Plants from Old

Most plants can be reproduced vegetatively – that is, a part of the plant itself may be detached and grown to produce its other parts so as to form a whole plant genetically identical with its parent. Vegetative increase occurs naturally, as with elm suckers or strawberry runners. It can also be induced by taking cuttings and by other means, and, certainly for a botanic garden, vegetative propagation is an essential practice for perpetuating valuable plants.

A particular advantage of a clone, as a group of genetically identical individuals is called, is that especially desirable forms can be rapidly produced in massive numbers. Against this, however, must be set the greatly increased risk of epidemic attack by pest or disease since resistance – or the lack of it – will be uniform.

Natural methods of vegetative propagation can be adapted as a means of increasing plants in cultivation. Many plants produce perennating organs and all gardeners will know how easy it is to increase stock of herbaceous plants

Many plants are able to reproduce themselves vegetatively by means of plantlets produced from roots, stem or leaves. This fern from New Zealand, *Asplenium bulbiferum*, produces masses of new plantlets on its fronds. Left to their own devices, these will eventually fall off and develop into new plants. They can also be removed at an early stage and grown on easily in a propagation house using a peaty compost.

More recently it has been found possible to induce plantlets (*in vitro*) from small sections of the Boston fern, *Nephrolepis*; this is a valuable technique already in use for mass-producing these important commercial pot-plants.
Photo: J. B. E. Simmons.

such as *Helleborus* or *Phlox* by simple division of rootstock. This technique can be applied to a very wide range of plants including tropical subjects, like the calatheas, which are best divided in early spring just as the new season's growth is developing.

Bulbs are in a similar category and often produce daughter bulbs, though they can be increased by other means. When dormant, rhizomes, such as those of the ginger family, can be split up into sections for multiplication. In contrast the tubers of *Gloriosa* produce but a single growth bud at their tip and if this is damaged no further shoot forms.

Orchids with perennial stems often possess pseudobulbs, simply tough swollen stems consisting of one or several internodes, which form both a valuable food reserve and a ready means of propagation when detached since there is usually a dormant bud on the node which can be induced into growth. Offsets or shoots without roots from rosette plants such as the bromeliads also provide a ready means of propagation.

Stems and leaves may also serve for propagation, as for example in the climbing tropical yam (*Dioscorea bulbifera*) which is grown in the Palm House each year and forms little tubers in the axils of its leaves. Flower-stems, too, as with some of the hybrid fibre-producing agaves and furcraeas, can be a source of bulbils. Sometimes a plantlet with young roots may form, as happens on the leaves of *Nymphaea micrantha*, a waterlily from west tropical Africa, and on the old flowerheads of *Hedychium greenii*, a red-flowered ornamental ginger relative from the Himalayan region.

In conventional propagation the stem-cutting is still a very frequently used means for a very wide range of herbaceous and woody plants, particularly hardy trees and shrubs. Since the late 1950s the use of mist-propagation has simplified the problems of rooting stem-cuttings and allowed more plants to be increased this way. Thus, from greenhouse species of fig (*Ficus*) to hardy maples (*Acer*), semi-ripe cuttings are carefully selected in season. Surprisingly, perhaps, soft-stemmed plants such as the begonias root more vigorously and grow on to produce more robust plants when rooted under mist than in a closed case—as previously used for virtually all types of cuttings.

Remarkably, the large scaly stems of the cycads, such as the African *Encephalartos* species in the Palm House, can be cut into giant sections and set in sand to regenerate since their stems are quite soft internally and contain large food reserves—but owing to the rarity and value of the specimens such a drastic means of propagation is rarely undertaken, naturally produced outgrowths or leaf bases being preferred. Similarly, however, many succulent plants, such as the large columnar cacti, can be rooted with ease from relatively large pieces of stem.

A number of small herbaceous plants can be propagated from leaves. A leaf with its petiole is necessary for African violets (*Saintpaulia*) and the rosette-forming peperomias; while only sections of leaves, cut transversely to include the midrib, suffice for some *Streptocarpus*. Leaf-cuttings of bulbous plants, such as the African *Lachenalia* or *Haemanthus* species, form bulblets along the cut base of the leaf, which can be grown on, and similarly the individual scales (which are modified leaves) of bulbs, such as the liliaceous *Drimiopsis*, make excellent cuttings.

Root-cuttings tend to be used where stem-cuttings prove difficult (as with *Romneya*, a beautiful Californian member of the poppy family grown in the Herbaceous Ground), but it is probable that root-cuttings could be used more

widely than is at present thought possible. Cut into small lengths of 2–5 cm (1–2 in), many root-cuttings can be prepared from a single parent plant. The attractive red-flowered *Plumbago rosea* from India is conventionally propagated in this way. A more unusual plant, the attractive West African shrub *Euadenia eminens*, has given a success rate of almost 100 per cent when propagated from root-cuttings, a method resorted to in desperation when propagation from stem-cuttings failed consistently.

The rooting of woody shoots while still attached to the parent plant by pegging them into the ground (layering) was once a fairly widely used technique for plants such as the magnolias and wisterias that proved difficult to root from cuttings. Although now largely abandoned as a commercial technique because of the high maintenance costs and low production rate, it still has a value in collections where a replacement for a rare specimen is required.

Under glass, where there are restricted beds or containers, pegging down branches becomes impracticable, but air-layering (where a selected shoot is partly cut or girdled, treated with an auxin and then surrounded by a moist ball of mossy compost wrapped in polythene) may be used to good effect.

The process of grafting, which includes budding, is one of conversion—that is, you have to start with one plant, the rootstock, and convert it to another by grafting on a different 'top' (scion). Thus, it is an expensive technique requiring skill and is used only when essential. With commercial crops, such as apples or rubber, where the rootstock contributes desired characters (disease

The giant bamboo, *Gigantochloa verticillata*, grows in the Palm House, where its huge shoots grow up to touch the roof, 15 metres above, in a single season. When the young shoots emerge, as illustrated, it is possible to increase the stock by removing a shoot with its underground stem and roots but, as is to be expected, this is a major operation. The rootstock is large and deep and, even with careful excavation and removal, the survival rate is low. Fortunately for Kew's propagators, the smaller bamboos and other tropical grasses, such as sugar cane (*Saccharum officinarum*) and lemon-grass (*Cymbopogon citratus*), are more easily divided and grown on.
Photo: T. A. Harwood.

Only one seedling of the spectacular hybrid tree *Brownea × crawfordii* resulted from a cross of two South American species, *B. grandiceps* and *B. macrophylla*. This unique specimen, which was given to Kew in 1888, proved difficult to propagate and remained in the Palm House as the sole representative of its kind until, in the 1950s, it was increased by air-layering.

resistance, for example, or control of size and yield), the rootstocks themselves are specially produced. For a botanic garden, however, it is more a matter of raising seedlings of the species concerned or a near relative, and then grafting scions of the particular form required on to the seedling stocks.

There are many different techniques used in grafting. With Kew collections, where stock and scion size are likely to be variable, side-grafting proves useful for the vegetative propagation of many plants that are difficult to root from cuttings such as *Aesculus, Daphne, Pinus* and *Quercus*. It can also be used as a technique for grafting the Australian banksias, correas and grevilleas. The latter show a wide range of compatability amongst species, but such knowledge tends to be empirical. In Syon Vista there is an ash tree (*Fraxinus angustifolia*) showing partial incompatability having been grafted at about 1 metre (40 in), instead of ground level, on to a common ash stock.

Another problem of grafting may be the suckering effect of a rootstock which if not tended can grow out and suppress the scion. This has happened with Kew's species rose collection, which were budded on to briar and *Rosa multiflora* stocks. For botanical collections it is now preferable either to raise plants as seedlings from wild-source seed or to establish the plant on its own roots by cuttings. There is also a current tendency to graft material of as juvenile a stage as possible.

Budding is a simple grafting technique and chip budding, where a bud with its 'chip' of bark and underlying woody tissue is mated to a matching incision in the stock, is valued for hardy trees and shrubs. At Kew one further old practice persists with cocoa (*Theobroma cacao*) propagated for intermediate quarantine work by means of patch-budding – a technique that requires the use of a double-bladed knife.

New Acquisitions

Kew as an institution is especially concerned with the study of the wild plant, and though the horticultural side of the gardens involves a limited use of some plants of cultivated origin, all new acquisitions for the collections come, as far as is practicable, direct from natural sources. Each specimen, as a plant or propagule or sample of seed, receives an individual number, which it retains permanently, and full details of its origin are recorded with provision made for gathering further information on the performance of the plant in cultivation and any scientific studies undertaken on it. Each of these acquisitions is called an accession and there are about 110 000 such accessions held in the collections at Kew and Wakehurst.

As we shall see in Chapter 14, collecting expeditions form an integral part of Kew's work, but collecting living material in the field is a more arduous task than is generally appreciated. Once safely in the Gardens this valuable material is not only raised for use at Kew but surplus seed, and later seedlings, are distributed to other centres, mostly in Europe and America, in exchange for material from their expeditions.

This process, and that of propagation generally, while enriching qualitatively the collections at Kew and elsewhere, has a more vital and fundamental value related to the now desperate need to learn more about the biology of the world's rapidly diminishing flora and the means by which rare or endangered species can be maintained.

J.B.E.S.

᛭ 10 ᛭
Trees and Shrubs
at Kew

Springtime, with its fresh leaves and abundant blossom, is perhaps the most popular season for visitors to Kew. But many thousands also come in summertime to enjoy the richness and historic maturity of the plantings. Autumnal colour rivals that of the spring, and even in winter hardy visitors appreciate the colour and texture of tree barks, the tracery of branches and the distant views. Yet probably few see the underlying theme and purpose of it all. Its arrangement is not accidental, but one composed through generations of planting to meet the needs of both landscape design and the plant sciences.

The northern end of the Arboretum is primarily composed of specimen trees spaciously set in lawns. In a forest the large trees lose their lower branches as they become shaded out, through keeping their crowns in the sunlight, but as isolated specimens without competition they can keep their branches right to the ground.

Beyond the Palm House, radiating out south and west towards the Pagoda and the River Thames, which bounds the western side of the Gardens, the trees and shrubs are all grouped, in denser plantings, by their families, following a forerunner of the Victorian Bentham and Hooker system of plant classification. The collections, which cover about 80 hectares (200 acres) and represent some 115 families, start near The Temple of Bellona and are completed by the olive and birch families (Oleaceae and Betulaceae) near the Tea Bar. The conifers are planted in the south-western part of the Arboretum and beyond them is the third element of the Arboretum, the 16 hectares (40 acres) of Queen Charlotte's Cottage Grounds, a semi-natural bluebell wood now maintained by replantings of native trees and shrubs.

Britain's favoured maritime climate allows a wide range of hardy woody plants to be grown and Kew, in the mild Thames valley, has an excellent representation of the range. Receiving on average only about 600 mm of rainfall each year, Kew suffers from drought at times. While trees such as the holm oak (*Quercus ilex*) and the Italian maple (*Acer opalus*), both from southern Europe, as well as the cedars and pines, obviously thrive, others such as the pocket-handkerchief tree (*Davidia*) from China, the eucryphias from Chile and Australia and the pseudotsugas (Douglas firs) from western North America and eastern Asia, grow far better in moister gardens. This, of course, is where Wakehurst Place, at a higher altitude on the Sussex Weald, with its greater rainfall and more moisture-retentive soils, has proved of such value in extending Kew's collections.

The soil at Kew is a river gravel, some 20 metres (70 ft) deep, over the top of London clay. Because of the proximity of the Thames, there is a reasonable supply of ground water for deeply rooted and well-established specimens – though, as is to be expected, shallower-rooted plants, such as

In a cool autumn, maples at Kew can provide a profusion of colour. Some species of maple grow in moist woodland whereas others, such as that illustrated, the Italian maple (*Acer opalus*), grow well in Kew's dry sandy soil. Photo: F. N. Hepper.

Despite its antique appearance, the Barron's tree transplanter was used successfully to transplant trees at Kew until the 1930s. To transplant, the tree was first prepared over one or two seasons by digging around to cut the spreading roots and by back filling with fine soil. The transplanter, which can be dismantled completely, was then assembled around the tree to be moved, then the exposed ball of roots and soil, wrapped and tied, was winched up into the transplanter. After carting it could straddle the new planting site, the specimen could be lowered into position and the transplanter be removed by dismantling.

rhododendrons, suffer badly in dry periods. These latter are also adversely affected by Kew's irrigation water, which is chlorinated for reasons of public safety, and quite alkaline from the salts absorbed from the chalk hills that form the Thames basin. In contrast, Kew's sandy soil is acid (pH 4.5 in places) which fortunately suits a great proportion of the collection, and it is a simple matter to add lime where required.

Development of the Landscape

Because Kew is so flat, trees are vitally important in giving the Gardens the dimensions of height and depth, of framing views, screening the undesirable, and forming a backcloth for the ornamental. Most of the trees that we now enjoy at Kew have been introduced over the last two centuries, more particularly over the last 140 years, with many of the more spectacular specimens, such as the magnolias, being planted in this century.

The ground on which the specimens grow has been altered many times. Looking at the Queen Charlotte's Cottage Grounds today it is hard to imagine that this was once the site of a palace garden (Chapter 1). In the far corner of the Cottage Grounds a temple's mount can still be found. The temple, 'a circular dome crowned with a ball and supported by Tuscan columns, with a circular altar in the middle', as described in 1769 in Chamberlain's *History and Survey of the Cities of London and Westminster* (p 627), has long since disappeared, along with the palace and almost all of the other garden features, save, topographically, for the riverside terrace (that overlooks Syon House and a historically little-changed prospect of the mud-banked tidal Thames) and the large depression near the Beech Clump and Azalea Garden that was once the Amphitheatre.

We have seen that the remover of these features was 'Capability' Brown (or 'untutored Brown' in the words of a poem by Mason in 1773 referring to the destruction of Kew). However, he added, while in the service of George II's grandson George III, at least one permanent mark to the flat landscape by directing at some time between 1760 and 1771 a troop of Staffordshire militia to excavate Hollow Walk, which later became the present Rhododendron Dell. Some of the mounts in the Gardens date from an earlier period and certainly Chambers made use of them in the 1760s for his embellishment of the Princess Augusta's garden, to which Kent also contributed. Most of the important garden buildings, such as the Alhambra and Temple of Aeolus, were sited on mounts as were many of the specimen trees, such as the elms that stood on the Orangery Lawn, until Dutch elm disease caused their death in the 1970s.

The Princess's garden at Kew also included paddocks and a large lake with an island. The Palm House Pond, in its present formal shape, is the modified remains of this lake, the main area to the south of the Palm and Waterlily Houses having been filled in around 1814. Today, however, this old lake site provides one of the moistest sites at Kew and contributes to the well-being of some of the Arboretum's largest specimens.

The formal Victorian landscape of Nesfield with its broad avenues and vistas, was overlaid on to the previous landscape of the Royal Gardens – which even up to the death of William IV, a century after Queen Caroline, was still being modified or added to, as exemplified by the construction of King William's Temple (1837), sited, of course, on a mount.

The vistas in the Arboretum have proved hugely successful features, being planted over a period of nearly thirty years, starting with Syon Vista in 1851 and ending with the Sweet Chestnut Avenue in 1880. Later more informal vistas were created by careful thinning and pruning of the existing plantings. The lake is also a Victorian addition; it was excavated between 1857 and 1861, then enlarged in 1871.

Other later developments, such as the addition of the Queen Charlotte's Cottage Grounds (1897), the formation of the Lily Pond (1897) and the Bamboo Garden (1899–1902) virtually concluded the landscape changes.

Development of the Tree Collections

Probably only two trees survive from the seventeenth-century gardens at Kew – a common oak (*Quercus robur*) at the eastern end of the lake, and a sweet chestnut (*Castanea sativa*), nearby to the south. The main botanical plantings date from the 1760s, when Princess Augusta was forming the embryonic botanic garden within her pleasure gardens at Kew – an embryo that ultimately grew to encompass the greater part of the old Royal Gardens, and eventually surpass them in fame and function. Many of the earliest specimens were presented by Archibald, the 3rd Duke of Argyll, from his noted garden in nearby Whitton.

The plantings in the original Arboretum of 1795, which was about 2 hectares (5 acres) in extent, were arranged by Aiton following the Linnaean system, with conifers sited in the north-east corner, near what is now the Main Gate. From this first pinetum one specimen survives: the large Corsican pine (*Pinus nigra* var. *maritima*) planted in 1814 and now some 27 metres (*c.*88 ft) high,

Though their flowers superficially resemble the tulip, the tulip trees (*Liriodendron*) are actually related to magnolias. Seedling trees do not begin flowering until they are about thirty years old and they may be aged fifty years before flowering freely. The specimen illustrated of the American tulip tree (*L. tulipifera*) is the largest at Kew and is over 200 years old. The area it stands in is now the Azalea Garden but it was once the site of the Forest Oval in King George II and Queen Caroline's garden at Kew.
Photo: F. N. Hepper.

The foliage, flowers and fruits of the trees and shrubs that make up Kew's extensive collection of woody plants mark every gradation of the changing seasons.

Right, top: in the Lily Pond, the swamp cypress (*Taxodium distichum*) grows with its roots in the water as it does in its native North American swamps. In the foreground are the brightly coloured winter stems of the golden willow (*Salix vitellina*).
Photo: J. Fielding.

Right, bottom: spring in the Arboretum brings blossoms like those of the small, pink-flowered hybrid *Magnolia* 'Leonard Messel'.
Photo: J. B. E. Simmons.

Opposite, top left: the Asian wisterias grow well at Kew. Old specimens of, for instance, the forms of the Japanese *Wisteria floribunda* are pruned back each year to gnarled stems and flower abundantly.
Photo: F. N. Hepper.

Opposite, top right: in summer, greenery fills the Arboretum, leaving only the extensive vistas to provide distant views.
Photo: J. Fielding.

Opposite, bottom left: early fruits on a striking mountain ash, *Sorbus hupehensis*, suggest the autumn to come.
Photo: D. M. Joyce.

Opposite, bottom right: this huge beech clump, shown in its autumn colours, is really a circle of trees formed from the rooted ground-level branches of several specimens.
Photo: F. N. Hepper.

The stone pine (*Pinus pinea*) produces large cones containing edible seeds and is characteristically flat-topped. In its native region, the Mediterranean, it usually forms a taller main stem. The low and architecturally pleasing branches on this much photographed specimen near the Ferneries may have arisen as a result of its earlier culture in a pot. Other pines in this area, several of which are multi-stemmed, all date from the 1840s and later, when the Arboretum was being extended. These include the Aleppo pine (*P. halepensis*), the Macedonian pine (*P. peuce*) and the Bhutan pine (*P. wallichiana*) south of the Palm House. Also in this northern part of the Arboretum are several fine deodar cedars (*Cedrus deodara*), the fittest survivors from a larger original planting in the 1840s.
Photo: T. A. Harwood.

though it has scarcely increased in height or girth over the last seventy years. From the other original royal botanical plantings several notable specimens remain. Of these the maidenhair tree (*Ginkgo biloba*) by the Ferneries is still in good condition, whereas the oriental plane (*Platanus orientalis*) near the Orangery and the *Zelkova carpinifolia* near the Main Gate are showing signs of senility, while the locust tree (*Robinia pseudo-acacia*) and Japanese pagoda tree (*Sophora japonica*) are but reduced relics of their former glory.

The botanic collection grew quite rapidly; Sir John Hill's *Hortus Kewensis* of 1768 listed 488 trees and shrubs growing at Kew, and a Royal Catalogue of 1773 included 791 species and varieties from 177 genera. The next phase of expansion for the Arboretum commenced in 1843, soon after the Gardens became a public institution, when an additional area of 18.8 hectares (47 acres) was added by permission of Queen Victoria. This area, now the northern part of the present Arboretum, was not planted to any systematic order, but as a mixture of well-spaced individual specimens. Today these have formed many fine trees, including the largest tree (in volume) at Kew, the chestnut-leaved oak (*Quercus castaneifolia*), 30.48 by 6.10 metres (100 ft by 20 ft) when it was measured in 1979.

The third phase of expansion followed almost immediately, in 1845, when a further 80 hectares (200 acres) were added, providing sufficient room for what was virtually a completely new arboretum. This third arboretum was planted systematically following, as already indicated, a forerunner of the Bentham and Hooker system of plant classification. After completion of the initial planting, in 1850 Kew had the most complete collection of any arboretum, with 2325 species and 1156 varieties and hybrids. Because it was not possible to know how all the specimens would thrive, nor to foresee the massive amount of new introductions that would arrive—particularly from China—in the early part of this century, some modifications of this layout became necessary.

Work commenced on the present Pinetum at Kew in 1870, and by 1872 some 1200 specimens had been planted with each species or variety being planted in small groups of from three to twelve specimens. The layout was systematic with, where required, subdivisions within genera for Old and New World species.

In 1894–6 the first of the Kew 'Hand-lists' for hardy trees and shrubs was produced, and it listed some 3000 species and varieties; the separate 'Hand-list' for conifers listing 227 species and 340 varieties. By 1902 the second edition of the list showed that the number of hardy trees and shrubs had risen to 4500 species and varieties, and in 1903 the conifers had also increased to 246 species and 451 varieties. The expansion continued and was accelerated by the addition of much new Chinese material. Thus by 1924 the third editions were listing 6300 species and varieties of trees and shrubs and 288 species and 398 varieties of conifers.

Subsequently the collections levelled off numerically and actually declined until recently. Because of atmospheric pollution, a new location away from Kew was sought for the conifers and, in conjunction with the Forestry Commission, Bedgebury, near Goudhurst in Kent, was selected in 1924 as the new site for the National Pinetum. From 1925 to 1945 W. J. Dallimore of Kew devoted much of his time to developing this new Pinetum with plants donated by Kew, as they are still to this present day, though the management of the Pinetum passed fully into the hands of the Forestry Commission in 1965 when Kew acquired Wakehurst Place.

The development of the Kew and Wakehurst Arboreta is now progressing rapidly, following the initiation of field-collecting programmes by the staff of the Living Collections Division. New arrangements for acquiring and distributing plant material have been made together with a fresh planting programme and a reorganization of the staff of the Arboretum at Kew. Initially the aim was to replace ageing trees of unknown origin by material from known wild sources, but in practice many new species have been added, such as, at Kew, a large number of *Eucalyptus* species, *Cupressus dupreziana* from the Sahara and *Quercus brantii* from the Zagros Mountains of Iran.

The Arboretum through the Seasons

Having assembled a woody collection from around the world within Britain's variable climate, it is hardly surprising that each year the Kew Arboretum brings its own variety of sequence and performance in flowering times and floriferousness. Throughout a reasonable winter some tree or shrub can always be found in flower. Perhaps if they flowered in summer, we should scarcely notice the pink-tinted blossoms of *Viburnum × bodnantense*, the bright yellows and reds of the strangely petalled witch-hazels (*Hamamelis*) or the delicate scent of winter sweet (*Chimonanthus praecox*), but in winter, when all else appears steadfastly dormant, these shrubs attract great attention.

In winter too the Heath Garden, near the Pagoda, provides a carpet of colour from the winter-flowering heath *Erica herbacea* (*carnea*), and its forms and hybrids with *E. erigena* (*mediterranea*), *E. × darleyensis*. Kew is really too dry for the successful growth of most ericas, which require watering during dry periods and a fairly regular replacement of group plantings when disease (*Phytophthora*) also takes its toll. The musk willow (*Salix aegyptiaca*), far from its native mountain water-courses in Armenia and Iran, is more content with the moister parts of Kew, and it is one of the first willows to herald the coming of spring by releasing a fine display of catkins. Other early harbingers providing a bold display are the massed yellow flowers of *Cornus mas*, the cornelian cherry from central and southern Europe and west Asia, and the closely related Japanese cornelian cherry (*C. officinalis*) from eastern Asia.

If they are not spoiled by the frost, the rose-scarlet blossoms of

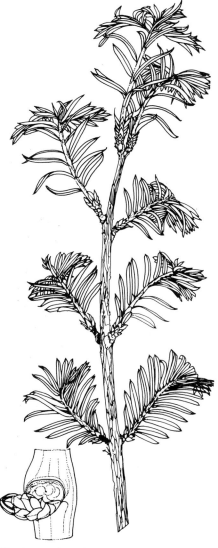

The dawn redwood (*Metasequoia glyptostroboides*) was introduced to Kew and many other Western gardens in 1948. Its discovery in western Hubei Province, China, in 1941 created great interest, since the genus had hitherto been known only from fossil remains. From this initial introduction a vast number of trees has been produced in cultivation. It is a deciduous conifer (like the swamp cypresses) and grows well in moist soils. Like many plants, it produces its seeds more freely in regions which experience a warm 'continental' summer. Drawing: Joanna A. Langhorne, Kew Artist 1973–80.

Rhododendron × nobleanum, an old hybrid from a cross made about 1832 between the pink or yellowish-white *R. caucasicum* and the red-flowered Indian *R. arboreum*, provide a welcome early beacon by the northern entrance to the Rhododendron Dell. Along with the crocuses, the first camellias open their blossoms in March. *Camellia japonica* and its cultivars grow very well at Kew, tolerating quite shaded conditions, though their early blossoms are often spoilt by frost. The hybrid forms of *C. × williamsii* are, however, the most floriferous and consistently out-perform their parents, *C. japonica* and *C. saluenensis*. Among other early indicators of relief from winter are the spring green shoots and flowers of the large old clump of the oso berry (*Osmaronia cerasiformis*), from western North America, near the Ferneries.

The season for most early-flowering trees and shrubs is rather variable. The Italian maple (*Acer opalus*) can give a startling display of pallid yellow blossom, but whether or not this is noticed appears to be related to the performance of the leading protagonists in the spring display – the magnolias. If it is a good year for them the delicacy of the maple's display is often overlooked, just as the clouds of yellow pollen floating in gentle breezes give a clue only to the observant that the yew trees are flowering.

For overtness, however, the spectacle of the April-flowering magnolias cannot be missed. Usually, though not always, the earliest to be seen are the white linear-petalled flowers of the Japanese *M. kobus* and *M. salicifolia*, which star the now large trees of these species at Kew. They head a sequence of flowering which includes the aged *M. kobus* 'Stellata' by the Ferneries and the dramatic flowering of the large dark pink form of *Magnolia campbellii* from the Himalayan region, equalled by the paler pink of its subspecies *mollicomata* from south-east Tibet and Yunnan, and surpassed by the many spectacular seedlings resulting from the cross (made at Kew in 1946) between these two. One year, late snow left the blossoms only slightly damaged as a pink cloud above a white crystalline carpet. The white candles of the yulan, *Magnolia denudata* (*conspicua*), from China, also open early on, and this plant is one of the parents of the very popular *M. × soulangiana* hybrids which are frequently seen in suburban gardens; its other parent is the later, purple-flowered *M. liliiflora*. Soulange's magnolia flowers in season between its two parents and is usually late enough to miss the hard frosts. Those magnolias that flower without their leaves or as their leaves emerge are all of Asian origin but there are also many other Asian and American species that flower in summer after their leaves have expanded, though they are missed by many visitors.

The flowering cherries are always spectacular at Kew. The early-flowering delicacy of the spring cherry (*Prunus subhirtella*) from Japan is closely followed by the floating white masses of its hybrid the Yoshino cherry (*P. × yedoensis*). Later still come the numerous and sumptuous forms of the Japanese flowering cherries, which are probably derived from several species, including *P. serrulata*, *P. spontanea* and *P. speciosa*, which is also the other parent of *P. × yedoensis*. Another hybrid to be noted at Kew, between the Lake and King William's Temple, is *Prunus* 'Okame', a carmine-rose hybrid raised by Collingwood-Ingram using pollen taken from the tender *P. campanulata* in the Temperate House to cross with *P. incisa*.

As spring advances the range of species in flower increases dramatically: orange *Berberis darwinii* from Chile; yellow, white and red brooms (*Cytisus*); *Cornus* 'Ormonde', which has spectacular white bracts; richly scented lilacs (*Syringa*); and the snowdrop tree (*Halesia*). Other attractive plants include

The azaleas of our gardens are mostly hybrids derived from both New and Old World species; they are actually deciduous rhododendrons. The forms with more strident colours are often difficult to place in a garden, but blended together *en masse*, as they are in the Azalea Garden, they make an undeniably arresting display. The many magnolias are planted in and around the Azalea Garden, where the shade they provide is useful to the azaleas, whose parents are mostly woodland plants. Photo: T. A. Harwood.

wisterias, with trailing, elegant flowers; *Ceanothus*, foliage hidden in a froth of blue blossom; and the Judas tree (*Cercis siliquastrum*), with its purplish pea flowers sprouting directly from old stems. Azaleas and rhododendrons create conspicuous masses of colour; gaudy Wilson azaleas near the Japanese Gateway and subdued, sweeter-scented ones in the Azalea Garden, hybrid rhododendrons in the Dell and species in the Woodland Garden off Cedar Vista. Bluebell time comes as a climax. Then it is worth strolling through the gardens on an evening when low-angled light emphasizes the sheets of blue that reach through to the Cottage Grounds.

With the late azaleas, the tulip trees (*Liriodendron*) put forth their flowers. Most of the specimens at Kew, including the giant of more than two centuries in the Azalea Garden, are the American *L. tulipifera*. Less common at Kew, and lacking the orange colour to its flowers, is the closely related *L. chinense* from China. More readily noticed, the Chinese beauty bush (*Kolkwitzia amabilis*) regularly produces a profuse display of pink *Abelia*-like flowers, but within the Arboretum, as the days lengthen, the quantity of flowering diminishes. Individually notable, however, is the golden rain tree (*Koelreuteria paniculata*) from the Far East and growing near the Ruined Arch, and the manna ash (*Fraxinus ornus*) from southern Europe and west Asia which grows near the Lake. Other summer flowers—the roses, hibiscuses, mallows, hebes and hydrangeas—are diminished somewhat by the wealth and grandeur of the summer foliage. Now is the time to witness Kew's magnificent collection of oaks in their full summer dress, including the giant chestnut-leaved oak near House 15, and nearby the thick-barked cork oak (*Quercus suber*) and the Chinese cork oak (*Q. variabilis*). In the collection beyond the Rhododendron Dell particularly notable species include from California, the live oaks (*Quercus chrysolepis* and *Q. agrifolia*), the Kermes oak (*Q. coccifera*) from the Mediterranean region, *Q. glandulifera* from east Asia and the American hybrid *Q. × ludoviciana*, with the similarly rarely seen in Britain tan-bark oak (*Lithocarpus densiflorus*) from southern Oregon and California and also *L. edulis* from Japan.

As rose hips colour and wild apples and pears scent the air, the European spindle-tree (*Euonymus europaeus*) splits its fruits to reveal red-arilled seeds. By mid-September, the start of the new academic year for schools, children or their willing parents are furtively searching for the season's crop of horse chestnuts—the discerning waiting longer for autumn's feast of sweet chestnuts (*Castanea sativa*), knowing the trees which bear the sweetest nuts, picking them from moist autumn grass to relish raw or roasted by an evening fire.

For connoisseurs of autumn colour, Kew has much to offer, as signalled by the blaze of red when the old *Cotinus obovatus* (whose naming is in doubt, it is probably a hybrid—but not its performance), by the Temple of Bellona, turns from insignificance to splendour. It is followed by *Prunus sargentii*, the hardy and vigorous Sargent's cherry from Japan, and the North American tupelo (*Nyssa sylvatica*), its lustrous foliage turning scarlet or yellow—and on through autumn's catalogue: the poplars, ashes, oaks, liquidambars, tulip trees, caryas, *Parrotia*, *Oxydendrum*, maples, copper beech and rusty taxodiums, with a climax in the first two weeks of November before, suddenly, there are bare twigs against grey skies. On pale sunlit winter's days visitors linger to admire the finer points of barks—the snake-bark maples, flaking copper *Acer griseum*, polished *Prunus serrula*, ghost-like *Stuartia sinensis*.

The conifers are of interest throughout the year, but when hoar frost or snow

The late-flowering Indian horse chestnut (*Aesculus indica*), has become increasingly popular as a garden plant. From an original introduction to Kew (the tree still grows by the Restaurant) a selection of an improved flowering form was made from amongst seedlings raised in 1928 and planted near the Main Gate. Grafts from this plant are now in commerce as *Aesculus indica* 'Sydney Pearce'–a cultivar named after a former Assistant Curator of Kew's Arboretum.

The closely related, but still rarely cultivated, *Aesculus wilsonii*, introduced from China by E.H. Wilson in 1908, *A. assamica* from the Himalayan region and many other species can also be seen at Kew.
Photo: F.N. Hepper.

A covering of snow, while adding delight, can also spell danger. When the snow freezes and accumulates on the evergreen branches of the great cedars the resultant increase in weight can be so great as to snap off huge limbs. Serious damage is not frequent but has been recorded in 1927 and in 1981.

At Kew the hemlock spruces (*Tsuga*) do not make large plants; they do better in the moist valleys at Wakehurst.
Photo: J. Fielding.

garlands their branches, then the sheer beauty of the cedars, pines and spruces can be breathtaking. The Lebanon and Atlantic cedars thrive at Kew, as do the second selected generation of deodar cedars. Many pines also grow very well. Notable ones include the white-bark pine (*P. albicaulis*), the bristlecone pine (*P. aristata*), the foxtail pine (*P. balfouriana*), the limber pine (*P. flexilis*), the Yunnan pine (*P. tabuliformis* var. *yunnanensis*)–Wilson's 1909 introduction from west China–and some large Bhutan pines (*P. wallichiana*). More unexpectedly the collection includes from the tender range of species the Mexican *Taxodium mucronatum*, some large *Podocarpus andinus* from Chile and the dwarfer *Podocarpus lawrencii* from Tasmania and south-east Australia and *P. nivalis* from New Zealand. Other relatively tender species represented at Kew are *Fitzroya cupressoides* from southern Chile (named after Captain Fitzroy, Darwin's captain on the *Beagle*), *Torreya californica* from California and *T. grandis* from eastern China, and some interesting *Cupressus*, such as *C. goveniana*, from California. In contrast to these plants there is from the other end of the tender/hardy scale the Siberian larch (*Larix russica* (*sibirica*)), from within the Arctic Circle.

Maintenance of the Trees

The 'old lions' of the Gardens, as the Victorians termed some of their older and favourite trees at Kew, need quite considerable attention. The surgery unit watches for signs of decay, wounds to be treated, branches to be braced and always, sadly, dangerous or diseased trees to be removed without damaging their neighbours. On Kew's poor soil, feeding with proprietary fertilizers or top-dressing with organic material certainly helps to extend the life of older specimens–the old Lucombe oak (*Quercus × hispanica* 'Lucombeana'), for example, has had a new lease of life subsequent to such treatment.

New planting is currently the order of the day. Although the cycle of renewal in an arboretum is of a greater duration than for herbaceous collections, or as nothing compared to the rapid recycling of some greenhouse plants, it requires, even more importantly, a carefully planned strategy of replacement. In the Arboreta at Kew and Wakehurst trees are lost each year by disease, gales or old age. At Kew, where the collection is almost three times the age of Wakehurst's, an average of about two hundred specimens are lost each year, and exceptionally, as in the severe drought of 1976 when Dutch elm disease and sooty bark disease became epidemic, up to 600 specimens were lost in both this and the succeeding year. As Kew's collection of woody plants numbers probably more than a quarter of a million individual specimens, the indicated loss is not significant in terms of landscaping, provided that at least an equal number are planted each year. In the past few years this scale of replanting for trees and shrubs has been achieved and exceeded at both Kew and Wakehurst, the positive balance being all the more necessary at Kew to make up for the overall decline that had occurred since the 1930s, and at Wakehurst as a function of the developing collections.

To perform its function as a national reference collection–for scientific study, as a genetic resource, a base for education and a public place of pleasure and information–the specimens must be authentic, fully documented, well cultivated and arranged, and accessible. Potentially these are competing aims, but when harmonized they create a truly great national arboretum.

J.B.E.S.

✧ I I ✧
Wakehurst Place
Kew in the Country

An hour and a half's drive south of Kew lies the rural estate of Wakehurst Place set high and proud on the Sussex Weald. Since its opening to the public under the control of the Royal Botanic Gardens in 1968 the beauty of this garden has become increasingly well known, with its spectacular landscape of streams, valleys and lakes, massive rock outcrops and a romantic Elizabethan mansion. The conditions it offers are ideal for a wealth of plants, amongst the most notable being rhododendrons, which benefit from an average rainfall of 821 mm (32.3 inches) – about half as much again as at Kew – and a varied topography with a wider range of soils running from sand to heavy loam.

The Elizabethan mansion, originally the home of the Culpeper family (of which the famous herbalist was a member), presents a splendid aspect when viewed across the water and closely mown lawns. Beside the Mansion Pond lies the artificial rock outcrop, with unusual plants like *Fascicularia pitcairniifolia*, a relative of the pineapple. Mature plantings of magnificent rhododendrons form an impressive backcloth to the scene.
Photo: T. A. Harwood.

As we have seen in Chapter 4, the gardens as they exist today were initiated by Gerald W. E. Loder (1861–1936, created Lord Wakehurst in 1934) and from the time he bought the estate in 1903 until his death thirty-three years later he worked to improve the great natural beauties of Wakehurst Place. Today it is possible to see much of his work coming to maturity, especially in areas such as the Heath Garden and the Pinetum.

The history of the Wakehurst estate is recorded back to Norman times. For generations the owners were concerned mainly with woodland and agricultural management. The real development of the garden occurred in the early years of this century and was greatly stimulated at that time by the wealth of plant introductions being made from the Himalayan region. This surge of new and exciting plants, including rhododendrons, magnolias and conifers, many needing moist, mild growing conditions, encouraged the development of woodland gardens in many parts of Britain – and Wakehurst was always well up with the leaders. Many of the original introductions of this period, from collectors like Farrer and Wilson and later by Forrest, Kingdon Ward, Rock and Yu, are among the mature plantings still to be found flourishing at Wakehurst.

The estate covers some 200 hectares (500 acres). On the map these look very scattered, but on the ground the 22.5 km (14 mile) boundary weaves naturally around fields of rich pasture, following the heavily wooded valley edges. The

Map of the Gardens of Wakehurst Place. The parts of the estate open to the public are shaped like a horseshoe, which comprises two steeply wooded valleys joining at Westwood Lake. The Gardens occupy only a portion of the extensive estate, which also includes managed woodlands and the new Loder Valley Reserve, which is not shown on this map.

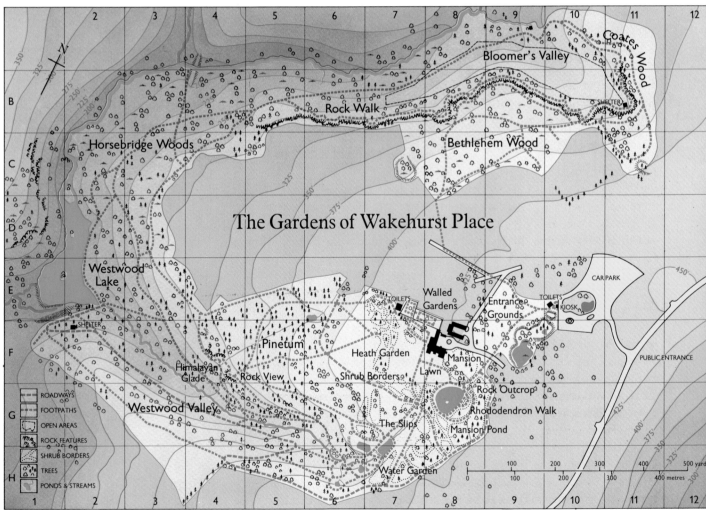

The Gardens of Wakehurst Place

public entrance to the garden lies on its eastern side, with the main axis of the estate running north to south following the lines of the streams that feed Ardingly Brook. The area of the garden open to the public occupies about one-third of the estate, and its focal point is the Mansion itself.

The aim of Kew's management since acquiring the estate has been to convert the garden to both scientific and public use as a botanic garden, while retaining everything of the old that contributed to its charm and character. At first the horticultural problems were of a rather commonplace nature such as renewing fencing, forming service areas from which staff could operate, creating nurseries for raising planting material, and providing a system of paths and rides to meet the needs of visitors and give access for machines. The ground staff of the garden undertook the bulk of the work on the formation and clearing of walks as well as constructing steps and access points. In addition there was a need for preserving some trees and thinning over-planted areas such as the Pinetum. Now, as one walks through the sylvan glades carpeted with bluebells, among the handsome specimen trees of the earlier planting period and the new growth of young plants, it seems as though it has always been so.

The acquisition of Wakehurst also required Kew to revise its policies for its mother arboretum and for the first ten years the pattern was of transfer, from Kew to Wakehurst, of specific collections. With time and experience the policies have clarified to the mutual benefit of both arboreta. The moister, cooler atmosphere of Wakehurst makes it a fine complement to Kew. For this reason *Rhododendron* was selected early on as a genus for extensive development at Wakehurst; similarly a successful *Nothofagus* (southern beech) collection has also been assembled. Problematically, though, the requirement for moist conditions is not precisely divided according to systematic relationships, but more to geographic origin. For example, Wakehurst has notable specimens from the southern hemisphere, whereas for many of these, such as the Chilean fire-bush (*Embothrium coccineum*), Kew has too dry a climate to allow their survival outside. Coincidentally too the area where these

Left: bluebells are conspicuous in many parts of the estate during late spring, but they are perhaps seen at their best in Horsebridge Woods in the shade of large specimen trees. This moist, steep-sided valley is ideal for conifers such as the giant fir (*Abies grandis*), currently the tallest tree at Wakehurst. Photo: F. N. Hepper.

Right: a plant of *Ozothamnus backhousei*, a member of the Compositae, growing in the Heath Garden. It was collected by Harold Comber (as No. 2237) in Tasmania during his collecting trip in 1929–30 and is one of many plants in cultivation of known provenance and bearing the field numbers of their collectors. Photo: A. D. Schilling.

From above Bloomer's Valley the Rock Walk leads through dense mixed woodland into Horsebridge Woods and down to Westwood Lake, which lies some 76 metres (250 ft) below the level of the Mansion. The Lake, from which water flows into the new reservoir, was formed in the nineteenth century by damming the Ardingly Brook.
Photo: T. A. Harwood.

plants thrive at Wakehurst is lacking in phosphorus – which of course is ideal for many Australian Proteaceae since they occur naturally in phosphorus-deficient soils. Thus a preference has slowly emerged for the use of geographic arrangements for the collections at Wakehurst. Following the still current development of southern hemisphere plantings on the site of the 'Heath Garden', and the development of the Himalayan Glade (linking the Pinetum and rhododendron plantings in Westwood Valley) the intention is also to concentrate North American plantings through Horsebridge Woods, and the Asian plantings through Westwood Valley, with a separate area for Japanese plants. This has the effect of not restricting Wakehurst by family or genus of woody plants, but allows it to more fully extend the range of genera cultivated by the Royal Botanic Gardens.

A Garden for the Connoisseur

The path to the Mansion leads visitors to the Top Lake past many interesting specimen trees – the round-leaved beech (*Fagus sylvatica* 'Rotundifolia') for example, and swamp cypress (*Taxodium distichum*) – set in a grassland with naturalized bulbs.

To the east of the Mansion Pond lies the 'Rhododendron Walk' with its mature plantings of choice rhododendrons in wide variety. In early spring the scarlet-flowered *Rhododendron barbatum* blooms here, followed a little later by its Himalayan relative, *R. arboreum*. The dwarf hybrid *R. × cilpinense* is another early flowerer and is especially well represented by a mass planting close to the viewpoint adjacent to the south-east edge of the pond. Far taller and with bright scarlet flowers is the hybrid *R. × shilsonii* which is a cross between *R. thomsonii* and *R. barbatum*. These early-flowering rhododendrons are followed by many others which produce a continuous succession of colour throughout the spring and summer.

Amongst this wide representation of the genus *Rhododendron* can be found other interesting plants, such as the conifer *Fitzroya cupressoides* from the moist mountains of Chile and Argentina. *Hoheria sexstylosa* is also here: it is commonly known as ribbonwood in its native home of New Zealand and produces countless white mallow-shaped flowers in July and August. Beneath the trees and larger shrubs will be noted a wide range of interesting ground-cover plants, many herbaceous, but some shrubby, such as the late-winter-flowering evergreen *Sarcococca hookeriana*, the variegated *Euonymus fortunei* 'Emerald and Gold' and the British native tutsan (*Hypericum androsaemum*). This last-named is purported to have many curative properties, the common name being a corruption of *toute-saine* (heal-all). It is an ideal subject for planting in areas of shade, is relatively tolerant of drought, and flowers from June until September.

Back north-eastward along the path close to the pond edge there is a fine example of *Magnolia wilsonii* from south-west China. This lovely species, which was introduced in 1908 by Henry Wilson, bears white pendulous flowers in late spring and is without doubt one of the gems of its genus. Further along the path will be seen the Chusan palm (*Trachycarpus fortunei*) which is also Chinese and is the only palm which can be considered truly hardy in the home counties of Great Britain.

As one passes the rock terraces at the head of the pond, attention will inevitably be drawn towards the interesting array of slow-growing conifers, choice ground cover plants such as *Geranium procurrens*, *Polygonum vacciniifolium* and *Potentilla ambigua* (*cuneata*), and a selection of dwarf maples.

Moving across towards the front of the Mansion the path skirts a mixed border containing *Camellia sinensis* (the tea plant of commerce), a very fine example of *Pittosporum colensoi*, a somewhat tender species from New Zealand, and the golden-leaved form of the red flowering currant (*Ribes sanguineum* 'Brocklebankii').

Beyond the formal lawns which flank Sir Edward Culpeper's Mansion the rich purple tones of a sixty-metre-long lavender hedge will catch the eye of mid-summer visitors. It was planted in the spring of 1974 to replace a tall and ailing yew hedge which cut the upper gardens in two, obstructing the view between the Heath Garden and the Mansion Pond. To make the hedge *Lavandula* 'Hidcote' was chosen for its attractive dwarf habit, for the value of its late and prolonged flowering, and because the introduction of the common lavender and the actual building of the Mansion date from the sixteenth century.

Not far from the Sir Henry Price Garden, described in Chapter 4, is the Heath and Southern Hemisphere Garden, where Gerald Loder put in so much of his time and interest. This area of closely aligned beds, interspaced by narrow grass paths, shows Wakehurst's botanical attractions to great advantage, particularly favouring plants from the southern hemisphere, most notably from the protea family, Proteaceae, and also the leptospermums or ti

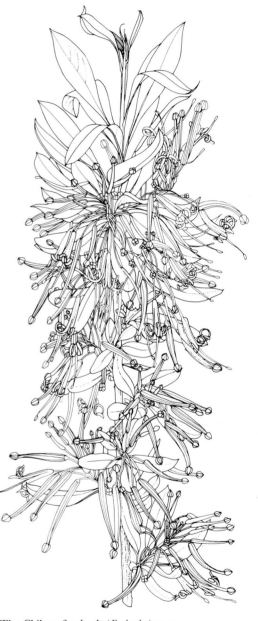

The Chilean fire bush (*Embothrium coccineum*), well named because of its startling scarlet flowers, is a feature of the Heath and Southern Hemisphere Garden in late May and early June. The hardiest form in cultivation in Britain is that collected in 1926 by Harold Comber in the Argentine Andes. Drawing: Joanna A. Langhorne.

Left: *Magnolia campbellii* was first collected by Joseph Hooker and named by him after Archibald Campbell, Superintendent of Darjeeling Botanic Garden. It is one of the noblest of hardy Himalayan trees and Wakehurst has perhaps the largest specimen in Britain. The pink-flowered form is usually seen in cultivation, though the white form is more commonly met with in the wild. It takes about thirty years to flower when raised from seed.
Photo: A.D. Schilling.

Bottom, left: the white bracts of *Davidia involucrata* (illustrated var. *vilmoriniana*), a native of China, have earned for it the names pocket-handkerchief or dove tree.
Photo: A.D. Schilling.

Opposite, top right: the large-leaved rhododendrons prosper at Wakehurst. One of the finest is *Rhododendron sinogrande*, from Tibet and neighbouring regions, with its dark green leaves, silvery grey beneath. Unfortunately the spectacular, but rather precocious, flowers are subject to damage by frost.
Photo: A.D. Schilling.

Opposite, bottom right: although *Rhododendron arboreum* is not particularly hardy at Kew, it thrives at Wakehurst. This tree species, with a wide distribution in the lower Himalayas, has numerous colour forms, including one with blood-red flowers which has contributed to many hybrids.
Photo: A.D. Schilling.

Right: one of the special features of Wakehurst is the presence of a number of Australasian Proteaceae growing outside. *Grevillea sulphurea*, sometimes referred to as *G. juniperinum* var. *sulphurea*, was introduced into Britain from New South Wales by the Kew collector Allan Cunningham. It was given an Award of Merit by the Royal Horticultural Society in 1974.
Photo: A.D. Schilling.

Below: the lush growth of water-loving plants reaches its climax in the height of summer. The Water Garden, constructed in 1974 near the head of the Ravine, combines both horticultural beauty with plant conservation, since many of the plants are uncommon British native species.
Photo: T.A. Harwood.

trees from the myrtle family. These latter, which come in a host of shades from white to red, seem almost overburdened with blossom each June. Members of the protea family from Chile, Australia and Tasmania can also be spectacular, for example the fire-bushes (*Embothrium* species), or the waratahs (*Telopea* species) and they are certainly fascinating as are grevilleas, hakeas and lomatias.

A good proportion of these intriguing plants were collected by Harold F. Comber, who was sponsored by several famous gardens to collect plants in the Andes of Chile and Argentina (1925–27), as well as in Tasmania (1929–30). Some still bear his collecting numbers such as *Sophora macrocarpa* (Comber 583) and *Pernettya prostrata* subsp. *pentlandii* (C. 1162). Other southern hemisphere plants grow well here: *Desfontainia spinosa* (with its holly-like foliage and red and yellow flowers), cassinias, hebes, helichrysums, hoherias (which regenerate naturally in great abundance), hymenantheras (woody shrubs from the violet family), olearias and pittosporums, to name but a few. Epacridaceae (the southern hemisphere counterpart of the Erica family) is also well-represented with, amongst others, *Richea scoparia* growing and flowering extremely well. *Weinmannia trichosperma* from Chile, with its dark green fern-like leaves, is the only hardy member of the family Cunoniaceae that is cultivated at Kew or Wakehurst, and while on fine foliage plants the beautiful bamboos of the genus *Chusquea* from the Andes must be mentioned. This area also contains many cultivated rarities from other regions of the world such as the Himalayan cypress (*Cupressus torulosa*) or, and just surviving, the Asiatic *Reevesia pubescens*, in the mainly tropical family Sterculiaceae, to which cocoa also belongs.

This original planting theme has been extended and enriched under Kew's management with new beds and plantings of both southern hemisphere plants and a wide range of dwarf and sun-loving *Rhododendron* species.

The Ravine to Westwood Lake
The series of ponds and terraced banks at the head of the Ravine (Westwood Valley) have been combined to make a large water garden feature. The planting programme for this area includes a wide range of water-loving plants of horticultural merit, as well as British native bog, marshland and water-plants, such as the narrow-leaved reedmace (*Typha angustifolia*), the sweet flag (*Acorus calamus*), the great water-dock (*Rumex hydrolapathum*), the beautiful pink-flowering rush (*Butomus umbellatus*) and the intriguing water soldier (*Stratiotes aloides*). As in other parts of the gardens, emphasis wherever possible is being placed on wild-collected material of known origin.

The stream that leaves this area flows on down to Westwood Lake through the Ravine which provides the home for the huge rhododendron collection numbering over 380 species, in addition to the many cultivated varieties (cultivars). Amongst the more interesting can be mentioned the red-flowered form of *Rhododendron arizelum* (Forrest 21861), a large-leaved species which originates from the mountain forests of Yunnan Province in south-west China. *R. succothii* from Assam and Bhutan, glows crimson-scarlet in early spring, as also does *R. mallotum*, which Farrer collected from Upper Burma in 1919.

The seldom seen *R. argipeplum* from the eastern Himalayas is another early-flowering species to be found in the collection. There are many species more tender than these which have been unaffected by the rigours of the Sussex winters and have grown to maturity here in favoured situations. Most notable are *R. facetum*, *R. stamineum*, *R. wilsonae* and *R. delavayi*—all from China.

Such are the near-ideal conditions in Westwood Valley that much natural regeneration occurs and it is possible to observe self-sown seedlings of many species, including *R. falconeri*, *R. sinogrande*, *R. fictolacteum*, *R. hypoglaucum*, *R. niveum*, *R. neriiflorum* and *R. glischroides* growing on the moss-covered banks.

Two of the many notable trees in the Ravine are a superb specimen of the elegant western hemlock (*Tsuga heterophylla*) now some 38 m (127 ft) high, and a fine specimen of the pocket-handkerchief tree (*Davidia involucrata*), which was introduced by Henry Wilson in 1904 and must surely be one of his most hard-won and worthwhile plant-hunting achievements. Close to the *Davidia* grows what is one of the largest specimens of *Magnolia campbellii* in Great Britain, and another plant adjacent to this and with similar claims to unique national stature is the rare Chinese laurel (*Persea ichangensis*).

Half way down this deep and wooded valley is an area of magnificent natural sandstone outcrops where re-landscaping has created a delightful glade planted with carefully chosen Himalayan species of plants, such as *Berberis concinna*, *B. gyalaica*, *Cotoneaster conspicuus*, *C. adpressus*, *Euonymus tingens*, *Potentilla arbuscula*, *Spiraea bella*, *Viburnum cordifolium* and a wide range of *Rhododendron* species.

The central area of the glade is set aside for an immense group-planting of *Berberis wilsoniae*, whilst the rock outcrops have been liberally planted with *Polygonum vacciniifolium* and *P. affine* for autumn effect. Existing large specimens of *Rhododendron falconeri* and *R. arboreum* already form an imposing and mature frame to this picture of the Himalayan temperate flora.

The long path that runs on the east side and around the head of the valley amongst the trees is called Rock Walk. It runs beneath impressive sandstone outcrops across whose vertical faces snake the contorted, clasping roots of trees with stems that appear almost to balance on the top of the rocks. The moist rock outcrops covered with damp moss permit the growth of 'aerial' roots over the surface of the rock in a spectacular manner. Photo: T. A. Harwood.

109

The remarkable curtain-like branches of Brewer's spruce (*Picea breweriana*), a native of California and Oregon, are best seen against the light. The Wakehurst trees were planted in 1915 and are larger than the one at Kew sent in 1897 by C. S. Sargent (founder of the Arnold Arboretum).
Photo: A.D. Schilling.

Conifers thrive well in the moist climate of the Sussex Weald. In the Pinetum at Wakehurst there is a tree of the rare Sikkim larch (*Larix griffithii*). The species was introduced into cultivation by Sir Joseph Hooker in 1848 and beautifully figured by W.H. Fitch in *Illustrations of Himalayan Plants* (1855).

The Pinetum

Planted around 1914, the Pinetum covers an area of 8 hectares (20 acres) and runs parallel to the south-west side of the Ravine, from which discreet views have now been opened to reveal the beauty of its conifers. The genera *Abies*, *Cedrus*, *Larix*, *Picea*, *Pinus* and *Tsuga* are well represented and include a number of rare and notable specimens. From the genus *Tsuga*, for example, the Carolina hemlock (*T. caroliniana*) is probably the tallest specimen in the country and equally notable is the Chinese hemlock (*T. chinensis*), which is only rarely grown in Britain. Some conifers, such as the Himalayan fir (*Abies spectabilis*), which has needles with a silvery under-surface, are by no means the largest of their kind in Britain, but are nonetheless an attractive sight. Among the uncommon conifers is *Libocedrus plumosa*, the kawaka from the north-west corner of the South Island of New Zealand, which is slow growing, and at about 5 metres quite large for a specimen in England.

Taiwania cryptomerioides is represented, but to be frank it is only on the borderline of hardiness, coming, as its name records, from Taiwan, and also from western China and northern Burma. Were it fully hardy, it would make a magnificent tree, as in its native home, where its timber is favoured for coffins. Amongst the 'tender' conifers the Mexican *Pinus patula* has in contrast, however, proved quite hardy at Wakehurst. The multi-stemmed specimen in the Pinetum is eye-catching with its cinnamon peeling bark and needles as much as 20cm (8in) long.

Other notable specimens must include the Himalayan larch (*Larix griffithii*), the Korean thuja (*Thuja koraiensis*), the very large Sargent's spruce (*Picea brachytyla*), which like the *Thuja* is amongst the 'top 20' of its kind in Britain, and a large *Cedrus brevifolia*, the Cyprean cedar, growing as well as in its native Troodos Mountain home.

In comparing conifers at Kew and Wakehurst it is interesting to note the specimen of *Keteleeria davidiana*, from China and Japan, which is now around 10m (33ft) in height, and quite content with life at Wakehurst, whereas at Kew it has to be confined to the Temperate House. In the reverse direction it can be noted that the beautiful *Picea smithiana*, with its pendant branchlets, is happier in the drier atmosphere of Kew, reflecting its more western Himalayan distribution, from Afghanistan to Nepal, where it occurs at altitudes up to 2700 metres (9000ft) in dry valleys.

Through the Woods

Westwood Lake acts as a junction for the two valleys which shape the Arboretum. While the Ravine may be admired for its rhododendrons, the other valley that leads through Horsebridge Woods and on into the grassy expanse called Bloomer's Valley must be noted for its many specimen trees, especially conifers. In this area are some of the tallest trees on the estate, including some large sequoias, notably *Sequoiadendron giganteum* (the sierra redwood) and *Sequoia sempervirens* (the coastal redwood). They are accompanied by a tall Serbian spruce (*Picea omorika*) and a lofty giant fir (*Abies grandis*) which at 46 metres (150ft) is at present the tallest plant on the estate.

Although Wakehurst Place lies relatively close to London, it is a very different and less noisy world and admirably complements the rich and historic collections of Kew.

A.D.S. & J.B.E.S.

⊰ 12 ⊱
Wildlife at Kew

Wild Flowers

Painted on a board inside each of the entrance gates to Kew is a notice to visitors: 'The public are not allowed to pick the wild flowers which are as much a source of enjoyment to visitors as are the cultivated plants.'

One might be forgiven for asking where wild flowers – weeds to most people – are likely to be found in a garden. But it does not take long to realize that Kew has large areas of rough ground where the native British plants flourish at will. In May the sheets of bluebells in the woodland are an awe-inspiring sight which would soon be ruined if everyone took a bunch home.

The bluebell (*Hyacinthoides non-scripta*) may be the most spectacular wild flower at Kew, but there are many others in the meadow areas and bushy places. Some are relicts of the original Thames valley flora now sadly nearly exterminated by urban development. In the sixteenth century William Turner, the father of English botany, who lived near Kew, knew the snake's head fritillary (*Fritillaria meleagris*) in the water meadows at Mortlake where it persisted until 1876. Today the meadow saxifrage (*Saxifraga granulata*) at Kew enjoys the more open areas among the daffodil bulbs, while the buttercup called goldilocks (*Ranunculus auricomus*) prefers shadier places in short grass.

Even the shade beneath an individual tree is sufficient for a mini-nature reserve. One of the joys of Kew is to see the true shape of the trees with their lower branches sweeping the ground or spreading out naturally. Beneath them there is often a terrestrial white halo of hedge parsley (*Anthriscus sylvestris*),

Left: the wildest part of Kew is the woodland to the west of the Pinetum. In spring, hedge parsley (*Anthriscus sylvestris*) flowers profusely in the light shade. With it grows another member of the Umbelliferae, the naturalized *Smyrnium perfoliatum*, which has striking yellow-green bracts.
Photo: M. Svanderlik.

Right: the foxglove (*Digitalis purpurea*) is a native British species and isolated plants occur here and there at Kew. It is encouraged to grow in colourful masses near the Lily Pond.
Photo: F. N. Hepper.

Among the many British woodland plants that occur in the shade of trees and bushes at Kew is the ground ivy (*Glechoma hederacea*), which trails along the ground and produces subdued mauve flowers in spring.

An uncommon species of open, grassy places is the meadow saxifrage (*Saxifraga granulata*), which is a relict of the original and now greatly depleted Thames Valley flora.

bluebells and ground ivy (*Glechoma hederacea*) with its subdued blue flowers discernible among the grass. Extensive areas of light shade in the arboretum are not mown until summer, when bulb leaves have died down. The problem is how to manage these sites in such a way that choice species are maintained – too much cutting exhausts them, while not enough at the right time of year encourages the growth of vigorous grasses, which overwhelm them. The light, sandy soil of Kew, being poor in plant foods, favours slender grasses such as the sweet vernal grass (*Anthoxanthum odoratum*) which scents the air with the nostalgic fragrance of new-mown hay. Fine-leaved fescues (*Festuca*) and coarser bent grasses (*Agrostis*), which have reddish inflorescences later in the season, are mixed with chaffy field woodrush (*Luzula campestris*) and yellow-headed composites such as cat's ear (*Hypochoeris radicata*), mouse-ear hawkweed (*Pilosella officinarum*) and dandelion (*Taraxacum officinale*). There is also red clover (*Trifolium pratense*), ox-eye daisy (*Leucanthemum vulgare*), bird's-foot trefoil (*Lotus corniculatus*) and the pale-blue germander speedwell (*Veronica chamaedrys*). Even the common daisy (*Bellis perennis*), though scorned by the purist, adds charm to the mown lawns.

On the grassy slopes between the trees on the mound that bears the Temple of Aeolus, drifts of wild daffodil (*Narcissus pseudo-narcissus*) have become naturalized. Their yellow trumpets often appear very early in the year as harbingers of spring. Much later in the spring in the dappled shade of the Pinetum there is a fine display of *Smyrnium perfoliatum*. This is a close relative of the celery-like alexanders and is actually an introduced species from southern Europe. It is fully naturalized at Kew, where its erect stems, clothed with brilliant greenish-yellow upper leaves, go well with the white of hedge parsley, the mauve of cuckoo flower (*Cardamine pratensis*), and the haze of bluebells inside and outside Queen Charlotte's Cottage Grounds. Grassy glades and winding paths are cut here and there to avoid visitors trampling on leaves of the bluebells since this has a bad effect on their flowering.

The Wild Plants of Queen Charlotte's Cottage Grounds

The wildest part of Kew is the 15 hectares (37 acres) of woodland around Queen Charlotte's eighteenth-century cottage. The consort of George III used to walk in the gardens and take tea in the thatched cottage she had built in the traditional style, at least in appearance. Inside, it contains virtually one room upstairs and another downstairs, and thus is quite impossible to use as living accommodation, but is now beautifully refurbished and open to the public at weekends.

At one time there were paths and ornamental buildings within the grounds (Chapter 1), but after Capability Brown's clearance of the previous layout trees took over. So, for over two hundred years, trees have grown in the Grounds, some spontaneously, others planted apparently at random, becoming wilder and forming a mature English woodland as the years passed by. No wonder Queen Victoria loved it, earnestly trusting 'that this unique spot may be preserved in its present and natural condition' when she passed it over to the Royal Botanic Gardens in May 1898 in commemoration of her Diamond Jubilee in 1897.

In recent years a definite policy has been evolved in order to enhance the value of the Grounds from the point of view of nature conservation. Careful management maintains a balanced community of British flora and fauna. In former years exotic and introduced shrubs had been planted, while sycamore trees (*Acer pseudo-platanus*) had self-sown themselves in profusion. Suppression of these unwanted species has been coupled with an annual clearance of brambles (*Rubus*) in certain areas to encourage native plants. Snowdrops (*Galanthus nivalis*), primroses (*Primula vulgaris*) and martagon lily (*Lilium martagon*) have become established in large, colourful drifts. Scattered plants of red campion (*Silene dioica*) show off their pink flowers against the rich colour of the bluebells which, together with the hedge parsley, beautifully scent the air during early May. The sun shining through the delicate, unfurling beech leaves casts deep shadows among the bushes beyond the bluebells. Later in the year the woods are ablaze with rosebay willowherb (*Epilobium angustifolium*) which is more welcome here than elsewhere in the Gardens.

A tangle of brambles, alder buckthorn (*Frangula alnus*), yew (*Taxus baccata*) and elderberry (*Sambucus nigra*) provide protection and food for birds and other creatures. Old branches remain where they fall from the trees since they provide an ideal habitat for fungi, insects and predatory birds that feed on insects. Grass seed is a useful source of food for migratory birds such as bramblings. Access to the public is only along a wide cinder track curving through the centre of the Grounds, so the bluebells and the wildlife are undisturbed through much of the area. New plantings of native trees can therefore be fitted in with the best of visual, scientific and conservation interests in mind. For example, a collection of willows (*Salix*) has been grouped near the riverside, where they thrive in the moister ground. Elsewhere, numerous hazels (*Corylus avellana*) have been planted in order to establish a traditional hazel coppice with oak standards. Cutting every ten years or so will encourage ground flora such as primroses, ground ivy and violets. In this way Kew is dynamic yet conservation-orientated with a diversity of flora encouraging a diversity of fauna. Since insects, birds and mammals depend on plants for their habitat and food, Kew is widely recognized by naturalists as an oasis of wildlife, and for many years records have been compiled and published from time to time in *Kew Bulletin*.

F.N.H.

Wild Birds

A few years ago a questionnaire revealed that more visitors come to Kew to see the ornamental waterfowl than the plants! Perhaps that was an exceptional day, but there is no doubt that the Lake and its birds attracts many a family party out to enjoy the amenities of Kew. More serious ornithologists can be spotted by their binoculars and note-book. At most times of year bird-watchers find Kew a rewarding place for wild birds.

From a bird's point of view the Gardens offer one particular habitat, and that is woodland. The species found are typical of any large area of woodland in the outskirts of London. The Pond and Lake offer water in addition, but there are no significantly large areas of open grassland or bushy country so that the species drawn to Kew are somewhat limited to woodland ones. Just outside the Gardens, however, the river bordering the western edge and Syon Park beyond attract a different set of birds, enhancing the interest of the whole area for the visiting bird-watcher. The lack of a footpath on the far side of the river coupled with the private nature of the eastern part of Syon Park undoubtedly remain essential ingredients of this relatively unspoilt district, disturbed only by the passing of motor-boats and aircraft.

In recent years over eighty species have been seen annually either within the

By mid-summer, parts of Queen Charlotte's Cottage Grounds are ablaze with the tall rosebay willowherb or fireweed (*Epilobium angustifolium*). Although formerly considered to be a rare species, it began to spread rapidly throughout Britain towards the end of the nineteenth century and is now a feature of woods, clearings and waste places.

These drawings were made by the Kew artist Walter Fitch for George Bentham's *Handbook of the British Flora* (1865), later editions of which were revised by Sir Joseph Hooker. Many generations of British botanists were brought up on 'Bentham and Hooker', the Fitch illustrations to which appeared as a separate volume. Bentham and Hooker also produced at Kew their monumental, three-volume *Genera Plantarum* (1862–83).

One of the tasks of the officially appointed Bird Keeper, is to look after the game birds such as the pheasant (above), as well as the ornamental waterfowl that are raised in special pens in the Arboretum Yard.
Photo: K. A. Boyer.

Water birds feature prominently around the Lake. While many are introduced species, others are indigenous, such as the mallard duck, the dabchick and the moorhen (below).
Photo: R. Hastings.

Gardens or just outside them – 1979 was an exceptionally good year with a round one hundred being recorded. Inside the boundaries of Kew up to forty-five species breed annually.

While the Gardens are botanically most attractive during the warmer months, it is the winter season that brings many of the commoner resident birds fully into view. Not only are they revealed by the bare branches, but also they are as tame here during the winter as at any place in Britain. The Rhododendron Dell and Queen's Cottage Grounds are two notable areas where an outstretched hand offering much-prized food will be descended upon by a host of eager tits, robins and even nuthatches.

Keen bird-watchers will visit the Gardens hoping to see particularly attractive or scarce species. Undoubtedly the star among these was the hawfinch, which of late has sadly declined at Kew. In the first three decades of this century it was seen only rarely, but it increased during the 1940s and a nest was found in 1949. Unfortunately the pair had chosen a service tree (*Sorbus domestica*) which was in full blossom in early May. It stood near the Main Gate and the numerous visitors passing beneath it caused the shy birds to desert. Subsequently they nested each of the following years up to 1956, with no less than three pairs breeding in 1952. Clearly this was their heyday at Kew. Up to twelve were seen together, but after 1956 nesting became less regular and gatherings were smaller. The last nest known was found in 1970, though a young bird was seen in 1974. Now they are a great rarity, only seen flying over Kew in recent years.

Another interesting breeding bird is the kingfisher. Though a regular visitor for many years, it was not found nesting inside the Gardens until 1972, when a suitable gravelly bank had been created during digging operations. Subsequently a larger vertical bank was made in the hope that they would return, which they did. Since 1975 they have nested every year and typically try to rear two broods, one in spring and one in summer. They are not always successful, largely because of human disturbance or predation by foxes, which try to dig down to the young in the nest tunnel. All through the summer they can be seen daily along the river, a spectacular dart of brilliant blue and red or a sudden small splash.

All three British woodpeckers occur regularly at Kew. The great spotted is commonest and is a characteristic bird of the Gardens. They may nest quite close to numbers of visitors, as did a pair in 1980 which chose a swamp cypress close to the Pond and No. 1 Museum. The green woodpecker is scarcer with maybe only one regular pair, so that they are seen less often, despite their large size and colourful plumage. The best area for them is the vicinity of the Queen's Cottage Grounds. The very elusive lesser spotted woodpecker can be met with regularly at times, especially in winter and early spring. It is most surprising that it has never been found nesting at Kew.

The Gardens attract three species of warbler which are likely to stay and breed. Commonest is the blackcap, whose song can often be heard in the Rhododendron Dell and Queen's Cottage Grounds. This is one of the few birds that is prepared to frequent rhododendrons. Chiffchaffs occur annually in the same areas as well as at the Lake, though they may not breed so regularly as the blackcap. Their simple song can be heard for a greater part of the summer. Scarcest is the willow warbler, which occurs every spring but may be a most infrequent nester.

Of the aquatic birds, the Canada goose is without doubt much the commonest. Introduced to Britain, they have become very much a feature of Kew's lawns, not to everyone's delight. It is hard to believe that they were relatively scarce until the 1960s. Nowadays their numbers are controlled but they continue to increase and one flock alone numbered 210 in August 1980. In contrast, duck numbers remain steady with a few pairs of tufted duck and pochard nesting each year. Until recently the little grebe was an annual breeder at the Lake and great crested grebes nested there in 1976 and 1978, rearing young both years.

No account of the breeding species would be complete without mention of the successful nesting of crossbills in 1967, when a pair reared at least one young. The species had last been found breeding in the London area way back in 1936; the locality in that year was remarkably also Kew Gardens. The nest was then in a lofty pine, about forty feet up, and five young were hatched. They had never been seen at all at Kew before that year.

During winter and the migration seasons of spring and autumn, a less predictable collection of birds turns up. They may number anything from forty to sixty species, including a complete gradation from the most predictable to the completely unexpected. The winter visitors are most regular in appearance. Within the Gardens they are represented characteristically by redwings which occur in groups feeding on the ground below the trees or on yews and crab-apples. Usually the gatherings are small but 'hundreds' were roosting in the Rhododendron Dell during particularly cold weather in February and March 1954. The related fieldfare is much scarcer, preferring open ground to woodland, except when roosting. Most are seen over-flying Kew.

Along the river, herons and cormorants are present daily for a large part of the year and are almost as characteristic of Kew as the Canada geese. Herons spend the day resting in the marshy part of Syon Park or feeding along the foreshore when the river is low. At night they are more active and some drop in at the Lake and Pond to feed. One or two even visit the little Aquatic Garden which is very well stocked with large goldfish.

While herons are present in the summer cormorants are only about between August and May, with the largest numbers in mid-winter.

Aside from the breeding species, the most regular duck at Kew today is the shoveler. This bird was once a rarity and was only recorded for the first time in 1953 but recently they have increased considerably.

Another visitor that turns up more often now is the sparrowhawk. This bird occasionally bred at Kew until pesticide poisoning took its toll nationwide in the early 1960s. After many years of rarity they are now returning and a male was even displaying in spectacular fashion near the Lake in April 1980.

Among less expected visitors that have been sighted in the Gardens are great grey shrike, waxwing and various duck, including, in August 1979, a garganey In addition to the waders that are seen along the Thames, there have been reports of red-necked and black-necked grebe, common scoter, smew, common tern and even, many years ago, a puffin.

Ornamental Birds

The birds introduced by man provide plenty of interest for visitors, complementing the attraction of the wild ones. No doubt the birds gain added appeal from the beauty of their surroundings. They must also seem rather more familiar than the many trees, shrubs and flowers with their apparently forbidding scientific names on every label.

Another British water bird is the coot, which builds a large raft for its nest. Adult coots have a conspicuous white frontal shield above their white beaks.
Photo: J. Lonsdale.

For many years black swans have been a feature of the Kew Lake, although there was a gap in the 1970s. Sometimes they raise a second brood during the short winter days, thereby maintaining the rhythm of their Australian homeland.
Photo: L. Sullivan.

The wildfowl collection at the Lake has been very popular for many years. Unfortunately it became severely depleted during the 1970s. The initial population crash occurred in 1970, when over a hundred birds died and were found to be heavily infested with leeches (which may not have been the direct cause of death). The majority of the survivors fell to an outbreak of botulism in the hot, dry summer of 1976 probably due to pollution of the water by excessive quantities of bread provided by visitors, who are now asked not to feed the birds. Unfortunately even the handful of birds remaining were not safe, with foxes making kills on winter nights when the Lake was frozen. The last barnacle goose and last black swan fell in this way on one night in January 1979. Later that year, rebuilding of the collection began, starting most appropriately with a fine new pair of black swans, a species particularly associated with Kew. They built a nest early the following winter, since that would be summer in their Australian homeland! By the summer of 1981 the collection had reached a respectable size once more, containing a variety of European and other duck.

Farther afield is a strange selection of introduced game birds. Golden and silver pheasants can be seen, particularly near the Temperate House, and at least one Lady Amherst's pheasant has been about there. The big silver pheasants sometimes wander over to the Restaurant to pick up food around the tables. Guinea fowl were new on the scene in 1980, haunting land alongside the Rhododendron Dell and elsewhere.

Not to be forgotten are the free-flying ring-necked parakeets, a species accidentally introduced into parts of London and elsewhere. Those that visit Kew spend the night on Chiswick Eyot, an island in the Thames. Groups up to four in number appear at Kew, rending the air with loud screeches as they tear about. Once alighted they can disappear from view if they stay silent. Their visits to Kew fall largely in the autumn and winter months.

Other Wildlife

It is not only the birds that hold interest for those seeking animal life in the Gardens. Butterflies are well represented for an area so close in to London, with sixteen species noted during the summers of 1979 and 1980. A very characteristic one is the speckled wood, found among trees where sunlight is penetrating in patches, a habitat that is obviously widespread at Kew. A good year was 1980, when they could be found in many suitable areas. The holly blue, a very active butterfly not easy to see well, is scarcer but appears in both its spring and summer broods; it seems to occur largely in the northern half of the Gardens. Commas are about in summer and autumn, well into October in fine weather, in many parts of the Gardens. They are much easier to watch while they feed sedately from flowerheads. Among the migrants, red admirals seem to be scarce but the 1980 invasion of painted ladies affected Kew, with about six sightings occurring that autumn.

Dragonflies are also attracted to Kew's waters and open spaces with nine species recorded in 1979 and 1980. The most obvious of these is the scarce aeshna (*Aeshna mixta*) which appears in August and September. It enjoys any sunny area, be it the Lake, an open grassy space or part of the Rhododendron Dell. Most of the dragonflies seen are wandering individuals but the common ischnura (*Ischnura elegans*) probably breeds at the Lake.

Mammals are represented by the conspicuous and destructive grey squirrel which becomes especially active and visible towards evening. Generally they

Opposite: most visitors to Queen Charlotte's Cottage Grounds go there during May when the bluebells carpet the woods in a spectacular display. Winter time, however, can be just as beautiful, when light snow picks out the tracery of twigs on the lime trees. These woods are now managed as a nature reserve to encourage British plants and wildlife by creating diverse habitats. The cut avenues provide long vistas.

117

The brown aeshna (*Aeshna grandis*) is one of the dragonflies that may be seen around the Lake in late summer.
Photo: K. A. Boyer.

Dog roses (*Rosa canina*) flower in June in the wildest part of Queen Charlotte's Cottage Grounds and along the boundary with the Old Deer Park golf course.
Photo. F. N. Hepper.

do not allow as close an approach as in inner London, although there was an outbreak of visitor-biting only a few years ago. Most summer days they are lost in the foliage but they can often be found in winter, when they are not only more exposed but probably spend more daylight hours feeding. Rabbits are also active during the day, particularly in the Queen's Cottage Grounds; short-tailed voles and hedgehogs are sometimes met with, too. Throughout the year, foxes are present. Some arrive in winter from the Old Deer Park golf course to the south and some have established earths in the Queen's Cottage Grounds and Rhododendron Dell. Many tracks may be seen in winter if snow is lying, and pigeon corpses are found close to bushes used as cover by the fox before pouncing. Great efforts are put into trapping and shooting these animals because of the deaths they cause among pinioned wildfowl and sometimes pheasants. Unfortunately fresh foxes have not been prevented from entering the Gardens despite a new fence along the golf course boundary. In the late 1950s a badger set was found in the Arboretum, but unfortunately the occupants could not be tolerated owing to their predilection for wildfowl. Several badgers were therefore transported to Kenwood where they were released in the more spacious surroundings of Hampstead Heath.

The 120 hectares (300 acres) of Kew in the urban region of Greater London clearly support a population of resident and visiting wildlife that will interest many British and foreign visitors. Fortunately the protected environment that this botanic garden provides should ensure that the diversity of wildlife is maintained.

R.B.H.

❧ 13 ❧
Wildlife at
Wakehurst Place

Geography and Climate

Wakehurst is very fortunate in being situated centrally in the High Weald of Sussex. In contrast to Kew with its flat landscape and dry soils overlying gravel, Wakehurst Place has a rich variety of landscape features.

The geology of Wakehurst Place gives rise to a dissected landscape containing ponds and streams, gentle and steep slopes, impressive rock outcrops and a wide variety of soils derived from sandstones and clays. The varied topography and the different rocks and soils have encouraged the development of a wide range of vegetation.

Climatic differences also influence the flora and fauna of the estate. Two of the most important factors are higher rainfall, 821 mm (32.3 in) per annum against 635 mm (25 in) for Kew, and very much cleaner air. Air purity can be judged most easily by the abundant lichen growth on many trees. A system has been developed whereby the degree of air pollution can be judged by the number of lichen species present. Kew falls into Lichen Zone 2–3, on a scale which runs from one to ten (one being the most polluted), Wakehurst Place is in Zone 7.

The Gardens and Arboretum

The intensively cultivated areas close to the Mansion hold a surprising quantity of wildlife. The high walls of the Mansion provide homes for house martins, sparrows and starlings. Spotted flycatchers regularly raise their young in the creeper-covered walls of the chapel. Many other common birds welcome the visitor to the gardens; some chaffinches, robins and great tits are so used to human attention that they will take food from an outstretched hand.

Wild plants in these areas tend to be discouraged. 'Weed' is the unfortunate term applied to any native plant which dares to raise its head in the immaculately maintained beds. Two interesting parasitic plants are, however, tolerated. One, *Lathraea clandestina*, the beautiful blue toothwort, is an introduced plant from Europe naturalized in the gardens. Normally associated with poplars and willows, this toothwort has far greater choice in a botanic garden and can be found on many other genera, maples being particularly favoured. The other is mistletoe (*Viscum album*), which can be seen on several trees near the Mansion Pond. This strange plant, so loved by ancient druids and present-day Christmas partygoers, is the only British representative of *Loranthaceae*, a large family of parasites with a worldwide distribution.

The management of much of the Arboretum is less intensive, grass is allowed to grow longer, trees are on the whole more mature and there is less disturbance. These factors favour a far wider range of species than is to be found in the garden areas.

Wild orchids have a particular fascination and of those recorded on the Wakehurst estate the common spotted orchid (*Dactylorhiza fuchsii*) (below) is most likely to be seen. The rarest is the violet helleborine (*Epipactis purpurata*), which inhabits the margins of woodland in the Loder Valley Reserve.
Photo: K. A. Boyer.

Over ninety species of birds have been recorded at Wakehurst Place, a large proportion of which can be observed in the Arboretum. Even comparative rarities such as the crossbill and hawfinch are regular visitors.

The wild flora of the Arboretum varies considerably, being dependent on soil type and degree of tree cover. Many of the grass areas hold a rich meadow flora. Parts of the Ravine are a good example; in spring drifts of lady's smock (*Cardamine pratensis*), are followed by masses of common spotted orchid (*Dactylorhiza fuchsii*), lesser valerian (*Valeriana dioica*), and sanicle (*Sanicula europaea*). Horsebridge and Bethlehem Woods are worth a special visit at this time to see the masses of primroses (*Primula vulgaris*), violets (*Viola* species), and bluebells (*Hyacinthoides non-scripta*).

Although every effort is made to preserve and encourage native flora and fauna in the gardens and Arboretum, occasionally there is a conflict with the needs of the botanical collections. Some of the larger mammals in particular can cause problems. Deer, rabbits and grey squirrels are present in some numbers and can cause considerable damage, especially to newly planted trees and shrubs. Steps are taken to limit the population of rabbits and squirrels but roving groups of fallow and roe deer are more difficult to deter. In spring roe deer often thrash the lower branches of trees and shrubs in their efforts to rid their newly grown antlers of the skin or 'velvet' which has nourished and protected them during development. Fallow deer shed velvet in August and add to the damage. This type of behaviour may be repeated later in the year as part of the rutting display. Worse is to come during spells of severe weather since deer will on occasion strip bark from young trees when food is scarce. As a matter of policy all new plantings in vulnerable areas are now protected by wooden 'deer cages' in an effort to minimize this damage.

Site of Special Scientific Interest
Both Horsebridge and Bethlehem Woods are included within a very much larger area designated as a Site of Special Scientific Interest by the Nature Conservancy Council. The boundaries extend from Sheepwash Wood on the

The British woodland flora is well represented at Wakehurst.

Left to right: tangles of the parasitic mistletoe (*Viscum album*) may be seen on mature host trees, including lime and poplar, near the Mansion.

Two attractive spring-flowering natives are the wood anemone (*Anemone nemorosa*), which has white blooms flushed purple, and the wood sorrel (*Oxalis acetosella*), which has white flowers and folding leaves.

Two British plants typical of wet places are the marsh marigold (*Caltha palustris*) and lady's smock (*Cardamine pratensis*). The former, which has shining golden flowers, is more restricted in its habitat than lady's smock, always growing in the wettest places.

From George Bentham, *Handbook of the British Flora* (1865), drawings by W. H. Fitch.

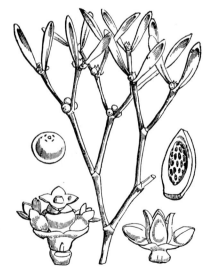

northern extremity of the estate to Tilgate and Platts Wood in the south. The site provides a protected refuge for many interesting plant and animal communities including several species with a very localized distribution; for example the scarce Tunbridge Wells filmy fern (*Hymenophyllum tunbrigense*) occurs within the SSSI and Horsebridge Woods is home to several species of rare mollusc.

The filmy fern (*Hymenophyllum tunbrigense*) occurs infrequently both at Wakehurst and in Britain as a whole. Since this delicate species cannot survive dry conditions, it is restricted to damp sandstone outcrops in deep shade. Drawing by Joanna A. Langhorne.

The Loder Valley Reserve

In 1975 the decision was made to develop an extensive tract of woodland previously closed to the public. After initial survey it was realized that the site had great potential as a conservation area. The rich variety of habitats presented an opportunity perhaps unique for a botanic garden in the British Isles. With the completion of the Ardingly Reservoir by the Southern Water

Butterflies such as the cabbage white, tortoise-shell and comma are often seen visiting flowers or on the wing, but the scarce purple emperor is seldom visible because it inhabits the crowns of oak trees.
Photo: K. A. Boyer.

Authority in 1978, the conservation value of the area was further enhanced. The flooding of the valley bottom by an arm of the reservoir resulted in an 18-hectare stretch of open water following the course of Ardingly Brook. In the summer of 1978 Kew hosted an international conservation conference which stressed the urgent need for botanic gardens to take an active part in the conservation of native flora. This strengthened the resolve of those concerned to develop the area as soon as possible. Work started almost immediately, enabling the reserve to be formally opened in July 1980.

The Loder Valley is planned to provide a protected reserve for the native plants of south-east England, with particular reference to the flora of the Weald. Provision is also made within the reserve for the conservation of a number of trees and shrubs not native to the area but threatened in continental Europe. The main objective is to provide suitable habitats for the continued success of complete plant communities. Three major habitat types are to be found within the reserve, woodland, meadowland and wetland. Each may be further subdivided into more specific environments. For example, the woodland consists of economic forestry plantings, 'natural' oak woods, coppice and scrub, each of which requires a particular management technique.

Woodland

Man has managed the woods for many centuries and taken timber in many forms as one of his most important raw materials. Traditionally much of the area was maintained as coppice with standards, a system of management that involves harvesting the coppice every few years on a rotational basis. The most important species exploited in this way to supply materials for building, industrial and domestic use were the common oak (*Quercus robur*) as standards and hazel (*Corylus avellana*) as coppice. Oak, which is so abundant in the area that it has been called 'The Sussex Weed', provided heavy structural timbers, while hazel supplied rods, poles and brushwood which were used to make a great variety of products. The cycle of clearance and gradual regrowth is of great value to certain plant and animal communities, providing, for instance, for many herbaceous plants normally suppressed by heavy shade. The upsurge

The creation of Ardingly Reservoir, which lies partly in the Wakehurst estate, has led to the designation of a nature reserve called the Loder Valley Reserve. It affords an opportunity to practise nature conservation in a variety of natural habitats.
Photo: A. D. Schilling.

of plant growth and the subsequent increase in insect population encourages many birds to colonize these areas. Because of the cyclical nature of coppice management plots are to be found at all stages of growth, some ideal for feeding, some for nesting and others approaching harvest. In the reserve a large area of long-neglected hazel coppice with oak standards is being reclaimed and managed in the traditional way.

The wetter areas of the woods have a very different composition. Oak will not tolerate waterlogged conditions and ash (*Fraxinus excelsior*), alder (*Alnus glutinosa*) and sallow (*Salix cinerea*) become dominant. The animal community changes also; conditions here suit birds such as the woodcock, which probes for food in the damp soils. Sallow is the host plant for the larvae of one of our most beautiful butterflies, the purple emperor, a rather rare species confined to southern England. The adult males are rarely seen as they spend much of their time soaring high in the canopy of the surrounding oak woods.

More recent plantings have tended to be forest plots of conifers, which provide a rapid timber return but do not support a great deal of wildlife. The plots are retained to provide a reliable source of timber for estate use.

The great crested grebe has rapidly taken advantage of nesting sites beside the new Ardingly Reservoir in the Loder Valley Reserve.
Photo: K. A. Boyer.

Meadow

Meadowland habitats are among the most threatened in Britain. In little more than one generation, the methods of grassland management practised for centuries have been revolutionized. The modern farmer has to maximize his grass yield in order to produce an economic return. High levels of nutrients and selective herbicides are employed to make this possible. This intensive cropping system, together with the decline of the old permanent pastures, which have been largely replaced by short-term grassland, has reduced many previously common species to rarities.

Within the Wakehurst estate Hanging Meadow is an isolated pasture which, until the reservoir was constructed, was completely surrounded by woodland. Difficult access had restricted its use to rough grazing since it was last cultivated approximately thirty years ago. The flora of the meadow is quite rich, over 130 species being recorded during initial surveys. A mowing policy has now been implemented which is designed to retain and encourage this great variety of plants.

The meadow is divided into two paddocks, in one of them controlled plant introductions of threatened species are being made. For example the cowslip (*Primula veris*) is now very scarce on the estate. It did, however, reappear in small numbers on ground disturbed during reservoir construction. Some of these plants have been moved into the safety of Hanging Meadow where, it is hoped, they will form the nucleus of a new population. During the summer the meadow is a patchwork of bloom, as clovers, vetches and ox-eye daisies abound amidst a haze of flowering grasses. The abundance of flowers at this time encourages numerous insect species. Butterflies, in particular, love the sheltered open aspect of the meadow and often can be observed in great numbers.

The Hanging Meadow above the Loder Valley Reserve is the kind of old grassland seldom seen nowadays. It contains a wide range of species, including many grasses and flowering herbs. In the damper areas, the pink- and sometimes white-flowered ragged robin may be quite common. A policy of careful mowing and the absence of fertilizers and herbicides help to conserve the 140 species so far recorded in this meadow.
Photo: A. D. Schilling.

Wetland

The most prominent wetland habitat within the reserve came as something of an unexpected bonus. At first proposals to flood the valley bottom in the area which now forms the eastern arm of the Ardingly Reservoir were met with a degree of apprehension. It was soon realized, however, that with sympathetic

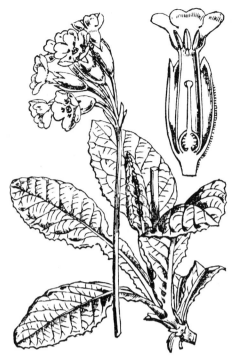

Measures are being taken to increase the population of cowslips (*Primula veris*) in the Reserve, following a decline in numbers in recent years.
Drawing by W. H. Fitch.

While some mammals, such as deer, are unwelcome in parts of the estate, others are encouraged. Dormice (below), which occur in limited numbers, have a localized distribution in southern England. They hibernate during the winter in a nest built on the ground in the shelter of tree roots or inside stumps.
Photo: K. A. Boyer.

treatment of the margins, the reservoir would become an asset rather than obstruct plans for this part of the estate. During construction the minimum of woodland clearance was undertaken. It was, of course, necessary to remove all timber from below the proposed top water level. Above this point, however, little was felled. As a result of this policy the eastern arm of the reservoir had an almost natural look from the time it was filled, in the winter of 1978. Since this time it has gradually matured and many plants and animals have become established in and around its waters. In particular, the numbers of wildfowl breeding on the estate have increased dramatically. Some, like the great crested grebe, nested there for the first time within months of the reservoir being completed. Several other wetland habitats can be found in the reserve. They may be less dramatic than the 18-hectare stretch of open water provided by the reservoir but are no less important. The Sussex ghylls are one example, deep channels that have been eroded into the steep valley sides by water draining from higher ground. These ghylls remain moist throughout the year, even during prolonged periods of drought, as they are fed by many small springs.

Moisture-loving plants such as water dropwort (*Oenanthe crocata*) and pendulous sedge (*Carex pendula*) abound in these areas and ferns, mosses and liverworts flourish in the damp shady conditions. Many animals and birds use the ghylls as secluded corridors when moving from one part of the reserve to another. Kingfishers often can be heard calling as they fly along the ghylls, long before they burst into view in a sudden flash of iridescent blue.

Management for Conservation

There appears to be a great deal of confusion in the minds of many people between the terms conservation, protection and preservation. It is not usually possible to protect a plant or animal species merely by throwing a fence around it and defending it from obvious dangers. There is a delicate balance in any habitat and small environmental changes can create a 'domino effect' radically altering the whole ecosystem.

Most supposedly natural habitats in Britain are in fact artificial systems maintained by man in a variety of ways. Unfortunately, recent changes in farming and forestry practice and the numerous pressures on land for other uses threaten many previously stable communities. Conservation, therefore, means wise management. Conscious decisions must be made as to how best to retain or encourage particular species. Within the reserve a range of management techniques are employed, each suited to a particular habitat. Some areas require the minimum of attention, for example, the climax vegetation of the Site of Special Scientific Importance in Tilgate Wood, which is allowed to regenerate without outside interference. The management policy here is to avoid disturbance to the site and to observe carefully any changes. In every other part of the reserve steps must be taken to prevent the vegetation reaching this climax stage in order to retain a variety of habitat types. Without regular attention, the meadows, coppice plots and scrub vegetation would eventually revert to oak woodland. In the same way, the animal population is influenced by the type of habitat management chosen. The number and variety of animal species can be held at an artificially high level by the provision of food plants, breeding sites and the control of predators. In short, in the interests of conservation mother nature sometimes needs a guiding hand.

J.L.

Botanical Research

Since Kew's establishment on a scientific basis,
it has been actively engaged in the discovery
of the immense flora of the world, its classification and naming, and the investigation of its
usefulness to man. To these activities have been
added many new disciplines, including biochemistry, cytogenetics and, with the growing
threat to natural environments, conservation.

Seed of *Petrorhagia velutina*,
greatly magnified

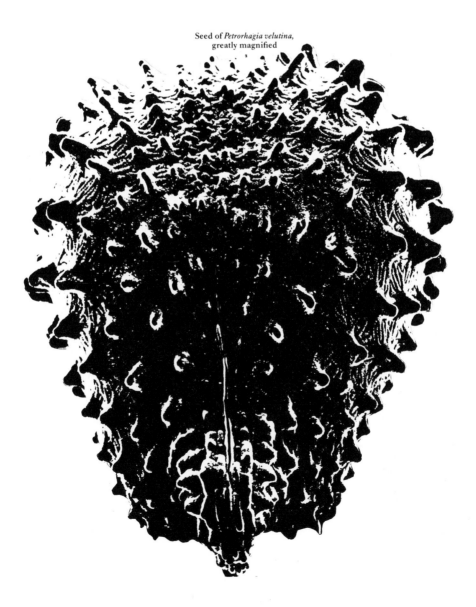

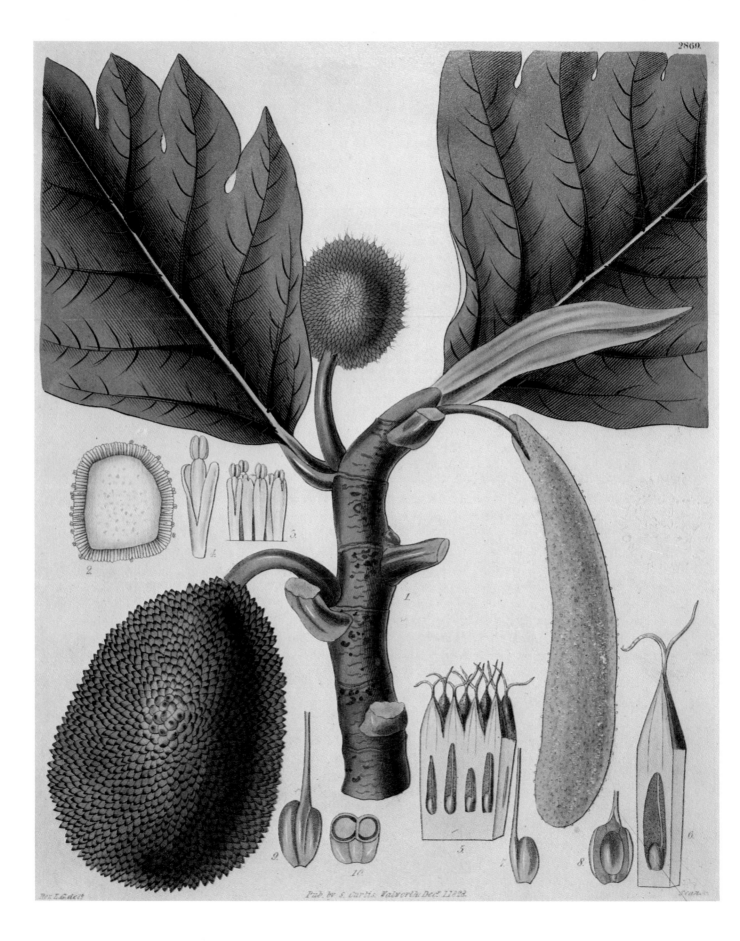

ᛯ 14 ᛯ
The Search for
Useful Plants

Ever since 1773, when Sir Joseph Banks came to Kew as the first 'director' of the Royal Gardens, the influence of Kew has been felt worldwide. Banks had just been round the world with Captain Cook and he knew from first hand of the exciting, untapped plant resources of distant lands. He set about sending collectors all over the world and the stories of their expeditions have often been told. The famous voyage in 1787 led by Captain Bligh on HMS *Bounty*, well-known because of the mutiny on board, was in fact primarily an expedition to collect breadfruit (*Artocarpus altilis*) from Tahiti for cultivation in the West Indies. David Nelson, a Kew gardener, who had been sent to make the collection, remained loyal to Captain Bligh in the mutiny of 1789 but perished on landing in Java eleven weeks after being cast adrift in an open boat by the mutineers. Breadfruit was successfully introduced into St Vincent a few years later by two other Kew men, Christopher Smith and James Wiles.

Botanical collecting expeditions brought to Kew a wealth of new plants. Banks initiated these ventures – and faced some criticism (probably unjustly) for hoarding botanical treasures at Kew. Bizarre and beautiful exotic plants poured in from South Africa where Francis Masson, to whose activity we owe the initial introduction to Britain of the Cape heaths (*Erica*), was based for several years (1772–4 and 1786–95).

It was not only from South Africa that new plants were sent to Kew. William Kerr went to make collections in China in 1803, while soon afterwards George Caley was sent to Australia, where he was succeeded by Allan Cunningham. Cunningham's appointment was made, together with the appointment of James Bowie, another Kew gardener, by Sir Joseph in September 1814 in a splendidly worded letter using phrases hardly to be expected in letters of appointment today. The salary was evidently so low that Banks felt he must encourage 'frugality' in spite of the 'liberality' of their employers. On appointment, both collectors proceeded to Brazil en route for South Africa, where Bowie remained, while Cunningham continued to Australia.

During the serious decline the Gardens suffered following the death of Banks and his patron, George III, in 1820, Kew failed to sustain its international activities. However, with the recovery of the Gardens that followed the appointment of Sir William Hooker as Director in 1841, Kew re-asserted its influence worldwide and its impact was soon felt in the field of economic botany.

The Hooker epoch at Kew coincided with a period of very active exploration and empire-building, during which much was discovered about the potential use of the flora of overseas territories. Dr Lindley, in his report of 1838, hoped that Kew would 'promote throughout every part of the Empire the interests of science', and this it certainly achieved, not least by the establishment of

Opposite: the breadfruit was formerly known as *Artocarpus incisa*, but it must correctly be called *A. altilis*. There are several varieties of it, most of which are seedless, but this one illustrated in *Curtis's Botanical Magazine* (1828, pl 2869) is of the warted, seeded form. The male inflorescence on the right is covered by many minute flowers, each containing a single stamen.

The plant is native in the western Pacific area, where the seedless fruits are an important source of carbohydrate, hence the idea that it could be similarly used in the West Indies. Captain Bligh's expedition in the *Bounty* to take plants there from Tahiti included the Kew gardener David Nelson, who perished after the mutiny.

Although Kew expeditions have been sent all over the world, few can have been on such a grand scale as that of Sir Joseph Hooker to the Rockies in 1877. Sir Joseph (seated, left), Professor Asa Gray (sitting on the ground), Sir Richard and Lady Strachen, Dr F. V. Hayden, and other notable people are shown encamped at Lavetas Pass, Colorado. It is interesting to see that the design of the slatted plant presses for the collection and drying of herbarium specimens has changed little since that time.

Sir Joseph and his father before him, as Directors of Kew, were both keen on economic botany, as well as on the more strictly scientific aspects. They accumulated a vast reference collection of plant products in the Museums and they assisted botanical gardens in the tropics to act as acclimatization stations for new crops, with Kew distributing living plant material.

associated botanic gardens in the tropics with acclimatization plots for new crops. As long ago as George III's time, Banks had suggested the provision of such a garden in Ceylon, and this eventually materialized with the appointment of William Kerr as chief gardener in 1812. Relations with the later garden at Peradeniya continued to be very close and even to this day the Superintendent is required to have been trained at Kew.

Both William Hooker and his son Joseph acted as catalysts, using their influence to promote botanic gardens and to staff them with men trained at Kew. For example, within five years of Sir William's appointment, William Purdie was recommended to supervise the garden in Trinidad, and later Walter Hill went to Brisbane Botanic Garden. Close links had long been forged between Kew and Calcutta from where Sir David Prain eventually moved in the opposite direction to become Director of Kew in 1905.

At Singapore, too, Kew was influential in the appointment of the first superintendent of the Government Botanic Gardens, James Murton. In turn, he was succeeded by Henry N. Ridley, who became famous for his pioneering work on natural rubber. The introduction of rubber from South America into tropical Asia and, prior to this, of quinine into India are the two classic stories of Kew's involvement in economic botany.

Bitter Bark Quinine
Nowadays quinine is little more to most people than a taste in a soda drink, but a century ago it was the most powerful medicine in the world for curing malaria, a disease from which millions of people suffered. Although malaria was much more widespread then than it is today, it is still a killing disease and is

evidently beginning to increase again since it is not responding as well as previously to synthetic medicines. Hence quinine is returning to favour.

This bitter drug is obtained from the bark of South American trees in the genus *Cinchona* of the bedstraw family, Rubiaceae. Its febrifuge properties were known to the Amerindians long before the powder was introduced into Europe in 1639. By the nineteenth century the demand for this medicine, imported under the names of Peruvian bark, Loxa bark and red bark according to species, was rapidly outstripping supply. The wild trees were felled during the collecting process and smaller and smaller ones were being stripped of bark with no thought of replanting or conserving them. In British India, Dr Forbes Royle of the East India Company had tried to encourage the planting of *Cinchona* as long ago as 1835, but it was not until 1854 that six plants obtained from greenhouses at Kew, Edinburgh and Chiswick were taken to India. Unfortunately they died in the cold conditions at Darjeeling, but this failure stimulated a further attempt to obtain seeds from South America and Clements Markham left his administrative post in India to organize collecting parties. By 1860 three groups of collectors were ready and Kew was geared up to receive seed and distribute seedlings raised in a specially built greenhouse. The Dutch, incidentally, already had collected seeds in Bolivia for cultivation in their East Indies, where quinine plants were successfully raised in 1854.

Markham's plan was for the three groups to explore selected regions in order to collect each species of *Cinchona* that yielded the different kinds of bark. Markham and his gardener assistant, John Weir of Kew, tackled Bolivia and Southern Peru, where yellow bark (*C. calisaya*) was known to grow, while an English resident of South America by the name of Pritchett was assigned the forests of Northern Peru. Ecuador was to be investigated by the eminent Yorkshire botanist Richard Spruce, who was already in the country collecting specimens for the Kew Herbarium and Museums.

The experiences of Spruce and his companions give some indication of the difficulties that had to be overcome. Spruce had been in the equatorial forests so long that his health was suffering, but he valiantly made his base at Limon on the west side of Mt Chimborazo where the red bark from *C. succirubra* was cut in the forests at middle altitudes. He was also looking out for *C. officinalis*, the source of Loxa bark, which was reported from the same region. Though Spruce had the help of Dr James Taylor, a lecturer at Quito University who knew the forests well, he was hampered by finding few bark cutters who were willing to guide him to suitable trees in the misty forests, and whenever he did find a tree the flowers were cut off in his absence while he was waiting for the seeds to ripen.

Spruce and Taylor waited for the Kew gardener Robert Cross to join them from the port of Guayaquil, where he had arrived in May 1860. But Cross became ill, and in any case travel inland was out of the question until the war between the coastal faction and the government forces in the Ecuadorian Andes was concluded. Eventually, in July, Cross reached the foothills after a hair-raising thirteen-day canoe journey through still hostile territory and made his way up to Limon. He set to work with Spruce, taking 1000 cuttings on 1 August, and many more subsequently. Spruce collected seed capsules and dried them off to avoid deterioration, then Cross sowed a proportion of them lest they did not survive the journey to Kew. By October all the seeds had been sent to Kew and elsewhere, but the plants remained with Cross until December. They were packed in baskets with damp moss and after an eventful

Polythene bags containing living plants are nowadays sent by air and have superseded the heavy Wardian case. Such cases were used very successfully for over a century for the transportation by ship of rooted cuttings and seedlings of plants of economic importance. These mobile greenhouses, invented by Dr Nathaniel Ward of London about 1830, could be placed on decks for long periods, the glass sides being opened only for occasional watering.

The bark of several species of *Cinchona* – a South American genus named after the Condesa of Chincon, wife of the Viceroy of Peru in the 1630s – yields bitter-tasting quinine, which reduces fevers, especially malaria.

The yellow bark (*C. calisaya*) was one of the species collected by Clements Markham and John Weir and sent to Kew about 1860. Quinine plantations were subsequently established in India and elsewhere.

From Bentley and Trimen, *Medicinal Plants* (1880, pl 141).

mule trek down the mountains Cross met up with Spruce at the river that was to take them down to the coast. A raft of twelve balsa logs '63–65 feet long, and about a foot in diameter' was obtained for the hazardous river journey; it was just the right size to accommodate the Wardian cases (portable greenhouses) with their 637 plants of *Cinchona*. Despite violent storms, which caused rapid fluctuations in river level, and the perils of travelling on a vessel that was at critical moments almost uncontrollable, the cargo was brought safely to the coast and dispatched to Kew.

Clements Markham, writing of his own experience, expressed justifiable surprise that any plants should survive.

> When the unprecedented length of the voyages and the numerous transshipments are taken into consideration, the wonder is that any of the plants should have been successfully conveyed from the slopes of the Andes in South America to the ghauts in Southern India, over thousands of miles, through every variety of climate, and subject to the risk of crossing the isthmus of Panama, of changing steamers at the island of St Thomas, at Southampton, at Suez and at Bombay, and of the journey through Egypt.

Indeed, some of the early shipments, including Markham's, failed to survive but the majority of Spruce and Cross's plants arrived in India in good condition. Nurseries were quickly established in the Nilgiri Hills by William G. McIvor, Superintendent of the Government Gardens at Ootacamund, where cuttings and seedlings were successfully grown.

The large quantities of seeds that had been gathered by the three expeditions were divided between the West Indies, Ceylon, India and Kew to avoid having 'all eggs in one basket'. In 1868 Robert Cross, after delivering the cuttings to India, actually returned to South America to collect seeds of missing species of *Cinchona*. Thus vast numbers of seedlings were raised at Kew and the young plants dispatched to India, where plantations were quickly developed following Markham's survey of suitable sites. A few years later, a life-saving dose of quinine was being sold for the equivalent of 'half a farthing' at village post offices throughout India.

Natural Rubber

Clements Markham also figures briefly in the story of rubber, for it was as a far-sighted official at the India Office that he envisaged vast rubber plantations in the Far East. However, the credit for realizing his vision lies with others.

Natural rubber (caoutchouc), which is still an important resource despite the widespread use of synthetic rubber, comes from various trees yielding milky juice (latex) growing wild in Asia, Africa and South America. It is now obtained almost entirely from the Para rubber tree, *Hevea brasiliensis*, a member of the spurge family, Euphorbiaceae.

In 1872 Joseph Hooker, inspired by a report on rubber-yielding trees written by John Collins, Curator of the Pharmaceutical Society's Museum, conceived a plan for the cultivation of *Hevea* in India. Unfortunately *Hevea* seeds have an oily area which goes rancid during transit and prevents them from germinating. Hence it was hardly surprising, though disappointing, that out of some 2000 seeds collected by a Mr Farris in Brazil in 1873 only a dozen germinated. Six of these plants were sent to Calcutta, but they failed when an attempt was made to grow them in Sikkim.

Joseph Hooker then arranged for further seeds to be obtained from Brazil, his collectors being Henry Wickham, a trader in rubber, and Robert Cross from Kew, who has been mentioned earlier. The true story of this enterprise has been wildly distorted and popular accounts indicating that Wickham dishonestly smuggled out the *Hevea* seeds are unfair both to the collector and to Kew. Nevertheless, his initiative in hiring an empty steamer to rush the seeds back to England before they deteriorated has elements of the melodramatic. The consignment of 70000 seeds, on reaching Santarem docks, Para, was presented to the customs officials by the British Consul as 'delicate botanical specimens' and immediate clearance was given. On arrival in England in June 1876 the seeds were sped by a special freight train from Liverpool to Kew, where greenhouses, hastily cleared of orchids, were made available for them. Germination of 2397 seeds was rapid and by August there were 1919 rubber seedlings on their way to Ceylon for distribution to the plantations.

The development of the rubber industry is complex but it is worth stressing the part played in it by Henry Ridley. The traditional method of tapping caused great damage to the *Hevea* trees. The trunk was cut in order to release the latex and the incision wounded the inner tissues (cambium) of the trees, progressively reducing the latex yield. Sir Joseph Hooker had sent two lots of seedlings to Singapore, a stock that Ridley increased in order to carry out his experiments. In 1888 he successfully developed a technique of excision, cutting away a thin slice of the outer stem in such a way that the cambium was not damaged and production of latex was maintained. In spite of official

The cultivation of Para rubber trees (*Hevea brasiliensis*) was first established in Ceylon with seedlings sent from Kew. In Malaya, the plantations – also from Kew plants – assumed great economic importance following the development of experimental tapping techniques by Henry Ridley in Singapore. The latex flows into a cup from the freshly cut outer stem.
Photo: F. N. Hepper.

Para rubber plants were raised at Kew following receipt of seeds from Brazil in 1876. The original 'pits' (above) – an early propagation greenhouse partly sunken to conserve warmth and humidity – were photographed early this century by an Assistant Curator, C. P. Raffill. Rubber seedlings are growing on the left-hand bench.

discouragement, during the 1890s he perfected his excision technique, which enabled trees to be tapped only six or seven years after planting. Instead of languishing and decreasing their yield, as had happened with trees cut by the old method, his trees flourished and maintained a flow of latex. Ridley, incidentally, retired to Kew in order to write his flora of Malaya and other botanical works.

The latter part of the nineteenth century had seen an increased demand for rubber – for footwear and clothing. The development of the motor industry, however, radically transformed that demand. Kew can take some credit for the fact that the Malayan rubber industry was ready to meet it.

Economic Botany Today

The existing reference collection in the Museums, together with those of the Herbarium and Library, comprise a vast resource of great economic potential. For many years a member of the Museums staff was an economic botanist but this post was discontinued in the late 1950s, with no likelihood of official reinstatement. However, in 1981 the potential importance of Kew's contribution to the economically important plants was recognized by a substantial grant from Oxfam spread over three years, in order to gain a better knowledge of plants suitable for improving the environment of arid and semi-arid regions of the world such as the Sahel zone of Africa. In these areas human existence is often marginal, threatened by sustained periods of drought, and the provision of new crop plants to satisfy such basic needs as fuel, food or forage, can represent a real contribution to the betterment of the millions of people who live there. The Kew-based project is looking for such plants, as well as those likely to help with dune stabilization, to provide soil cover, pole timber, gums, resins – in fact anything that might be useful in such areas.

F.N.H.

Economic Plants in the Gardens

Many of the plants mentioned in the Museums exhibits may be seen in the Gardens, either out of doors or in the greenhouses, where some of them have special explanatory labels. At one time there was a separate Herb Garden beside Cambridge Cottage, but it is no longer continued as all of the species occur in the Queen's Garden or in the Herbaceous Ground. Hardy spices, culinary herbs and medicinal plants are well represented in the Living Collections, while at the other extreme of size are the timber trees growing throughout the Arboretum.

Tender species have to be grown under glass. In the Temperate House there are the *Citrus* fruits (such as oranges, lemons and grapefruit), which bear reasonable crops despite the shade. Other less familiar fruits in this house include the tree tomato (*Cyphomandra betacea*) and naranjillo (*Solanum quitoense*). Both belong to the potato family (Solanaceae) and come from South America. Nearby is a plant of great interest and potential economic value, the jojoba (*Simmondsia chinensis*), a relative of the box tree. This low-growing shrub of semi-desert conditions is exciting conservationists because its seeds yield oil similar to that of the sperm whale. If jojoba can be brought into commercial cultivation the use of its oil would help to conserve whale populations.

A better-known shrub is the tea plant (*Camellia sinensis*), which is also grown

Many plants of economic importance are grown at Kew, especially in the greenhouses. One of these, to be found in the Temperate House, is the tree tomato (*Cyphomandra betacea*). In New Zealand, where it has become an important crop, growers have coined the name 'tamarillo', as its fruits have only a superficial resemblance to tomatoes. They are rich in vitamin C, have a rather acidic taste and can be used in preserves or eaten raw.
From *Curtis's Botanical Magazine* (1899, pl 7682).

in the Temperate House. Its small white flowers make it an attractive plant but, of course, in plantations it is maintained as a clipped shrub since it is the young shoots that are plucked and treated to produce Britain's national beverage. An exhibit on tea and coffee production can be seen in the Museum.

Rice, taro, yam, bottle gourd, luffa and melon are to be seen in House No. 15 in season, and cotton in House No. 10. Pineapples occur with the bromeliads in the T-Range and sisal with other succulents in House No. 5. The Palm House, however, is the principal home of many tropical plants of major economic importance, such as bananas, coconut, cocoa, coffee, ginger, papaya, rubber, yams and the palms already mentioned. There are also a great many species of minor importance but of great interest, like the sources of arrow poisons, which are also being investigated for possible medicinal use. One of those grown is the tropical African *Strophanthus kombe*, the seeds of which contain active chemicals. Essential aromatic oils are extracted from a variety of plants, especially the lemon-grass (*Cymbopogon citratus*) seen growing here and its oil is displayed in the Museum.

Pests, Diseases and Intermediate Quarantine

While all plant material arriving at Kew from overseas undergoes quarantine inspection for pests and diseases, intermediate quarantine is a special service related to tropical crops. Advances in tropical agriculture have been much marked by the development of many important crop plants in areas or continents far from the crops' origins. The cultivated cocoa of West Africa, for example, originated in South America, the Arabian coffee plantations of South America derive from a plant that is native to the mountains of Ethiopia, the Para rubber of S.E. Asia is native to Brazil and tea from Asia is grown in E. Africa.

Over and above the suitability of soil and climate in their new homes, an important underlying reason for the success of these crops is that they have been isolated from the pests and diseases that evolved with them – which if introduced to the plantations could have a disastrous effect. One example is leaf blight of rubber (*Microcyclus ulei*), which occurs in South America but is not

133

yet present elsewhere. Tropical plantation crops are particularly vulnerable to epidemic pests and diseases. Sri Lanka, now so famed for cultivating tea, was once as famous for its coffee prior to the arrival of the African coffee rust (*Hemileia vastatrix*) in 1869; this disease is now widespread on coffee in Africa and Asia and since 1970 has become established in South and Central America.

This serious concern over the introduction of potentially harmful pests or diseases is the reason for the existence of intermediate quarantine. The countries growing these crops still need to introduce new varieties and material for breeding work – new clones of cocoa (*Theobroma cacao*) from the West Indies to West Africa, for example. For cocoa the advantages of having intermediate quarantine in a cool temperate country is that if a tropical pest or disease is accidentally introduced it can very easily be contained and controlled since it cannot exist outside the greenhouse because of both climate and a lack of suitable host crop plants. Hence the continuing demand for Kew to provide this service to overseas countries, with current work involving cocoa, sugar cane plants and oil palm seeds. This responsible task, financed from outside Kew, is very demanding of knowledge and skill and though it usually complements the work of the Living Collections Division at Kew it naturally has also to make use of special facilities for handling the material being quarantined.

Worldwide Dispatch of Plants

The distribution of living plants from Kew is almost a daily operation, around five hundred consignments every year going worldwide for an enormous range of purposes. For example, in 1980 material was sent to forty-seven different countries. A lot of material is provided for other national or international collections and selected new introductions are made available to the nursery trade. Apart from introducing ornamental plants to other centres for ultimate amenity purposes in garden and town, there is now an increasing emphasis on plants of economic and scientific value, especially rare species. Dispatched items include seedlings of possible timber trees to forestry research institutes; wild species for fodder breeding programmes; material for fundamental crop research; material for comparative palaeobotanical studies and material for biochemical studies (often now associated with the evaluation of the medicinal properties of plants). Among other items are minor economics, such as cassia bark or ipecacuanha, for cultivation in Third World countries; samples of rare plants to be used as food for crop pests in entomological research; and rare plants of conservation value to be jointly established in other centres to increase their chance of survival until the reintroduction to original habitats becomes a possibility. As the natural areas of the world decline and resources become more scarce the world demand for these uses of the collections at Kew is bound to increase.

J.B.E.S.

Voyages of discovery were hazardous and lengthy when ships depended on unreliable winds. Before modern medicines were available West Africa was called 'the white man's grave', but the 1854 Niger expedition with Dr Baikie in the *Pleiad* (right) was notable as being the first one during which quinine was taken twice a day. There were no deaths from malaria.

Dr Baikie's next expedition to West Africa in 1857 met with disaster when *The Dayspring* foundered on rocks in the Niger near Jebba. However, while waiting for rescue in 1858, the botanist Charles Barter made a large and important collection of plants, which are now in Kew Herbarium. Barter died the following year and was succeeded by Gustav Mann, another man from Kew who sent back living plants and seeds, as well as herbarium specimens.

✦15✦
Modern Plant-Hunting Expeditions

The Scope for Botanical Expeditions

Television has brought the exuberant world of animal life into our sitting-rooms. But plant life has had less popular appeal, at least until colour TV gave it a chance. Occasionally plant-collecting expeditions appear on the screen, yet most people find it hard to realize that new plants remain to be discovered. Even gardeners may think that the numerous plant-hunting expeditions of the last two centuries have discovered everything.

Books about such expeditions, such as those by Frank Kingdon-Ward and Alice Coates, make fascinating reading, especially when they deal with well-known plants of horticultural interest. Scientific expeditions, however, are seldom written about, yet there is more plant-hunting and field-work now than ever before – and much of it is sponsored by Kew. The character of expeditions may have changed from the traditional image of a three-masted schooner carrying intrepid explorers to remote lands for arduous foot-treks, to sleek jets taking scientists to join motorized safaris. But the intentions of the collectors remain the same – to forward botanical knowledge as effectively as possible.

The collection of seed, herbarium specimens and living plants for scientific study are among the objectives of modern expeditions from Kew. Each expedition is planned to use the knowledge and interest of its members to best advantage. Truly natural plant communities are increasingly hard to find owing to human pressures and changes in land-use. Therefore such a diversity of vegetation as occurs in parts of Afghanistan is not often to be found. Some valleys are still forested, while the foothills are rich in herbaceous plants and the screes up to the snow-line support interesting alpines highly adapted to their harsh environment. Photo: C. Grey-Wilson.

There is a new sense of urgency in view of the rapid destruction of plant life throughout the world.

Why Are Expeditions Necessary?

Collectors are not necessarily expecting to find new species, and in any case unless the scientist is a specialist he is unlikely to recognize a previously unknown plant in the field. Nevertheless, there still remain many species waiting to be discovered and named. The scale of the problem varies according to the region. Tropical African plants are reasonably well-known, yet during the twenty-four years from 1953 to 1976 some 8000 new species were described. If one moves across to the Amazon Basin, where the flora is much richer than that of Africa, the totals increase immensely, although figures are not available for quotation. Places like the plateau of Roraima in Guyana still yield many previously unknown species. It has been estimated that very few of the plants occurring on the numerous table-top summits of south-east Venezuela are named. A similar richness of flora occurs in tropical South-East Asia.

As the world's flora becomes better known general collections are not required from well-collected areas nor are roadside gatherings of common weeds from populated districts. On the other hand, by carefully selecting those districts little visited by botanists in, say, Africa, general collections of plants can yield useful material and important information about their distribution. Yet much of Papua New Guinea remains poorly known since the terrain is rough and the diversity of species immense. In Brazil, too, vast areas are poorly known botanically, hence the several Kew expeditions to Bahia State.

Nowadays field-work is usually directly related to projects in hand, such as regional floras and monographic treatments; the need for anatomical or genetic material; or for seeds and plants to study alive. Each botanist gains first-hand experience of the living plants and their ecology. In observing the variation of plant populations he may collect representative samples for study in the Herbarium. For example, a recent expedition to Malawi resolved a longstanding problem over the taxonomy of *Clematopsis*, a genus closely related to *Clematis* and *Anemone*. Various attempts to classify the forms of *C. scabiosifolia* from dried specimens alone had proved unsatisfactory, but once the variation in the field was studied it was possible to reconcile the herbarium treatment with the out-of-doors observations and apply the names correctly. Two distinct species were recognized and five subspecies of *C. scabiosifolia* distinguished.

Soil types often have an influence on the species composition of the vegetation. Much remains to be done on this kind of research but it has been found that in southern tropical Africa metal-rich rocks support certain species of Scrophulariaceae, the foxglove family. In fact, these are now being used as indicators for possible mining exploitation. In Borneo the peculiar rock composition of parts of Mt Kinabalu was found to account for significant differences in the occurrence of palms. Similarly, in the Malay Peninsula the limestone hills near Kuala Lumpur support the palm *Maxburretia rupicola* and other threatened species of plants listed in the *Red Data Book*, which are being exterminated owing to quarrying for stone.

The Organization of Expeditions

The financing of expeditions depends to a certain extent on the project. Not

Clematopsis, a genus in Ranunculaceae, is widespread in the tropical African savanna but its range of variation is confusing to herbarium botanists. Recent field study in Malawi, however, has led to the recognition of two distinct species as well as five subspecies of *C. scabiosifolia*, which should now be known as *C. villosa* (below).

This figure by Margaret Stones was prepared from a Nigerian plant for the revised edition of the *Flora of West Tropical Africa* (1954, 1:63), written at Kew. Skilful and accurate drawings of this kind are a feature of taxonomic publications; they include in a limited space the more important morphological features of the plants concerned. Line drawings are usually preferable to photographs and cheaper to reproduce.

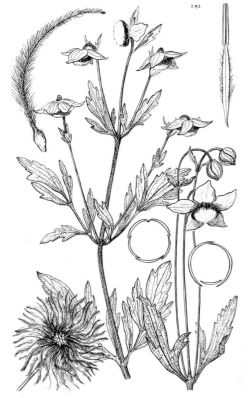

until the 1970s were expeditions treated as an integral part of the Kew staff's work and therefore financed officially by the Ministry of Agriculture. Prior to that the few expeditions had each to find funds from private sources or from trusts. This still applies in some cases as the official funds are insufficient to meet all the demands. In 1980, for example, the Australian Orchid Foundation invited an orchid specialist from Kew to do field study of *Dendrobium* in Papua New Guinea, Solomon Islands and Vanuatu.

Kew expeditions greatly benefit from the willing co-operation of the nationals of the various countries who provide facilities and expertise that formerly never existed. Such co-operation is to mutual advantage. The pattern of activity is nowadays one of mutual assistance between partners who benefit each other. However, recent political changes across the world have made botanical expeditions to several countries extremely difficult or even impossible, even though some areas have become more accessible.

From time to time Kew is called upon to advise on certain matters which necessitate overseas visits. This is not the place to deal with the numerous conferences and meetings attended by the Director and other members of staff since this chapter is concerned primarily with plant collecting expeditions. But it should be mentioned that such conferences are often coupled with field-work, which provides the opportunity for collecting and gaining valuable field experience. Occasionally a botanist may be attached for a time to a project, such as an enquiry into how to develop the cultivation of climbing palms (rattans) for the furniture industry in Sarawak, or a study of the legumes of Papua New Guinea. Members of the Kew horticultural staff (Living Collections Division) are also called on to advise on overseas botanical gardens. During the last decade close liaison has been built up with gardens in Venezuela, Mexico, Iran and Malaysia, enabling the advisers to carry out field-work in the vicinity.

Careful timing of expeditions is important if herbarium material is required, since it is imperative to be in the field when plant growth and flowering are at their best. Seed-collecting expeditions, of course, have to be timed for later in the season. In the drier countries rainfall is notoriously erratic and opportunity has to be taken of good rainfall. In 1975 a Kew expedition to North Yemen was suddenly brought forward a year in order to take advantage of an exceptional rainy season while, in the same year, the early rains were so late in Kenya that an expedition had to rearrange its programme to take advantage of the wet season in Tanzania. A previous expedition to that country, in 1956, had selected a remote area in the Songea district, which had to be reached before the rains made travelling impossible, with unsurfaced roads becoming quagmires, bridges being washed away and river ferries ceasing to operate. The two botanists rushed to Songea just before their communications were cut. Once there, they were able to collect intensively in the district, finding many new species, as well as gathering additional distribution records for the country.

Who Goes on Expeditions?

Formerly it was exceptional for any but the Herbarium taxonomists to travel on plant-hunting expeditions. But in recent years they have been joined by scientists from the Jodrell Laboratory and Wakehurst Place, and also by horticultural staff.

Research at the Jodrell Laboratory has included an integrated study on aloes

Succulents and other plants that do not dry well to make herbarium specimens need to be preserved in alcohol. Photography helps to record form and possibly colour and to distinguish between the habits of similar species, such as these two species of *Euphorbia* (*E. parciramulosa* and *E. ammak*) growing in North Yemen.
Photo: F. N. Hepper.

The high humidity of tropical rain forest hinders the preparation of herbarium specimens. Presses are, therefore, interleaved with corrugated airers and placed over a source of dry heat. In the Gunong Mulu National Park, Sarawak, expedition members erected a canvas canopy to keep rain from the drying equipment. Polythene bags are used for living plants required for cultivation and further study. Photo: G. Lewis.

Even seemingly unpromising arid areas can yield interesting plants. In the semi-desert of Somalia, *Aloe rigens* var. *glabrescens* was one of the plants found during a survey of the aloe populations. Living plants were collected for scientific study at Kew. Photo: P. E. Brandham.

(*Aloe*) of Africa. Several expeditions have therefore taken place to East Africa, Somalia and Kenya, as well as South Africa, in order to collect material for cultivation in the research collections. Study of populations in the field has thrown light on the hybrid origin of some aloes. Another long-term study on the mainly tropical family Commelinaceae, which includes the tradescantias, has necessitated much field-work in Mexico and elsewhere; it has yielded information on the classification of the family and on the mode of chromosome evolution. The plant anatomists at the Jodrell who have been working on the structure of Liliaceae have collected material in East and South Africa and in Argentina. Staff from the Seed Bank at Wakehurst Place have also sponsored expeditions in order to collect large quantities of seed for storage. Visits have been mainly to the Mediterranean region, but also recently to Kenya in an attempt to widen the study of seed storage to include tropical species.

Field-work enables members of the horticultural staff to see their plants in the wild in order to understand the conditions in which they thrive. Thus during a botanical tour of Iran two members were surprised to find huge trees of *Parrotia persica* and *Diospyros lotus*, which were much larger than any grown in British gardens. It will be interesting to see whether trees grown at Kew from their gatherings will show marked differences in size or appearance. Members of the horticultural staff have also collected seeds in the Greek mountains for growing in the Rock Garden. Ferns have been gathered in New Guinea, mountain plants in the Himalayas, succulents in East Africa and cacti in the Americas to renew and enlarge the holdings of live plants. The results of this policy of growing plants of known origin are already having a profound effect on the representation of many herbaceous species. As for trees and shrubs, these take longer to mature but ones raised from wild-collected seed are gradually replacing many already at Kew of unknown provenance.

Most of the accounts in this book refer to flowering plants and ferns but Kew also has an important section based at the Herbarium dealing with fungi (mycology). One mycologist is concerned with plant diseases and the quarantine of incoming and outgoing material, while the other three are taxonomists dealing with the larger fungi. Their studies have taken them to East and South Africa, to Australia and to the Caribbean to collect material for their taxonomic papers and handbooks on the fungi of the regions concerned.

What Transport is Used?

As indicated at the beginning of this chapter, advantage is taken of air travel to reach an expedition's starting point, though much of the heavy equipment may be sent by sea or by air freight. Once assembled the expedition members use whatever means of transport is available or most suitable. Four-wheel drive motor vehicles are essential for at least part of the journey. Occasionally unexpected problems are encountered, such as happened in 1953 when the red painted lorry used by an East African expedition aroused violent opposition from the local people in the Usambara Mountains. It transpired that a scientific research laboratory established in the region regularly obtained blood from the inhabitants in order to monitor malarial and other parasites, hence the opposition to the incoming blood-red vehicle, much to the surprise of the occupants!

Trekking on foot and climbing are still necessary, but the new roads in many of the developing countries enable plant-hunters to visit places hitherto inaccessible, or that until quite recently might have taken weeks of perilous

In rugged terrain, such as occurs in Afghanistan, expeditions may have to use animal transport (left). The timing of expeditions depends on their objectives. Usually they coincide with the maximum flowering period but seeds required for cultivation or the Seed Bank can only be obtained later in the season.
Photo: C. Grey-Wilson.

The vegetation of the cliffs and plateaux of Mt Roraima, Guyana, is rich in endemics and many species are still unnamed. To explore this region, a Kew expedition trekked through dense tropical forest before ascending a difficult cliff path that needed a sure foot and a good head for heights. Progress was eventually blocked by a sheer rock wall. The summit plateau can only be readily reached by one ascent route from Venezuela.
Photo: D. Philcox.

Botanical expeditions from Kew depend on various means of transport, especially motor vehicles, but crossing rivers in Africa (above) can be hazardous. Light aircraft are sometimes hired to reach remote places, while a hovercraft (right) was used on an expedition exploring the vegetation of Lake Chad.
Photo: F. N. Hepper.

Opposite: biological field studies help to elucidate the taxonomy of difficult groups of plants. For example, it was the discovery in 1971 of the mint relative *Eriope exaltata* in the interior of Bahia, Brazil, that prompted R. M. Harley to prepare a revision of the tree species that were formerly assigned to *Hyptis*. This revision, published in *Hooker's Icones Plantarum* (1976), was illustrated by Mary Grierson.

Sir William Hooker started the *Icones* in 1836 as a periodical devoted to describing and figuring new or interesting plants. The editorship still resides with the Keeper of the Herbarium.

travelling to reach. On the other hand places not linked by roads are now becoming more difficult to visit owing to the lack of people to carry the equipment. Few are willing to act as porters and those who are require high payment. One expedition that did use porters was in 1958 in north-east Nigeria before these problems arose. For several months some twenty porters were used, but on one occasion they failed to meet the botanist at a certain village. For five days he had to send messages across the mountains by the hands of villagers before locating them far away. Fortunately they had been fed on credit by a kindly village head pending payment, and the botanical specimens were retrieved intact.

More recently an expedition to New Ireland in 1975 found the coastal-dwelling inhabitants reluctant to venture into the interior forests. Porters were essential for transporting all the expedition's food, plant presses and stores as the mountainous region lacked roads. It was difficult to persuade men to leave their gardens, and some feared evil spirits in the mountain forests. Other problems were encountered by the porters with the Mt Roraima expeditions between 1971 and 1980. That remote, afforested terrain of Guyana is saturated and slippery. The approach to Mt Roraima is steep and ends with a climb up the rock walls that needs a good head for heights, even without a heavily laden pack.

Various expeditions have used boats, hovercraft, light aircraft and helicopters. Boats were required for access to the Aldabra Islands and the Solomon Islands. A hovercraft was used for the Trans-Africa Hovercraft Expedition in 1969 sponsored by the Royal Geographical Society, traversing West African rivers from Senegal to Lake Chad. The latter is an immense shallow lake, in fact so shallow between the islands that a motor boat would have its propeller fouled by water weed. A hovercraft, however, is immune to such problems since it floats above the surface and can hover while the botanist collects submerged material. Light aircraft are frequently used for short journeys within the expedition area, but helicopters have seldom been used by Kew expeditions. One occasion was in Oman in 1976, when the use of a military helicopter enabled a botanist to reach a plateau to obtain material of a previously undescribed wild carob, which was later named *Ceratonia oreothauma*, only the second species of *Ceratonia* known.

Biological Studies

Field studies have been invaluable for understanding the taxonomy and biology of a wide range of plants, such as *Hyptis*, a mint relative with numerous species in Brazil. Although *Hyptis* provide excellent dried material (unlike succulents) field observations greatly supplement herbarium specimens in such a genus where there are numerous similar species. Hybridization was

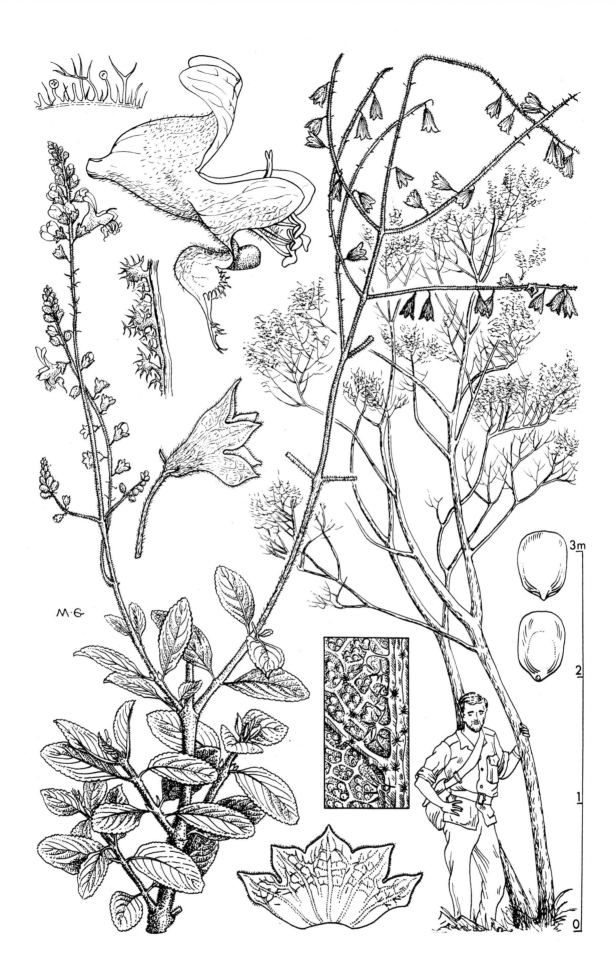

M·G

suspected and easily proved in the wild populations. Habit and subtle colour differences which are observed in dried specimens were clearly seen in fresh plants. The biology, such as pollination methods, could be studied only in the field, as well as the habitat preferences of each species. All this goes to show that a specialist is able to make fuller notes and better observations than a casual collector who is unfamiliar with the niceties of the genus.

Photography and collection in preserving liquid are essential for certain groups of plants that do not lend themselves to normal herbarium drying techniques. Notable among these are the cacti and succulents, which have been studied by several expeditions to tropical Africa and tropical America.

Regional Floras

Kew has a long tradition of writing handbooks (floras) describing the plants of different regions of the world. The botanist engaged on such work usually has an opportunity to visit the region of his interest in order to collect further material.

Since the Second World War there has been a special interest in tropical Africa. The *Flora of West Tropical Africa* has been revised and two massive projects, *Flora of Tropical East Africa* and *Flora Zambesiaca*, have been initiated at Kew or in conjunction with other institutions. Numerous botanists have visited Africa in connection with these floras.

Islands, too, in various parts of the world have been visited by Kew botanists collecting material for use in the preparation of particular floras. Thus Mauritius, Réunion and Rodrigues, as well as the Aldabra group, in the Indian Ocean, have been visited on several occasions. Many herbarium specimens were also gathered during expeditions to Cyprus and the islands of Trinidad and Tobago for their respective floras.

Beside the floras sponsored by Kew itself there are many sponsored by other institutions to which staff members contribute. Sometimes the organizers enable the botanists concerned to undertake field-work in the area. For instance, the Smithsonian Institution of Washington has sponsored the Flora of Ceylon, and the Flora of Hassan, India, and several members of the Herbarium staff have been involved and able to visit these countries.

The species of balsam (*Impatiens*) are difficult to understand from herbarium specimens alone. Sir Joseph Hooker, who studied them in the latter part of his life, regarded them as 'unmanageable plants'. A recent revision of the African species was coupled with field work which led C. Grey-Wilson to realize that part of the difficulty was due to hybridization. Hybrid swarms with markedly differently shaped flowers (A–Q) in Tanzania were found to be the progeny of the two species *Impatiens austrotanzanica* (R) and *I. gomphophylla* (S). Drawing by C. Grey-Wilson in *Kew Bulletin* (1980, 35:198).

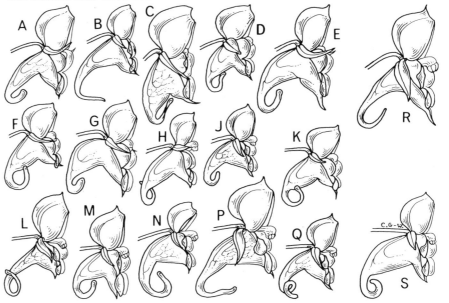

Urgency for Field-work

An additional urgency for field-work has been provided by a general awareness of a changing ecological situation – and one that is likely to have permanent, irrevocable and even disastrous results – namely, environmental degradation (see Chapter 20). Everywhere natural vegetation is being lost at an alarming and increasing rate, with pressure on every kind of habitat. Plant communities and their constituent species are threatened by modern machinery and chemicals which can wipe them out. Natural forests are being cut and burnt with insufficient time being allowed for natural regeneration to take place, or they are being cleared for agriculture, with the consequent total extinction of the plants and animals that inhabited them. Piecemeal degradation of habitats by local people is almost as detrimental as clear-felling. Valuable potential resource plants are being lost even before they are known. Therefore, botanists need to collect and study material from natural habitats before they are lost for ever.

Nature conservation and plant collecting may appear to be mutually opposed objectives, but this is not the case unless the species are very rare or collecting is on a commercial scale. The botanist collects on a very small scale and with discretion. While the effect of scientific collection on natural habitats is negligible, it is through study of the material obtained that a knowledge of the flora and vegetation is gained. Having obtained that knowledge it may also be possible to do something about the protection of the environment.

Several Kew expeditions have had as their main objective the conservation of nature – usually assessing the botanical content and potential of certain areas of interest. A report resulting from a visit to Seychelles in 1961 had important consequences for the flora and the subsequent declaration of nature reserves on some of the islands. The Aldabra Islands, which also lie in the Indian Ocean, have been subject to intense study during the last two decades. In the 1960s scientists were appalled at the proposal to build a military airfield there with the prospect of the elimination of the wildlife – these low-lying coral reefs are famous for their giant tortoises and vast numbers of seabirds. However, little was known about the flora until it was studied by botanists under the auspices of the Royal Society, which has now established a reserve and research station there.

Another study in connection with conservation was undertaken in the Philippines for the International Union for the Conservation of Nature. Here a Kew specialist on the genus *Begonia* studied the presence and frequency of its species as an indicator of the state of the herbaceous element of the forests they inhabit. Much of the forest has been cleared and the ground flora has gone with it. However, the observations proved how important are the undisturbed relics of high forest remaining in valley bottoms and on steep slopes for the continuation of the herbaceous plants that were often entirely lacking in secondary regrowth forest. Similar conclusions were reached in Brazil by a Kew botanist who won a Churchill Scholarship in 1981 to study the conservation of the forests in the north-eastern parts of the country. All these studies yielded important plant material for the benefit of local institutions as well as for Kew.

Returning to Kew

Collecting the material is only part of the task. All the live plants have to be kept going from the day they are dug up. They have to be transported from remote

Contrasting not only in colour but in shape of corolla, *Impatiens sulcata* (top) from Nepal has pouched bee-pollinated flowers, while the Tanzanian *I. walleriana* (bottom) has a flattened corolla pollinated by butterflies. *I. walleriana*, often called busy Lizzie, is a favourite house plant and is one of the many species featured in the *Impatiens* collection in Kew greenhouses.
Photos: C. Grey-Wilson.

The flora of remote islands is often of great interest to botanists, as many of the plants are to be found nowhere else. Such endemic species occur in considerable numbers on Socotra, which lies off the Horn of Africa. The dry conditions might seem to be unfavourable to plants but there are many bizarre adaptations of frankincense trees (*Boswellia*), the cucumber tree (*Dendrosicyos socotranus*) and dragon trees (*Dracaena*), including *D. cinnabari* (right). Some of the island's endemics are grown at Kew, following a botanical expedition to Socotra in 1967.
Photo: A. Radcliffe-Smith.

spots, transferred from vehicle to house, possibly grown on in a local garden and then flown home as quickly as possible. Formerly ships were equipped with portable greenhouses, known as Wardian cases after their inventor. Polythene bags and air transport have made a great difference in recent years but there are still hazards. For instance, tropical plants cannot stand the chilling of freight holds at high altitudes and so they must go in the passenger compartments. Living plants must not be crushed or sprayed with noxious fumes by an over-zealous sanitary official trying to keep out the plague. Many a consignment has been ruined by neglect in a customs shed while awaiting clearance.

Dried material has its problems too. Out in the field it is a full-time occupation drying the plants, especially under camp conditions when the expedition may be moving frequently. In a moist, tropical climate portable stoves are essential for quick drying, otherwise mildew attacks the specimens which turn black and disintegrate. Since it is policy to collect numerous duplicates for distribution on an exchange basis to other institutions, an expedition soon runs up vast numbers of dried specimens that have to be kept dry and free of insects – termites are a particular hazard for fresh herbarium material. The sheer bulk of dried specimens can easily overload the expedition vehicle and ways have to be found of sending it back to a suitable base, such as the local university. The shipment home may not be as critical as for living plants but it can be as frustrating if local officials insist on inspection or additional documentation. Once out of the botanist's hands there is no way of knowing whether the dried material is left lying outside during a rainstorm or subjected to such rough treatment that it shatters to pieces. A moment's carelessness can undo the work of days or even weeks.

It is satisfying when the plant material finally arrives at Kew in good condition. The expedition, with all its hard work, interest and excitement, has been a success, fulfilling its aim of adding to Kew's vast storehouse of scientific material and knowledge.

F.N.H.

The Classification and Naming of Plants

One cannot walk far in the Gardens without noticing the names, since labels hang from every tree or are positioned among the plants. These labels are carefully scrutinized by knowledgeable visitors, but the Latin intimidates the less knowing who would prefer the names to be in English. Alas, this is the problem, few of the plants growing in botanic gardens possess a common name. The few there are can be misleading in different parts of the world even as close as England and Scotland where 'bluebell' means *Hyacinthoides* in the former and *Campanula* in the latter.

The botanists at Kew and elsewhere use Latin names because they are internationally recognized. Latin was the historic language of education and science and for centuries it has been used for the names of plants and animals. Although they seem complicated one soon becomes familiar with Latin names, as any gardener knows when he speaks about his *Chrysanthemum* plants and *Rhododendron* bushes, hardly realizing that these are their scientific names which fit into a system of classification.

From our earliest days we have become accustomed to classifying things. A young child quickly knows a dog from a cat, but it is only later that he goes to the next stage and distinguishes by name a spaniel from a terrier. So it is with plants; we group them together and yet distinguish them as separate species. Species are gathered in genera, and genera in families, like with like. Thus all the daisies, such as *Chrysanthemum* and *Aster*, are grouped into the daisy family Compositae (or Asteraceae), while the heath, *Erica*, and the well-known *Rhododendron* go into the heath family, Ericaceae. Species are given two basic names, much as people have a surname and Christian names – Smith, John or Smith, Mary. If we take *Rhododendron arboreum* as an example, we see that *arboreum* refers to one particular kind or species of *Rhododendron*, tall-growing and tree-like, hence the specific epithet from the Latin *arbor*, a tree. Below species rank there are subspecies, varieties and forms – and cultivars which are usually selected varieties raised in cultivation.

The classification and naming of the 250 000 species of flowering plants in the world is still a necessary and very important function of many botanical establishments throughout the world, with Kew playing a major role. Those who engage in it are called taxonomists, their study being known as taxonomy. Kew is especially well placed for the accurate classification and naming of plants, having a wealth of reference material in its Herbarium, Library and Museums collections, as well as live plants in the Gardens, and a highly skilled staff. Taxonomists use mainly herbarium specimens for comparison, and handbooks or other literature for descriptions, keys and illustrations.

Plants do not always reach Kew with their names on them so how do the names arrive on the labels? A surprising number of people are involved and it

Hunter House, an eighteenth-century building facing Kew Green, is the entrance to Kew Herbarium and Library. The house was occupied by the King of Hanover until his death in 1851. Following the donation in 1853 of the collections of W. A. Bromfield, the Herbarium and Library were founded in Hunter House. George Bentham, a well-to-do botanist of great renown, presented his own collections in 1854 and, after the death of Sir William Hooker, his enormous herbarium was purchased. Since then, four wings have been added.

The Library, which for just over a century was kept in crowded rooms in this house, was transferred in 1968 to part of the spacious fourth wing. It contains several hundred thousand botanical works, as well as plant illustrations, maps, travel books and archives. Photo: T. A. Harwood.

The tropical Asian snake gourd (*Trichosanthes cucumerina* var. *anguina*) is cultivated for its edible fruit. It was grown at Kew as long ago as the eighteenth century, when G. D. Ehret drew it (right), and it is still often grown in House No. 15.

A worldwide taxonomic study by C. Jeffrey of dried material in the Herbarium and living plants in the field has yielded a new classification of the important cucumber family (Cucurbitaceae), to which the snake gourd belongs. A confusion of names has been cleared up and accounts for floras published.

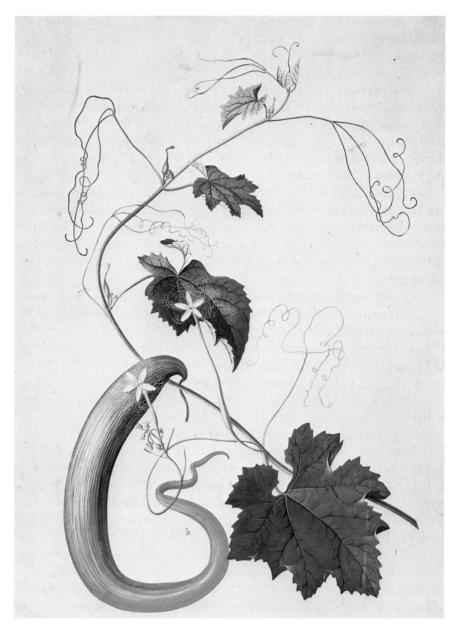

touches the heart of a great deal of the scientific work at Kew and in the Herbarium in particular.

We have seen in Chapter 15 that collecting expeditions are constantly bringing back dried specimens and living plants. The latter may take a year or more to flower at Kew and it is only then that naming can be attempted, because classification is usually based on the structure of their flowers. The flowering specimens are sent across from the Gardens to the Herbarium where they are dealt with by the taxonomists, each plant being accompanied by its accession card carrying details of its origin and any other information. The names and the related accession data are stored on a computer, which is of increasing importance as an information bank.

Botanical Literature and Plant Identification
In order to identify a plant the taxonomist needs to consult the Herbarium material already in the reference collections. He may be able to make the

identification simply by comparing the plant with the dried specimens already named, although usually he will need to use a book of one sort or another. Illustrated works are particularly helpful, but are not always available, especially for less decorative plants. Perhaps a garden encyclopaedia will suffice or he may have to search out the latest monograph published in a learned botanical journal. About 10000 such monographs and papers on plant taxonomy are published worldwide every year. To facilitate retrieval of the right publication, the Library compiles an annual index to this literature called *Kew Record of Taxonomic Literature*. Detailed references to new plant names are provided in *Index Kewensis*.

In European, North American and many other industrialized countries one can find numerous botanical books to aid the identification of 'wild flowers' and trees. One can even choose from a wide selection of profusely illustrated handbooks according to taste and pocket, ranging from beginners' guides and simple children's books to botanical specialist books and erudite technical works for the serious student.

This rich supply of botanical information is available in most of the temperate countries but unfortunately in the majority of tropical countries the situation is very different. They usually lack even the basic works, in spite of the fact that the tropics support a large proportion of the world's species. Many of these are still very poorly known even to botanists. Brazil, for example, is estimated to have at least 80000 species, many still unknown to science, while the whole of Europe has only about 13000, of which some 2000 occur in Britain. So here we have something of a paradox with those parts of the world which have the fewest species being well known and well supplied with identification works, while those regions with the most numerous species lack publications! It is a situation Kew is helping to put right. In fact the botanists in the Herbarium have been working on handbooks (called 'floras') of flowering plants, ferns and fungi for more than a century, yet the need for basic works to cover the plants of developing countries still remains acute. Unfortunately such handbooks have to be heavily subsidized as they are not commercially viable. They take many years to produce and constantly need to be revised in the light of further research on the classification and geographical distribution of plants. For example, the multi-volume *Flora of Tropical Africa*, one of the 'Colonial Floras' designed to cover the British Empire, started publication in 1868 and continued until 1937; the *Flora of Tropical East Africa* began publication in 1952 and is likely to continue until after the end of this century.

Although much of the work on the classification of plants at Kew might seem to be academic, it has important practical applications, since floras are basic working tools for a wide range of interests and disciplines. Take, for example, the use of Kew-prepared floras by agriculturalists in tropical countries where they need to know the names of their weeds before control methods can be worked out. Similarly, foresters need names for the trees they are using for timber. Although local names are often applied to timber, a positive scientific designation is necessary at some stage and certainly in publications and for international circulation. Moreover, since tropical forests are composed of very many different species of trees – unlike temperate forests which are dominated by one or two species, such as oaks or pines, to the exclusion of most others – the forester and forest ecologist require at hand the botanical information which a flora provides to enable them to identify the trees and associated species.

In Africa, there are some 500 species of *Crotalaria*, a genus that has undergone a major revision by R. M. Polhill in connection with floras sponsored by Kew and other botanical institutions.

Margaret Meen's painting of *Crotalaria incanescens* was executed in May 1784 and based on material raised at Kew from seeds sent from South Africa by Francis Masson.

147

AFGHANISTAN, Badakhshan-Wakhan: Sast-e-Bala
banks of Ab-e-Panj. Alt. c. 2900 m.
Borders of cultivated fields.

Sprawling, trailing or semi-climbing shrub.
Leaves deep-green. Flowers chrome yellow,
filaments purple-brown or reddish.

23 July 1971

.C Grey-Wilson & T F Hewer   No.1386

Clematis hilariae S.Koval-
evch. var Burseanum
Grey-Wilson   MOLOTYPUS
DET   C.Grey Wilson   1980

HERBARIUM KEWENSE
IRAN/AFGHANISTAN EXPEDITION 1971

Clematis orientalis L sens.lat.
Det. C. Grey Wilson   1972
Coll. C. Grey-Wilson and T. F. Hewer, No. 1386

A well-collected herbarium
specimen comprises the vital
parts of the plant—flowers and
fruits—as well as some leaves
attached to the stem. A label is
essential; it carries field notes,
the collector's name, serial
number and other details.

Identifying Herbarium Specimens

Parallel to the writing of floras and taxonomic research, the Herbarium provides an important service by naming vast numbers of dried flowering plants, ferns and fungi sent by other botanical institutes, organizations or individuals. For example, zoologists in several parts of Africa are studying chimpanzees and gorillas for which the identification of their food plants is important. Elsewhere, medical researchers are concentrating on potential cancer-curing drugs obtained from plants for which they need names.

Every year the Kew Herbarium receives some 50 000 specimens, of which a considerable proportion are unnamed, while others are presented as named duplicates by other herbaria. This system of distributing duplicates from one herbarium to another is an excellent means of building up collections and of making information and material more widely available. The distribution also safeguards against total loss or destruction, such as occurred in Berlin when some two million specimens of great scientific value were burnt during the Second World War. Fortunately there are duplicates of some of these specimens at Kew and elsewhere. Nowadays more use is being made of photography to record herbarium sheets, although photographs cannot be as satisfactory as the specimens themselves.

One may ask how such a mass of new material is dealt with in Kew Herbarium. Incoming specimens must be free of insects that feed on dried plants and this is now done by deep-freezing them for 48 hours at $-18°C$. Formerly they were fumigated with methyl bromide but this process exposed the staff to risks and has been discontinued. When the specimens are in the Herbarium the staff of the General Services Unit prepare lists and distribute the specimens to the several sections, where botanists name them—by comparing them with material already held or by using any suitable flora or monograph—often a lengthy process since accuracy is essential. The correct names are then carefully listed and sent to the collector or to the institution that sent the specimens to Kew. The specimens themselves are glued on to standard-sized sheets of cartridge paper $42 × 26.7$ cm ($16\frac{1}{2} × 10\frac{1}{2}$ in) together with labels giving full field information, before being filed away in systematic order in the Herbarium cabinets among the five million sheets already there. Dry herbaceous plants lie flat on the sheet, but specimens cut from trees have bulky twigs that take up much space. This means that there is a constant demand for additional storage accommodation in the Herbarium for specimens, including those in spirit jars and dry fruits in boxes.

Identification at the Jodrell and Museums

The Herbarium is by no means the only part of Kew in which identification of plants takes place, since both the Jodrell Laboratory and the Museums are involved. At the Jodrell, the identification of timbers, tree roots and other plant material carried out by plant anatomists has important practical applications. By cutting very thin sections of the wood and staining them with suitable dyes the various tissues show up under the microscope in a way that an experienced scientist can recognize as characteristic of a particular species. A large reference collection of microscope slides of specimens from all over the world enables the botanist to compare and check the identity of the new material.

In recent years many requests for the identification of tree roots were received by plant anatomists at the Jodrell Laboratory. Roots often cause subsidence of buildings with unsuitable foundations on shrinkable clay soils,

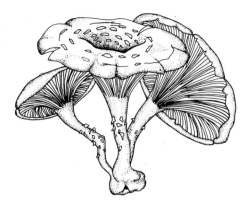

The larger fungi are also studied in Kew Herbarium. The mycological section identifies specimens from all over the world and fungus floras have been written for several countries, especially in the tropics. *Lentinus squarrosulus* (above) is an example of one species included in D. Pegler's *Preliminary Agaric flora of East Africa* (1977).

Many older gatherings are present in Kew Herbarium, including historic specimens, such as some collected on the Galapagos Islands by Charles Darwin. One of these specimens (below) is of a plant now named *Darwiniothamnus tenuifolius* (Joseph Hooker originally worked on Darwin's Galapagos plants).

Kew Herbarium is especially rich in type specimens—those on which new plant names are based. They are distinguished by being placed in red-bordered covers.

Gallapagos Islands,
(James Island,)
begin. of Oct. 1835: C. Darwin.

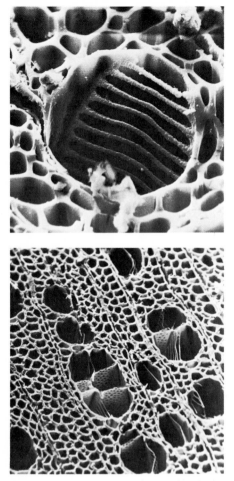

Carbonized wood (charcoal) from archaeological sites often retains many of the microscopical details of fresh wood. These can be seen readily using a scanning electron microscope.
Top: alder (*Alnus glutinosa*) charcoal from a Romano-British site (× 500) retains a characteristic scalariform perforation plate.
Bottom: modern wood of the same species (× 100) provides a comparison where the five bars of several perforation plates can be seen.

and blocked drains. In such cases the identification of the roots causing the trouble provides vital evidence. As a by-product of these enquiries, an analysis of the identifications has resulted in the publication of a booklet informing architects and landscape designers about planting distances and trees with troublesome roots.

Sometimes wooden objects are received for routine identification. A few years ago an African carved wooden head was examined by taking a small sliver from the base where no damage could be done. In due course the carving was returned to the sender and some time afterwards it was realized that this piece was actually an art treasure which was sold for a large sum.

Ancient material, such as timber from a Saxon farm or charcoal from a Roman villa, is also often submitted. Charcoal retains its cellular structure and the original timber can be identified. However, it needs a different preparation technique as the brittle charcoal cannot be sectioned or stained nor examined by transmitted light. It has to be fractured by snapping so that the cellular structure of the cross ends and radial surfaces shows up clearly when examined by reflected light under a binocular microscope.

As well as timber, other ancient plant material from the Egyptian tombs is sometimes sent for identification. For instance, a collection of wreaths, seeds and fibres from Saqqara dating from 300 BC required a variety of examination techniques. The leaves and flowers in the wreaths were so well preserved that a hand lens was sufficient to check their identity. The outer rim of the wreath, as shown by identification in the Herbarium, was composed of leaves of the *Mimusops* tree and decorated with inserted cornflowers (*Centaurea depressa*). Hot water and chemical treatment of the fibres and microscopical examination was necessary to see whether they came from palm, papyrus or grass.

Seeds, too, are sometimes sent to the Kew Museums for identification. These have included seeds used decoratively as beads such as the extremely poisonous red and black seeds of the climbing tropical pea *Abrus precatorius*, the scarlet bean *Adenanthera pavonina*, grey Job's tears from the grass *Coix lacrymi-jobi* or even whole fruits of a small *Raphia* palm. Some seeds are much more difficult to identify, including drift seeds picked up along beaches.

Public health and customs officials often make enquiries about small objects found in packets or cans of food. These usually prove to be seeds. In some cases a court case may even hang on their identification, especially of imported items, since taxable goods are sometimes imported under misleading names in order to escape duty. Scientists at the Jodrell Laboratory are frequently called on to make microscopical examination of powdered substances that prove to be a cheap adulterant of an expensive product. Identification is possible because the cellular structure of the plant's outer layer (the epidermis) survives grinding and is characteristic enough to be recognizable by an experienced plant anatomist. The police know that even a plant fragment or seed adhering to a suspect's clothing may provide important evidence in a court of justice.

Sometimes plant names have to be changed. When this is done it must be in conformity with the rules laid down by the International Code of Botanical Nomenclature. Though it is a source of vexation when a well-known name is discarded for another it is evidence that the classification and identification of plants is a live science constantly re-assessing old material in the light of new information.

F.N.H.

⊹ 17 ⊹
Co-ordinated Research Studies in Crocus

Behind the scenes there are many examples of research which involve the cooperation of several departments of the Royal Botanic Gardens. We could take orchids, which are well represented in the living collections and have a wide appeal to the public; moreover, they are of great interest to specialist orchid growers and are studied by taxonomists in Kew Herbarium. Or we could look at the tropical African aloes, which are less well known except to collectors of cacti and succulents, yet studies in the Jodrell Laboratory have had a spin-off in the shape of commercially acceptable house-plants. There are other projects, too, but for space considerations we must limit this chapter to one example.

It may seem, to the casual observer, that there are perhaps three sorts of *Crocus* – one blue, one white and one yellow! This is, however, far from being the case and at Kew we have in recent years carried out a survey of the genus which shows that there are as many as ninety species, plus a great number of variants of each of these. We have found that with *Crocus* it is unsatisfactory to attempt to define each species in terms of its general external appearance and our research programme is accordingly a combined effort between several of the Gardens' departments. Since the publication in 1886 of George Maw's monograph, the major work of its time on *Crocus*, many new species have been

Crocus biflorus is a very widespread species varying enormously throughout its range from Italy to Iran. Studies at Kew show that fourteen subspecies can be recognized within this area and this photograph shows subsp. *nubigena*, found near Bergama in western Turkey. Its blackish stamens make this a particularly striking variant. *C. biflorus* is already known as a fine garden plant and introductions of new forms may be a valuable spin-off from the research programme. Photo: B. Mathew.

151

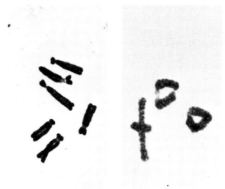

The very extensive chromosome studies of *Crocus* at Kew have assisted greatly in our taxonomic assessment of the genus. It is important to know the number of chromosomes in each species, and their relative shapes and sizes. The six chromosomes of *C. olivieri* subsp. *balansae* can be clearly seen in the left-hand illustration. On the right, they are shown in the type of cell division known as meiosis.

discovered and much information has been accumulated. From the outset of Kew's programme it was clear that the genus was in need of careful review; the project has now utilized the expertise of our growers, taxonomists, cytologists and plant anatomists.

In the field *Crocus* species are distributed in the Old World only, in Europe and western Asia, from Portugal eastwards to Russian Central Asia and from Poland southwards to Libya and southern Jordan, a vast area covering a great range of climates and habitats. Although Kew, as an international botanical garden of long standing, possessed a very good herbarium collection of dried specimens of *Crocus* species, these were mainly rather old and carried little information about the precise conditions under which each species grew in the wild. The living collection, too, was far from comprehensive and many of the corms were of unrecorded origin. For our review of the genus it was clear that new collections would be needed to provide good herbarium material and detailed information about the natural habitats and general behaviour of wild populations of *Crocus*. In addition, in order to understand more fully the make-up of each species and its relationship to others, chromosome studies would be necessary. To make a cytological survey of the genus, living material is required, since chromosomes can be counted only in rapidly growing tissues such as root tips or young flower buds. The material used for this purpose must ideally be of wild origin because of the possibility of hybridization or mutation having taken place in plants from cultivated sources. Previous to the Kew *Crocus* project some work of this type had been carried out, but of a fairly limited nature since it was based mainly on the material which was currently available from commercial sources.

In addition to recording habitat and distribution we wanted to answer some specific questions. How do wild populations maintain or increase their numbers? How do pollination and seed dispersal take place? What is the natural variation within each species? To a large extent the aims of the project have been achieved but inevitably, with a detailed survey such as this, unforeseen problems arise as rapidly as others are disposed of, not the least being the bewildering array of chromosome numbers found. One pleasing fringe-benefit of our work has been the introduction of some aesthetically worthwhile plants into cultivation, and a visit to the Kew Alpine House in the early spring or autumn will confirm this.

The ideal method of carrying out the project would have involved the investigation of all the wild populations of each of the ninety species, with samples being brought back to Kew to enable the various scientists to follow their particular lines of research. This, however, was clearly impractical. Many of the species are distributed over enormous areas and to gather samples from each population of one species alone would involve hundreds of individual collections. Add to this the fact that in many localities there is more than one species, with flowering times varying from autumn to spring, and the number of visits necessary to explore thoroughly even one of these *Crocus*-rich regions becomes vast.

The compromise solution to the daunting task of building up the *Crocus* collection for the study was based on selecting those areas likely to prove most rewarding. Obvious places to visit were those where several species were known to occur, this information being readily available from existing herbarium material and literature. Any species which were known to present particular problems to the botanist would also have to be studied in the wild, and it was decided that particular attention would have to be paid to seeing those which had not previously been observed in the living state, these often being rather rare or occurring in places difficult of access. It was recognized, too, that in addition to the visits to known areas of interest there would have to be some to regions where there were no previous records in order to determine distribution patterns and to make, it was hoped, new discoveries. During the last decade a series of *Crocus*-collecting expeditions has been undertaken, ranging in duration from one or two weeks to a few months. Since the Balkans and Turkey contain a large number of species, many of them endemic to relatively small areas, these are the regions which have received the most attention. Two examples give an indication of the way in which these excursions have been undertaken.

The first example concerns a yellow-flowered Balkan species, *Crocus cvijicii*, which was reported from the mountain of Galičica in the border area of southern Yugoslavia, Albania and Greece. One attempt to locate this had resulted in the unceremonious removal of the botanist concerned from the area by a border patrol. Some time later, when an account of *Crocus* was being prepared for *Flora Europaea*, another dried specimen of this species came to hand, giving the information that it was collected in May near the last of the melting snow on Mount Vermion in northern Greece – well away from the then 'touchy' border areas. Such was the enthusiasm of the Kew crocologists to acquire living material of this little-known plant that a foray was planned for the sole purpose of collecting *C. cvijicii*. Only 48 hours after leaving England the goal was attained – there as predicted was *C. cvijicii*, forming a yellow rim around the last of the snow patches on the summit of Vermion. Notes, photographs, herbarium specimens and living samples were taken and in another 48 hours some corms were back in England in sufficiently good condition to provide material for our cytologists to make the first chromosome count to be recorded for this species.

On another occasion it was decided to study the autumnal species of north-eastern Turkey, for there were questions to be resolved concerning *C. suwarowianus*. For example, was it really distinct from the very similar-looking *C. vallicola*? How closely related was *C. scharojanii*? And what pollinated these autumn-flowering plants? All three species were located and through repeated observations a clearer view of their distributions and habitats was obtained. Certainly *C. vallicola* and *C. suwarowianus* were structurally distinct from each other – their distinguishing features could be checked thoroughly using hundreds of specimens. They grow in close proximity and almost certainly are mimicking each other in outward appearance, perhaps to attract the same pollinators. A bonus came in the information gleaned about the habitats. Although all three species occurred in the same general area it was found that *C. scharojanii* preferred the wet turf immediately alongside mountain rivulets; *C. vallicola* grew nearby but in slightly drier mountain grassland and rarely hybridized with the former, while *C. suwarowianus* occurred only on rather bare places that experienced a considerable period of drought in summer. It was clear that this last species, although resembling *C. vallicola*, was in fact very closely allied to *C. kotschyanus*, a species observed later during the same expedition growing in similar conditions on dry exposed mountainsides. As if this were not enough for one *Crocus*-hunt, a species of bumblebee (*Bombus alagesianus*) was recorded pollinating *C. suwarowianus* – of interest because few of the pollinating insects of wild *Crocus* have been recorded – and in addition

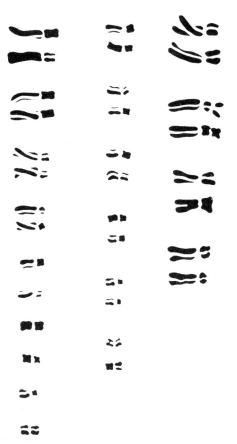

It is helpful to the cytologist to pair off chromosomes and display them in rows in order to compare the overall patterns in different species. Such a karyotype pattern, as it is called, is shown for three different *Crocus*. The eight chromosomes of *C. flavus* and twelve smaller ones of *C. angustifolius* are clearly shown, together with a set of fourteen, some of which do not form obvious pairs. This karyotype belongs to *Crocus* 'Golden Yellow', which is a sterile hybrid between the other two species; unpaired chromosomes are usually an indication of sterility.

To make a thorough study of all *Crocus* species, living material had to be acquired, but some species are rare, and were known only as dried specimens when the project began. The yellow *C. cvijicii* (above) was eventually tracked down near the melting snow patches on Mt Vermion in Greek Macedonia, but the lilac-blue autumnal *C. karduchorum* (below) proved much more elusive, having previously been collected only once in 1859. With the assistance of Turkish botanists, a population of it was finally found near Lake Van in eastern Turkey, thus enabling taxonomic studies of the species to proceed.
Photo: B. Mathew.

the rare endemic of the Lake Van region, *C. karduchorum*, was found in flower. This also belongs to the same group of species and it had been collected only once since the original gathering by Kotschy in 1859, so that some living material for cultivation at Kew for cytological purposes was more than welcome.

The less exciting and sometimes boring business of recording the distribution of each species is no less important. There are memories of dawn to dusk (and well after, by torch and car headlights) searches for populations of *Crocus niveus* and *C. boryi* in the Peloponnese, tedious at the time but of great value in helping to produce maps to indicate the precise geographical range of each.

To cover the areas which could not be visited by Kew staff a correspondence was built up with botanists and keen amateurs in the United Kingdom and other countries. Many valuable details and additional collections of living corms were gathered in this way, Kew's fine international reputation being largely responsible for the success in this particular part of the venture.

The material accumulated in this fieldwork was considerable. At one time the living collection numbered over 1000 different samples, representing nearly all the species. Over half of the ninety species have been seen in the natural state by Kew staff and the remainder have been acquired through other sources and cultivated at Kew so that living material of these too has been available for observation. In the course of the project, several new species or subspecies have been described, some of them very striking plants that may prove to be of considerable decorative value.

The responsibility of maintaining the living collection of *Crocus* lies with the Alpine and Herbaceous Section of the Living Collections Division. This section tends and propagates a basic stock of each species so that plants are available for research purposes. When in flower plants are also used to enhance the display to the public. Certain activities of the scientific staff necessitate the dissection or disturbance of the plants during their growing period, and this is often detrimental to their continuing healthy existence. Some species grown at Kew are rare in the wild and others have been obtained with some considerable difficulty and are therefore to some extent irreplaceable – thus, their conservation in cultivation is an important point and the staff of the Living Collections Division has a difficult balance to maintain between supplying material for experimental purposes and at the same time ensuring that the species is not lost. This is not always easy to achieve and has been known to stretch relationships between the various interested parties.

In addition to the basic work of growing and propagating the plants in the collection, the *Crocus* project has involved three other departments within Kew: the Herbarium, where the classification from the morphological point of view is studied, the Cytogenetics section and the Plant Anatomy section in the Jodrell Laboratory. The Library too is inextricably involved in that it contains most of the literature concerning previous work on the genus. To think of the work of these sections as separate projects would be misleading, for the findings of one might well have a bearing on the decisions of another, or suggest a line of further investigation.

Taxonomy: the Study of Classification
The herbarium botanists are concerned mainly with the external structure of plants and accordingly this part of the *Crocus* study has involved making

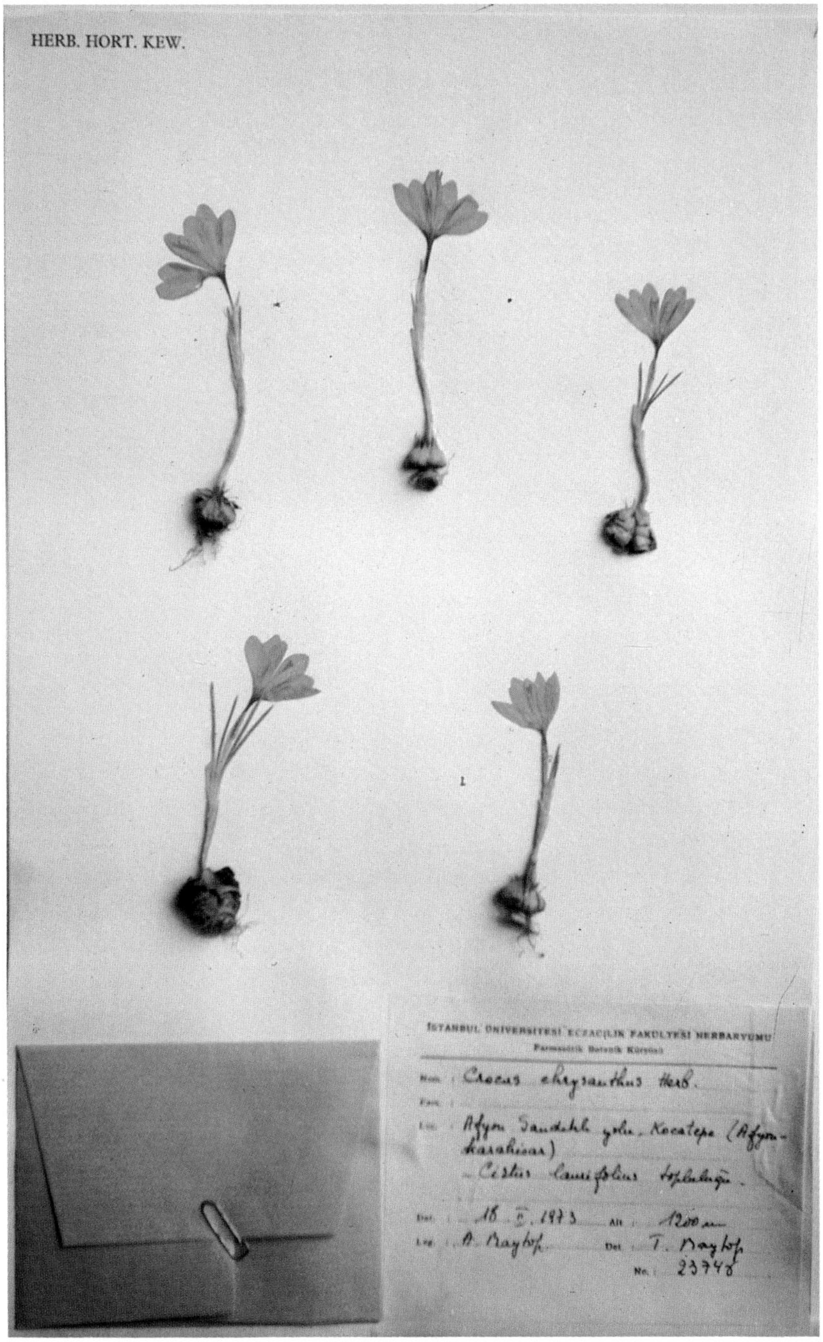

Crocus chrysanthus, of which a well-preserved herbarium specimen is shown, is the wild species from which many colourful spring *Crocus* have been raised for garden display. In the wild it is always yellow-flowered but through selection and hybridization with *C. biflorus* there is now a wide range of white, cream, yellow and blue cultivars.

Although living material provides the most extensive and accurate information about plants, it is essential that dried voucher material is stored away for future reference. Well prepared, this can be a lasting record of the morphological features of the plant, as well as supplying, through the attached field notes, such details as the locality, habitat, altitude, and the flowering period. Good specimens lose few of their characters over hundreds of years. Kew, like other large herbaria, holds many collections of each species from different localities so that the amount of variation in morphology can be assessed, and the exact distribution patterns determined.

painstaking observations and measurements of all the material available, both living and dried. In the case of herbarium specimens, although Kew has by far the most comprehensive collection in the world, material has also been borrowed from several of the other major herbaria in order to reduce the risk of overlooking something important.

In addition to the features which are very obvious to even the most casual observer, such as the flower colour and flowering time, there are a great many other characters which can be used to distinguish between the species. For example, the tunics, or coats, which cover the corms to protect them from desiccation and damage, are variously constructed so that they appear to be either fibrous or papery. In the former case the fibres may be netted together

Crocus corms are covered by protective tunics of varying types, some papery, some with parallel fibres, some netted, some smooth and leathery. The tunics shown here belong to *C. cancellatus*, in which they are very coarsely netted and consist of two halves, a basal one and an upper tunic. Each year a new tunic is produced, pushing the older ones to the outside, so that in the example shown the age of the corm can be easily estimated by the number of tunics.

like a fishnet in varying degrees of coarseness, or they may be parallel to each other. The papery types of tunic can vary, depending upon species, from a thin membranous quality to tough and almost eggshell-like.

It is not the purpose here to go into the taxonomy of *Crocus* but the reader can perhaps already begin to see how the work builds up. Taking just the corm tunic characters and combining them with flower colour and an autumn or spring flowering period gives us a whole range of species possibilities: yellow spring flowers and coarsely netted corm tunics; purple flowers in autumn and papery tunics; white autumnal flowers and shell-like tunics; purple spring flowers and parallel-fibrous corm tunics; and so on. There are, of course, many other characters as well to add to this amalgam – for instance the absence or presence of leaves at flowering time and the number, size and cross-sectional shape of those leaves, the detailed features of the bracts, the length of the flower tube, the shapes, sizes and colours of the perianth segments or tepals, the relative proportions and colours of the separate parts of the stamens and the degree to which the style is branched into separate stigmatic arms. The fruiting state, too, is important to observe, for some species produce their seed pods at soil level where ants distribute the seeds, while other species have capsules carried well above ground level on a long slender stalk. The seeds have been found to vary enormously from species to species in the features of their surfaces and a study of these using the scanning electron microscope has revealed a wealth of patterns which can be added to the rest of the knowledge about each crocus. The surface architecture ranges from long spiral papillae to a 'cobbled street' appearance, or nearly smooth, sometimes with pores similar to the stomata of leaves.

All these factors are considered by the taxonomists and cytologists and are coupled with the rest of the available data concerning such disciplines as ecology – the study of conditions under which the plant occurs in the wild. In fact any information which might be of significance is considered, whether it be the soil type, the altitude and aspect of the site, the rainfall of the region or the temperature regime through the seasons of the year.

156

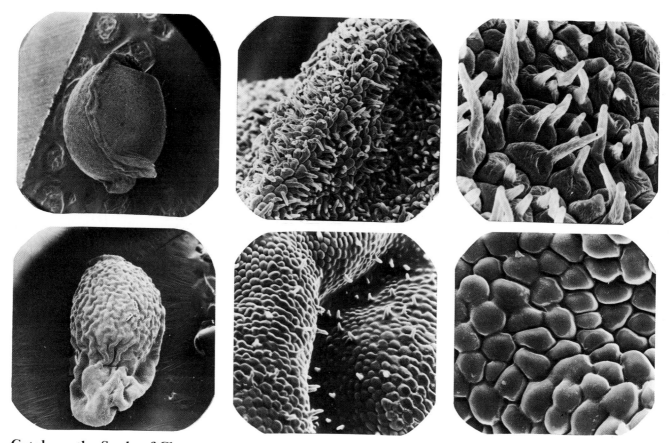

Cytology: the Study of Chromosomes

Though an apparently technical and scientific branch of botany, the study of plant cells and, in particular, of chromosomes, the parts of the cell nucleus that carry hereditary information, provides valuable evidence of the relationship of one species to another and clues to evolutionary development. A few basic points may help to clarify this account of Kew's cytological survey of *Crocus*. Firstly, as a general rule, the chromosomes in the body cells (diploid cells) of each species are characteristic in number, size and shape. Secondly, in sexual reproduction there is a complex process of cell division (meiosis) resulting in the production of gametes with half the chromosome complement of the diploid cells, the full complement being restored on fertilization.

When the cytological survey of *Crocus* was started in 1969, a large number of chromosome counts had already been published but based mainly on plants from unspecified or horticultural origin. Though it was clear from this early research that *Crocus* was an extremely variable genus both in chromosome number and karyotype morphology (that is, the shape and sizes of the chromosomes within each cell), it was not possible to tell if this reflected the state of the genus in the wild. Since the beginning of the survey, more than one thousand collections of wild *Crocus* have been examined and the results show that the genus is even more variable than was at first supposed, with chromosome numbers (for diploid cells, as are other counts given here) ranging from six to sixty-four. Some taxa (that is, species or other closely related category) were found to be stable, with a consistent number and arrangement of chromosomes. These include *C. flavus*, with eight chromosomes, and *C. boryi*, with thirty. Other taxa, however, showed 'intraspecific variation'. For instance, in *C. speciosus* subspecies *speciosus* the number of chromosomes can

Seeds of *Crocus* vary widely in their overall shape and in the degree of development of their various appendages. A more detailed study of seed surfaces using the scanning electron microscope has revealed that there are a great many interesting features which can be used as taxonomic characters.

The seeds of *C. cartwrightianus* (top row) and *C. fleischeri* (bottom row) are compared in magnifications of 12 and 15 (left), 170 (centre) and 510 (right). The seeds of *C. cartwrightianus* are completely covered with long twisted papillae, like minute hairs, while those of *C. fleischeri* are colliculate, that is like a cobbled street. The pair of illustrations in the centre shows the caruncles of each species. Sometimes the caruncle, an outgrowth from the seed, has a different surface pattern to the rest of the seed.

Crocus 'Golden Yellow', which heralds the spring, is one of the best and most easily grown. Here at Kew it is very successful and attractive in grassy areas. This well-known plant, which has been cultivated for over 200 years, was of unknown origin but our cytologists and taxonomists have been able to establish that it is a hybrid and have confirmed its parentage as *C. flavus* × *C. angustifolius*.

be six, eight, ten, twelve, fourteen and eighteen. Furthermore, there are two different karyotype patterns for those with ten chromosomes and also for those with twelve. There are, therefore, in this one subspecies eight variations of chromosome constitution (cytotypes).

Although a range of chromosome numbers within a genus is not unique in monocotyledons – amongst others it is also found in *Iris*, *Ornithogalum* and *Scilla* – *Crocus* demonstrates an extreme form of intraspecific variation. To explain it, particularly in the higher numbers, one has to consider the possibility of polyploidy (increase in the number of whole chromosome sets). Study of the chromosomes in developing pollen grains and embryos as well as root tip meristems has shown that chromosome doubling (autopolyploidy) occurs very rarely in *Crocus*. It is thought, however, that hybridization followed by chromosome doubling (allopolyploidy) has played an important part in the evolution of this genus.

While the work on *Crocus* chromosomes has concentrated on wild species, an attempt has been made to ascertain the origins of some of the cultivars. By examining the chromosomes and comparing them with those of the wild species it has been possible to see which of the cultivars have been selected from the wild and remained relatively unchanged in cultivation, which are hybrids and which are polyploids.

The colourful autumn-flowering cultivar *C. speciosus* 'Globosus' has fourteen chromosomes identical to those of wild material from the Caucasus.

158

However, *C. speciosus* 'Conqueror' has seventeen, very similar to those found in the Crimea, which have eighteen, suggesting that this cultivar originated from material gathered there but has subsequently become chromosomally slightly aberrant in cultivation. The common yellow spring *Crocus* of our gardens, known variously as 'Golden Yellow', 'Dutch Yellow' or 'Large Yellow', has fourteen. The chromosomes showed that this was a hybrid between *C. flavus* (eight) and *C. angustifolius* (twelve), with all eight *C. flavus* chromosomes instead of the reduced number of four; it is referred to as a triploid hybrid. Since the two species do not meet in the wild, the hybrid must have originated in cultivation at a very early date, 'Golden Yellow' having been grown for over 200 years.

Further hybrids were discovered in the *C. chrysanthus* cultivar group both between this species and *C. biflorus* and between different cytotypes of *C. chrysanthus*. For example *C. chrysanthus* 'Advance' (nine) is a hybrid between *C. chrysanthus* (ten) and *C. biflorus* (eight). *C. chrysanthus* 'Canary Bird', on the other hand, while also having nine, is a hybrid between two different cytotypes of *C. chrysanthus* with ten and eight. In the wild these different taxa grow in distinct geographical or ecological regions and only hybridize when brought together in cultivation.

The large Dutch purple and white spring crocuses are derived from *C. vernus* (sixteen), a native of Europe, and are polyploid. Again, this state is thought to have arisen through cultivation and selection and has resulted in their larger size and vigour.

Study of Embryology and Breeding Systems

The unusual diversity that has been found in chromosome numbers and karyotypes within species of *Crocus*, which often cannot be correlated with morphological or anatomical differences, has led us to suspect that some species may adopt reproductive methods which differ from the normal course of sexual reproduction. It may be that some species can set seed asexually. With this in mind the breeding systems and embryology are currently under investigation at Kew, in conjunction with the staff of the cytology section. The relative fertility of pollen and the growth of pollen tubes have been studied, and also interesting structures in the ovules have been observed. The significance of these structures has yet to be established, although some of them may be connected with incompatibility reactions. It is proposed to try and cross individuals of the same species which have different karyotypes, and to study the karyotype and embryo development of the resulting offspring. Problems arise in getting sufficient material to study, particularly owing to lack of coincidence of flowering times of different species, and because relatively few of the ovules in an ovary actually develop into seeds.

Study of Leaf Anatomy

The study of the leaf anatomy of *Crocus* has arisen out of a general survey of vegetative anatomy in the iris and lily family, which will eventually be published as a major work on the anatomy of the monocotyledons. Previously there have been a limited number of descriptions of individual species and two surveys of the genus, both of which have remained unpublished.

The work is done using both the light microscope, to look at leaf sections and leaf surfaces, and the scanning electron microscope, to study leaf surfaces. The basic anatomy of the *Crocus* leaf is relatively uniform, with very few exceptions.

The leaves of *Crocus* have a central 'keel' and two lateral 'arms', which show in these transverse sections. In *C. cancellatus* (top) the arms are shorter than in *C. speciosus* (bottom) and have prominent abaxial ridges. Both leaves have two prominent vascular bundles in the keel, and one at the end of each arm, as well as a row of smaller bundles in between. The keel has a central area of large colourless cells which cause the characteristic white stripe down the centre of *Crocus* leaves.

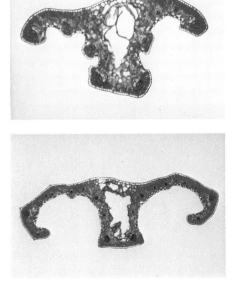

Stomata, the small pores on the plant surface through which gaseous exchanges occur during photosynthesis and respiration, are important features of leaf anatomy. A scanning electron micrograph reveals the stoma (× approximately 1070) on an abaxial leaf surface of *Crocus cartwrightianus*. Wax particles are present on the surrounding epidermal cells.

A preliminary study of *Crocus* pollen grains, the example shown is of *C. cancellatus* (× 600), has revealed that there are probably three different types. This line of research could possibly lead to a greater understanding of the evolutionary trends in the genus.

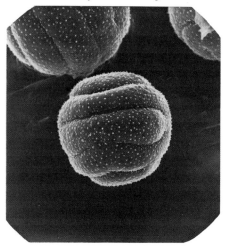

If we look at a cross-section of a leaf, it consists of a central part, or 'keel', and two lateral 'arms', which often have their ends inrolled towards the keel. The central area of the keel consists of large clear cells, and this area accounts for the characteristic white stripe which can be seen along the centre of *Crocus* leaves. The arms contain most of the green cells (containing chloroplasts) of the leaf. Conducting tissues (vascular bundles) are present in a single row along each arm, and around the underside of the keel, with two large bundles in the two keel corners. Stomata, which are pores in the epidermis through which exchange of gases and water vapour takes place, are usually found mainly on the inrolled under-surface of the arms.

There are some variations in this basic structure. For the most part these variations correspond to differences in external appearance and may be useful in helping to determine relationships between species. For example, the outline of the cross-section of the leaf is often characteristic in a species or group of species. *C. cancellatus* has one or more prominent ridges on the leaf under-surface between the keel and arm tip. *C. sativus* and related species have squared corners to the underside of the keel. This group of species also characteristically have groups of fibres extending from the main vascular bundles to the epidermis, which is unusual in other *Crocus* species. Other variable characters include the number of layers of cells in the arms, the orientation of the vascular bundles, the shape of the epidermal cells surrounding stomata, and the presence or absence of hair-like projections. Only two species differ fundamentally from this leaf structure. *C. scardicus* has chloroplast-containing cells and a vascular bundle extending across the upper side of the keel, so that the large clear cells in the centre do not reach the epidermis and there is no corresponding 'white stripe'. *C. cancellatus* has a series of ridges and grooves on the under-surface of the leaf, instead of the single keel and two arms.

There is very little variation within a single species. The leaves do not generally show differences corresponding to the karyotype differences which have been observed in the cytological investigation although in *C. speciosus* there is a variation in the size of surface cells that may show some correlation with differences in chromosome numbers.

Palynology: the Study of Pollen
The palynological section which is housed in the Herbarium has to date not made detailed studies of *Crocus* pollen. A preliminary survey shows, however, that this might be of value. The pollen is generally rather large, spheroidal in shape with a finely spinulate and usually finely perforate skin or tectum. There are three distinct aperture types and a more complete investigation of these could provide some additional taxonomic information. It may also be possible to comment on their evolutionary significance.

This, then, is our example of how the various sections within Kew can combine their talents to study a group of plants, in this case a genus which is known to most people who are interested in plants. For this reason the results are being published not only in scientific journals but also in the form of a monograph, illustrated by an aesthetically beautiful but botanically accurate colour painting of each of the ninety species.

B.M., C.A.B., P.R., S.J.O., I.K.F.

❖ 18 ❖
Kew's Educational Role

One of the principal roles of botanical gardens is public education. Kew is admirably suited to this and the best teachers are the plants themselves in all their infinite variety. Whether it be plants weird and wonderful in their growth or behaviour; or those useful to man; those from tropical forests; or desert cacti or trees of British woodlands – they are all there at Kew. In addition to these living plants, there are botanical exhibits in the Museums and Orangery.

Kew Museums

Public museum displays today are highly professional productions involving great skill and much time, and those at Kew, both permanent and temporary, are no exception. They have to tell a story using words, pictures and botanical objects in a way that is interesting and intelligible both to the ordinary visitor and to the student. The Kew Museums are more than a place to go on a rainy day; they are rich treasure houses containing timbers and resins; fruits and seeds; fibres and textiles; paintings, photographs and models; and much more besides.

The Orangery provides a fine setting for an exhibition giving visitors the historical background to Kew and introducing them to the various departments. The exhibits show something of the scientific work going on behind the scenes, the importance of this research and the extent of the world's dependence upon plant-life. For more than a century Kew has pioneered many aspects of botanical research and amassed a wealth of living and preserved plant material. Both at Kew and at Wakehurst Place, where there is an introductory exhibition in the Mansion, the public are given the opportunity to find out what has been and is being done in these fields.

Another portion of the Orangery is devoted to temporary exhibits. The theme is suggested, perhaps, by a forthcoming botanical anniversary or the special interest of a member of staff, and the idea has then to be implemented. Usually research into the topic leads to other museums or botanic gardens where further ideas and techniques may be gleaned. Eventually this is translated by the designer into working drawings to be executed by the Museums' experienced craftsmen, who operate in a well-equipped workshop. As the exhibit takes shape the Museums' artists apply their skill to the necessary drawings and paintings and photographers supply enlarged captions and prints. Meanwhile the Museums' collections and archives are searched for suitable demonstration material, or, if necessary, items may be specially bought. In an exhibit on the botanical explorer Richard Spruce (1817–93), for example, quinine bark and objects of ethno-botanical interest from the Museums' reference collections were shown, with some of Spruce's South American field notes used as captions.

An active educational programme by the Museums includes tours for organized groups, especially of children, with guide lecturers. Leaflets and quiz-sheets give information about plants to be seen at Kew, as well as stressing how vital plants are to human existence.
Photo: T. A. Harwood.

The Orangery, dating from 1761 to Sir William Chamber's design, is one of the finest buildings at Kew. Typical of greenhouses of the seventeenth and eighteenth centuries, it has windows only on one side, which make its interior unsuitable for many plants. Supplementary illumination was provided in winter during the 1960s before it was converted for use as an orientation and exhibition centre with bookstall.

Opposite: carnivorous plants are a constant source of interest to visitors, especially the young, who are fascinated by the hanging pitchers of the tropical *Nepenthes*. Special displays explain the structure and functioning of other carnivorous plants, such as those North American species featured in Marianne North's painting. Probably the best known of these is Venus's fly trap (*Dionaea muscipula*), at the front; on the right is the yellow pitcher plant (*Sarracenia flava*), and the common pitcher plant (*S. purpurea*), with reddish veins, is central. At the back, showing 'windows' in the arched hood, is the Californian pitcher plant (*Darlingtonia californica*).

Research on carnivorous plants at Kew began more than a century ago with close co-operation between Joseph Hooker and Charles Darwin.

Sometimes these temporary exhibits are incorporated into the permanent display in Museum No. 1. Others are used at society meetings, or go on exhibition at other museums in this country or even abroad. Not all are suitable for travelling, however, since many of the objects from the Museums used in these displays at Kew might deteriorate or be damaged in transit.

A new permanent museum is planned for Kew but at the time of writing the principal exhibition area is Museum No. 1, opposite the Palm House. This purpose-built museum, which was opened in 1857, incorporated large windows to let in as much daylight as possible and handsome display cases. The very features that were virtues when it was built have made the Museum difficult to adapt to modern display techniques. Nevertheless, the exhibits themselves are fascinating and one can learn a great deal from them, particularly about plants useful to man.

The world's first museum of economic botany was opened at Kew by Sir William Hooker in 1847. He had brought together specimens from expeditions around the world, industrial raw materials, such as resins and fibres, and anything else of botanical interest, either donated or purchased. These items were housed in the low building opposite the Aquatic Garden and the public display remained almost unchanged until about 1960, when the building was closed to be used for reference material. By modern standards the exhibits were crowded and overpowering in their profusion but they aroused great interest among visitors in Victorian times.

The present Museum No. 1 includes displays relating the stories of such important economic plants as rubber and such beverages as tea, coffee and cocoa. There is information on the origins of cultivation and cultivated plants and a display providing an explanation of inheritance and plant breeding based on Mendelism. Medicinal plant products feature prominently, including gums and resins, and the section on vegetable dyes incorporates a fine model of a nineteenth-century Indian indigo factory. Among curious items are bark fibres from the South Seas and basket materials and arrow poisons. An exhibit that differs from all the others contains living specimens of British wild plants and includes a glass-topped box of mosses.

A few years after the opening of Museum No. 1 the Orangery was converted into a Museum to house timber and wooden objects. This arrangement continued until 1957, when Cambridge Cottage, which already housed a Museum of British Forestry, was adapted as a museum of wood and wood products. Today, besides having an exhibit of British-grown timber, there are wooden objects of all kinds from many parts of the world, including walking-sticks, violins and carved elephants. Informative exhibits deal with the use of timber in house-building and ship-building and in the manufacture of newsprint.

The material that is on public display in the Kew Museums gives an indication of the exceptionally rich reference collections (used by staff and researchers only) which comprise nearly a million specimens of a wide range of plant products from all corners of the world, many of historic as well as scientific interest.

Living Exhibits
The Living Collections Division arranges several special exhibits in the greenhouses. These include displays of orchids and carnivorous plants, the latter being especially popular with young people and teachers. To help them

understand how carnivorous plants catch and digest insects a detailed explanation is provided above the growing plants. Drawings and photographs illustrate the mechanisms of well-known sundew (*Drosera*) and butterwort (*Pinguicula*), with enormously enlarged photographs of the glandular hairs shown under a scanning electron microscope.

Modern Labelling

The atmospheric conditions in the greenhouses present a problem for those responsible for the displays, in that the materials such as paper and timber normally used for exhibits are subject to damage by rot. The modern solution is to use non-rotting plastic panels for the wording and illustrations. These are applied by screen printing, using an ink of the same plastic material in a solvent that eats indelibly into the plastic surface.

In the open air there are several educational displays with appropriate labelling. The bulb garden distinguishes the various monocotyledonous families, all of which have bulbs and corms as storage organs. Nearby the species of grasses are grouped according to their natural relationships. There are, however, limitations to this principle of grouping in making displays since one cannot have tall species obscuring small ones. There are already one hundred large labels of this kind in position throughout the Gardens, the latest ones appearing in colour, all of course resistant to rain and sunshine.

The ordinary labels that accompany every plant at Kew are much smaller and basically provide the scientific name. Not many years ago these labels were made of lead with the plant names hammered into the soft metal; though very durable, they were difficult to read and became increasingly expensive and likely to be stolen. Since the Second World War they have been progressively replaced by laminated plastic labels, which are reasonably durable and more legible. The engraving machine cuts away the black surface layer to expose the white one beneath so that the name stands out clearly. The modern labels are also more informative. In addition to the scientific name they show an accepted English name where one is available. The botanical family to which the plant belongs is included in the top right-hand corner, while on the right at the bottom an indication is given of the part of the world in which the plant is native. Labels also include coded information about accession and the source of the material. Kew has so many accessions of plants that some 12000 of these labels are required annually.

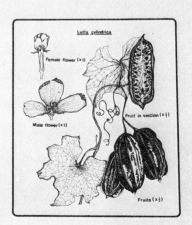

Educational labels of weather-proof material are increasingly used in the Gardens.

Information for Visitors

An increasing number of booklets and guides are available for purchase, while a free leaflet sometimes accompanies exhibits and displays. These handouts and quiz sheets have proved to be very popular, especially with school parties, as they give children an incentive to study the exhibits in order to complete their sheets.

Different aspects of Kew are shown by arrangement to groups of students by the Museums' guide lecturers, who are kept very busy from spring to autumn. Some 5000 people a year are given guided tours. Even in winter the lecturers' services are frequently in demand, both for tours, and also for talks on Kew to outside organizations.

Self-guided tours of the gardens at Wakehurst Place are encouraged by the use of a printed Garden Trail. This is similar to the familiar nature trail, attention being directed to interesting plants in numbered sequence along a specified route. This idea is being developed at Kew to guide visitors around, for instance, the collections of economic plants and conifers.

Requests are constantly received for tours of those parts of Kew not open to the public but such visits would cause serious interruption to the scientific work. Open Days are therefore arranged, usually in alternate years, enabling invited groups to see behind the scenes. Special exhibits are staged, with members of staff on hand to explain their work, while talks are given in the Lecture Theatre by specialists on a wide range of subjects. Invitations to the Open Days are sent mainly to universities, colleges and senior biology forms at local schools, which respond by sending several thousand people. A visit such as this provides an insight into the workings of Kew but, perhaps more important, it gives young people ideas for their own careers and some means of appreciating the value of plant-life to the world.

Marianne North Picture Gallery

A great effort has been and is being made to modernize the Kew Museums. But one that will remain unchanged as it stands is the Marianne North Gallery. This handsome red-brick building was designed by James Fergusson, an architect friend of Miss Marianne North (1830–90), whose unique collection of her own 832 oil paintings she presented to Kew, with the Gallery, in 1882. The impression on entering the Gallery is quite overwhelming, partly because of the range of colourful flowers displayed, partly because of the sheer quantity of

The Marianne North Gallery displays hundreds of the artist's oil paintings, which she presented to Kew in 1882. Quite apart from their botanical interest, these paintings are a remarkable record of the extensive travels undertaken by this Victorian artist.
Photo: T. A. Harwood.

Horticultural diploma students spend about thirty per cent of their time engaged in academic studies, with the rest of the year devoted to practical work concerned with maintenance of the Gardens.
Photo: T. A. Harwood.

paintings hung from knee level to well above head height without so much as a finger space between them. It is how Marianne North chose to present them a century ago and it is how they will be kept. A collection of great botanical interest, depicting plants of many parts of the world, they are indeed a tribute to her artistic skill but even more, perhaps, to her intrepid spirit in an age when travelling alone was a very unlady-like pursuit.

The School of Horticulture

Kew and Wakehurst offer unique and unlimited opportunities for learning about plants in all their aspects. Except in one area, however, formal teaching is not Kew's role. Of course most members of staff train their junior colleagues, a very necessary handing down of knowledge acquired through their own experience. But the Royal Botanic Gardens exist primarily for research and curation of plant material, not as a teaching establishment.

The one very important exception is the teaching of horticulture. Sir William Hooker first had the idea of providing a library for the use of young gardeners, and later some lectures in the evenings to improve their education. The present School of Horticulture provides a full-time, three-year course culminating in a Kew Diploma, which is highly regarded throughout the world. The course is not geared to teaching the production of cabbages, though students are expected to tend a demonstration vegetable plot, nor does it provide the training in high finance required by the man with his eye on a top-level commercial position, though a sound training in management planning and budgeting is included. The students for whom the course is best suited are those interested in the study of plants for gardens and parks and in learning how to grow them. New students must already have had considerable experience, over at least two years, in practical horticulture with some initial professional qualifications. They must also have good academic qualifications, approximately equal to those required for university entry, to enable them to benefit from the lecture courses and thus acquire a wide range of knowledge.

As other chapters in this book make clear, the influence of Kew in other countries, particularly in the tropics, has long been marked. In former days many Kew-trained staff established and maintained gardens in British territories all over the world; some still do go abroad. Among each year's intake of twenty students at the School of Horticulture are some from overseas. The links established by these nationals who come from the ends of the earth to learn about plants at the Gardens help maintain the international scope of Kew's activities.

F.N.H.

The labels in the Queen's Garden, which bear apt quotations from early herbals, reinforce the seventeenth-century character of this garden.
Photo: T. A. Harwood.

166

❧ 19 ❧
The Seed Bank and
Biochemical Research

The Establishment of the Seed Bank

The exchange of seeds between botanic gardens has a long tradition. The acquisition of seeds by Kew from elsewhere continually increased the wide range of plants for both research and horticultural display. In return Kew had to make seeds available to other gardens. During winter, when there was less work to be done outside, the seeds collected earlier in the year from fruiting plants in the Gardens were sorted, listed and offered to research institutes by means of a seed list (*Index Seminum*). Ordered seeds were dispatched in early spring before the sowing season commenced.

In 1969 a seed unit was established at Kew where seed could be held under refrigerated conditions for several seasons. With the annual routine cycle of collection, listing and distribution now broken more seed samples could be held without increasing the number of staff.

At the same time as the seed unit was being developed concern became widespread across the world at the rapid disappearance of many natural habitats owing to man's direct interference and the consequent threat to the

The characteristic shape and surface modelling of seeds often only becomes apparent when they are highly magnified. Seeds of the red campion (*Silene dioica*) and related genera in the campion family have been used to investigate the relationship between germination behaviour and distribution in the wild. The germination of this species is improved by alternate warmth and cold.
Magnification × 80.

167

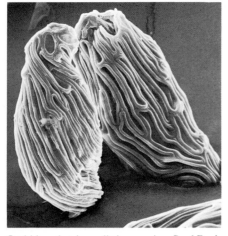

Orchid seeds take up little space in a Seed Bank as they are minute. These seeds of *Vanda tricolor*, a species from the East Indies, were photographed under a scanning electron microscope and are enlarged some 335 times.

Throughout the world, many orchids are at great risk owing to changing habitats and over-collecting. The retention of seeds in a bank, such as that at Wakehurst, has great potential for the conservation of threatened species.

survival of many plant species. Less obvious, but no less serious, was the reduction taking place in the genetic diversity of crop plants as the primitive, but more varied, land-races grown in traditional agriculture were replaced by advanced and carefully selected varieties. Paradoxically, many of the desirable features bred into these élite cultivated varieties had been selected initially from such primitive material.

Kew is obviously well placed to play a large part in promoting long-term storage of seeds in a seed bank of wild species, and at the same time to develop research capability to investigate problems of seed storage and germination. The seed unit was therefore amalgamated with the Physiology Section of the Jodrell Laboratory and in 1973 the Section moved to Wakehurst Place, where it is now housed in a purpose-built Seed Bank with well-equipped laboratories, workshops and offices; part of the Mansion is also used.

One of the advantages of a seed bank is the small amount of space required for storage. Each seed occupies very much less space than the parent plant. This is true even of large seeds such as broad beans (*Vicia faba*) – 50 000 beans would occupy no more than a standard-sized dustbin; twice that number of the tiny grains of timothy grass (*Phleum pratense*) would occupy less space than a salt cellar. Fortunately there is no conflict with nature conservation interests since most plants produce a great number of seeds each season. The collection of only a small proportion of these seeds would therefore not endanger the survival of the species as there would still be enough uncollected seeds for dispersal in the wild.

As to the practicality of the storage of seeds, it is known that their life-span (longevity) can be prolonged in an organized and mathematically predictable way by reducing both the moisture content of the seeds and the temperature at which they are stored. When held at moisture contents of five per cent and at the deep-freeze temperature of $-20°C$, cereal seeds live much longer than they do if kept at room temperature without drying – indeed, viability may be extended to hundreds of years. Research suggests that the same would be true of some eighty per cent of seeds of the world's plants.

Thus by exploiting the relatively small volumes occupied by large numbers of seeds and the ability to prolong their longevity for considerable periods of time, the collection and storage of seeds of a large number of species (without risk to their future survival) becomes economically acceptable.

The Scope of the Seed Bank

The collection and banking of seeds from the plants already growing in the protective custody of the gardens is of little value from a conservation point of view, since these seeds are always likely to be easily obtainable. Therefore, the Seed Bank has taken on the role of maintaining the seeds of wild species collected from adequately sampled wild populations of known provenance. The width of this objective meant that some selection was inevitable to make the collections meaningful. Initially the Mediterranean vegetation, which is severely threatened by the expansion of the tourist industry, was chosen for collecting activity, with species of the grass and pea families being selected for special concern owing to their potential usefulness. More recently attention has begun to turn towards the semi-arid and arid regions of Africa, South America and the Middle East in view of their potential for agricultural development. Efforts are also made to include collections from the British flora with special attention paid to those species, such as the bluebell, which, even though common in Britain, have a restricted world-wide distribution, or species from habitats that are of local occurrence, such as those found on shingle beaches.

Assigning priorities for staff's collecting activity has not resulted in the exclusion of seed collections from other areas. Already collections can be found within the bank that have been made in Antarctica and the Aldabra Atoll in the Indian Ocean, along with many of the islands and highlands in between.

The Use of the Bank
Maintaining seeds of wild species in long-term storage can be seen as an act of faith for the future. Indeed, a cursory glance at the 5000 collections presently held at Wakehurst Place would not reveal many recognized economic plants and may cast doubt on the value of this endeavour. Yet from the requests received, there is more than an eighty per cent chance that any collection will be requested once a year. Many of the requests received from throughout the world are for material on which pure research is to be conducted. Most of this research may seem at first sight to have little direct bearing on the future welfare of mankind. However, much of it will provide insights into plant behaviour which man can exploit for his own purposes. Seeds from the collections at Wakehurst Place have been used in an unexpectedly wide range of applications, including the Blood Transfusion Service, cancer research, soil stabilization and forage crop breeding in Britain, New Zealand and the Middle East, as well as agricultural research. More recently considerable interest has been shown in the potential of some collections to act as sources of chemicals either for pharmaceutical or industrial application. What properties will be sought amongst the collections in the future cannot be predicted but, if past experience is taken as a guide, we can be certain that many plants will prove to have valuable and perhaps surprising uses.

It may be noted that the Royal Botanic Gardens is by no means alone in maintaining collections of seeds for long-term storage but can be seen as an adjunct to a major international initiative, promoted by the International Board for Plant Genetic Resources of the UN Food and Agriculture Organization, to form an international network of such banks for most of the well-known crop species. Many banks restricting their interest to known crop plants can now be found throughout the world, some just beginning, others, like those in the Soviet Union, the United States, Japan, West Germany and Italy, being well-established.

Research on Seeds
At present, the research effort is divided between investigations into problems of seed germination and seed storage. Not all of the problems investigated are directly related to the Seed Bank activity. None the less, the understandings which accrue are often valuable in developing better bank practices. In germination studies, considerable effort over the recent past has been put into understanding what controls the substantial differences in germination behaviour which can be seen in many species. Thus seed collected from different localities throughout the species range, or from the same locality in different seasons or even from the same plants grown in the same season under slightly different micro-climates, have different germination characteristics. More recently attention has turned to the interplay between the germination conditions and the expression of viability in seeds with no dormancy. The study of both these phenomena is of great benefit when defining appropriate

Using the drawer system in the Seed Bank, it is easy to find each seed collection kept in bottles in the sub-zero temperature. The Bank contains thousands of samples gathered from many parts of the world.
Photo: J. Dickie.

germination conditions for material held in the bank as well as contributing to the wider understanding of seed germination.

In seed storage the lowest moisture content compatible with longevity is unknown. While studies to elucidate this factor will be of value in improving our understanding of the basic processes which control longevity, they will also be of practical value in indicating how bank stocks can be kept alive for the longest time possible, thereby making more effective use of the effort involved in collecting, documenting and identifying these collections as well as testing their viability. The same is also true of the investigations into the storage

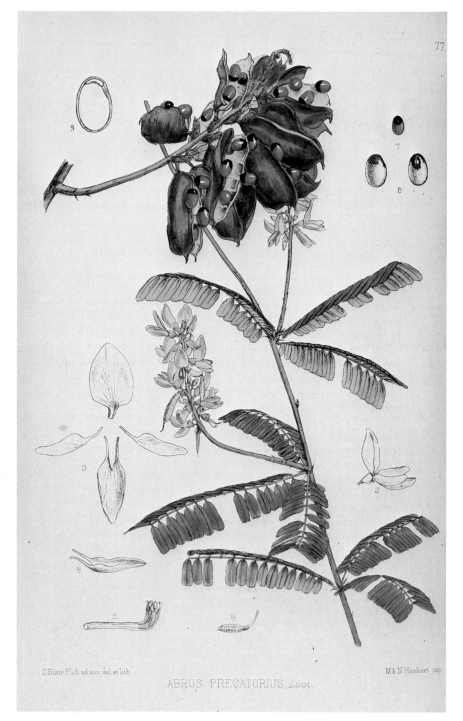

Leguminous seeds feature prominently in the Seed Bank collection, in part because of their potential economic importance and also because of Kew's research interest in the family. Biochemical studies have identified secondary compounds that are toxic to predatory insects, while taxonomic interest has centred on tropical African legumes for floras and monographs – works which are of fundamental importance for the identification of plants.

The conspicuous red and black seeds of the African climber *Abrus precatorius* are poisonous to humans, yet they are often included in necklaces, where they constitute a potential danger to children.
From Bentley and Trimen, *Medicinal Plants* (1880, pl 77).

characteristics of timber trees, where the knowledge contributes greatly to our understanding of seed survival in the wild and is also directly applicable to forestry practices.

The work carried out at Wakehurst Place can be seen as being directed towards either the design or production of a kind of botanical 'safety belt' worn in the hope that its absolute worth will never be tested.

R.D.S.

Research on Chemical Defence in Plants

Higher plants, unlike most animals, are unable to evade potential predators by running away. Often, however, plants and their seeds contain chemical compounds which are poisonous to or inhibit feeding by such predators. One of the research projects in the Jodrell Laboratory concerns the identification of such chemical defence compounds in seeds. A study is being made of the ways in which these compounds affect seed predators, such as fungi, insects and mammals.

The majority of chemicals that support life are the same in all living creatures, but the defensive chemicals of plants are of a different kind, and normally play no part in life-supporting chemical reactions. However, they may have adverse effects on the life chemistry of organisms that do not contain

Chemicals from plants are an increasingly important resource and, as relatively few species have been investigated, the potential is great. The chemistry of the opium poppy (*Papaver somniferum*) is well known. Its capsule contains a latex which dries to a brown gum known as opium. In 4000 BC the Sumerians referred to this as the 'joy plant', since opium eases pain and creates a feeling of euphoria. Opium has since been used in medicinal preparations for a wide variety of illnesses, from coughs to dysentery, but continued use leads to addiction and dependency, with inevitable social problems. The most important constituent is morphine, one of the first medically active chemicals to be isolated in a pure form.

The biochemistry section of the Jodrell Laboratory is carrying out active research on the chemistry of plants.
Photo: F. N. Hepper.

Cancer, the most feared and most baffling of human maladies, is not a disease only of modern life. Traces have been found in a million year old skeleton, and in some Egyptian mummies. Over the centuries, some 3000 plant species have been used by doctors and others to treat cancer, usually with little success. The Madagascan periwinkle (*Catharanthus roseus*) is one of the few plants from which clinically useful anti-cancer chemicals have been obtained. The search for others continues. Photo: F. N. Hepper.

them. When we use the term 'poisonous plant' or 'medicinal plant' what we mean is that the defensive chemicals of that plant interfere with our basic life chemistry, adversely in the case of poisons or beneficially with medicines.

Since the dawn of history man has depended on plant chemicals to make his short life more comfortable by using raw materials such as rubber, resins and indigo dye; crop protection chemicals like pyrethrum dust and nicotine spray; or drugs such as opium. This dependence was briefly minimized and remarkably reduced during the late nineteenth and early twentieth centuries when, with the rapid development of the chemical industry based on coal, and later oil, came the laboratory synthesis of many chemicals, such as the sulphonamides and DDT, which had far-reaching social effects. Man seemed capable of synthesizing everything he needed and plant chemicals were almost forgotten.

This age of arrogance was brief. By the 1950s serious problems were evident, particularly in connection with crop protection chemicals. DDT, for example, was not broken down in the soil and its accumulation led to serious ecological disturbance.

Today we are turning again to plants in a desperate search for insecticides and drugs – desperate because, although tropical forests are the repository of most chemically unexplored plants, they are being destroyed at an alarming rate in order to satisfy man's need for farms and firewood. Possibly there will be little natural forest left by the end of this century. The crops which feed our burgeoning population have been deliberately bred to be high in food value and low in defensive chemicals, which must now be supplied externally. Wild plants are the most likely source of biodegradable crop protection chemicals.

In the Jodrell Laboratory scientists are exploring the chemicals of wild plants, especially tropical members of the pea family (Leguminosae) and the aloes. Plant material is crushed, macerated with suitable solvents and filtered. The extracts are examined by thin-layer chromatography for the presence of interesting new kinds of chemicals, which are then isolated in a pure form. They can then be tested for a wide range of properties, such as pharmacological or anti-insect effects. This information is then published in scientific journals for the benefit of others.

A knowledge of plant chemicals can help in the classification of plants, when differences of external form (morphology) are inadequate. For reasons of economy, all species do not accumulate a wide range of defensive chemicals, but specialize in one or two appropriate to their ecological niche. Closely related plants tend to contain the same or similar chemicals. Conversely, plant classification based on morphology only can often indicate alternative sources of interesting chemicals.

For millions of years the chemical genius of wild plants has ensured their survival in the face of intense competition from other plants and predation by animals and micro-organisms. Chemicals, however, are no defence against that most rapacious of all predators, man, and his bulldozers. Unless we heed the voice of the conservationist, the chemical secrets of plants will be lost for ever within a few decades, and with them the information we need to ensure our own survival. Wild plants are our past and our future. Forget this and we become accessories in a collective folly every bit as disastrous in its consequences as nuclear war.

L.E.F.

❧ 20 ☙
Kew and
Plant Conservation

The Need for Conservation

Only one plant of the beautiful lady's slipper orchid (*Cypripedium calceolus*) survives in England. The combination of beauty and rarity proved its downfall. Vigorously protected and zealously guarded today, its survival still in the balance, the lady's slipper orchid has become a symbol of worldwide concern to save threatened plants for tomorrow. Helping to prevent plant extinctions is a major priority at Kew. Botanists returning from expeditions to remote regions tell of the destruction of vegetation on an unprecedented scale. There is a strong feeling that time is running out and something must be done to protect the flora that remains.

The threats to plant life are so great that if present trends continue, a large proportion of the world's flora may become extinct before the end of this century. The greatest threat of all comes from the world's still exploding human population: in 1975 there were 4090 million people, and by the year 2000 there will be at least 6180 million, assuming birth rates continue to drop, and even then the population will still be increasing by more people each day than it is at present. People need food and in the search for more land to grow crops and to graze domestic animals, natural vegetation is the victim. New methods of growing food that use far less land and other resources are still at the experimental stage, even for countries with the most sophisticated technology.

The economic advantage to man must be recognized as one of the most important reasons for maintaining the diversity of plant life.

Habitats in Crisis

The biggest losses of plant species are occurring in the tropical rain forests, home of as much as 30 to 40 per cent of the world's stock of plant species. The tragedy here is that many rain forests are being felled for minimal and often short-term economic gain. In parts of the New World tropics, some forests are literally burnt to create pasture for beef cattle. The valuable timber is reduced to ash. In many areas the pastureland that results is only productive for a few years because of low soil fertility. In a tropical forest, in contrast to a temperate-zone forest, most of the nutrients are locked up in the vegetation rather than available in the soil. This explains why rain forest, the most lush and luxuriant vegetation on earth, typically grows on very poor soils which often cannot support northern-style agriculture if the forest has been cut down. Large areas of forest are cut for shifting agriculture that again may only be successful for a short time, before burgeoning pests take over and before the soil nutrients that remain are simply washed away by heavy tropical rain.

Keeping the plant cover is essential in many tropical regions to maintain productivity and prevent erosion. Meanwhile in many drylands the cutting of

The elegant lady's slipper orchid (*Cypripedium calceolus*) is a European plant that in Britain has been uprooted and picked to such an extent that it is now on the verge of extinction in the wild. New propagation techniques for temperate and tropical orchids may help to reduce the destruction caused by the collection, often illegal, of wild plants for the horticultural trade.
Tankerville Collection, Kew Library.

173

The indiscriminate destruction of forest by clearing or by fire (above right, in Kenya) is a major threat to plant communities and individual species in many parts of the world, particularly in the tropics. Even in upland areas of Africa, only remnants of the virgin forest survive, such as the Tanzanian Mazumbai Forest (above left).
Photos: F. N. Hepper.

virtually every tree for firewood and excessive grazing by domestic animals is destroying vegetation so that only an unproductive desert, bare of plants, remains. The tragedy is that in the day-to-day search for food, people are having to destroy the very resources on which their future will depend. Not only are the plants becoming extinct – and some of them could be potential sources of food and medicines – but in some regions the ability of the land to produce food is also beginning to fail. The United Nations Conference on Desertification estimated that 'regions already in the grip of desertification or at high to very high risk cover 20 million sq km – an area twice the size of Canada.' This is why Kew's project to find new crops for arid lands from the native plants of the region is so important.

Many island floras, too, are in critical danger. Islands, especially in the tropics, often support many endemic species, that is, plants not found anywhere else in the world. At the last count, the Canary Islands, had 514 endemic plants, while Madagascar, New Caledonia and Hawaii have endemics numbered in thousands. Endemic plants occurring in small areas are especially prone to extinction. On small islands the pressures on land for building and agriculture are intense, and this increases the likelihood of extinction. Grazing by introduced animals, such as goats, can also play havoc with native flora that may have evolved in the absence of herbivores and so may not have many of the defence mechanisms – spines, poisons, resins for instance – which characterize those continental ecosystems such as the African plains that are dominated by large mammals.

It is grazing and cutting of the native forests which has brought to the verge of extinction the endemic flora of Rodrigues, a small island in the Indian Ocean. Out of thirty-four known endemic plants – and there may have been more that we will never know about – at least nine are extinct and a further twelve in imminent danger of extinction. Perhaps the saddest case of all is Hawaii, where extinction is perfectly avoidable – Hawaii being part of the United States, there is no need for the islands to be self-sufficient in food or timber or to ruin the environment by encouraging tourists beyond carrying capacity. Already 273 endemic plants have become extinct and many of the

174

others are in danger. Perhaps the greatest danger now is the rampant and rapid spread of introduced plants such as guava and *Lantana*, which have got out of control.

Loss of habitat in Britain is no less significant. However, the endemic flora is almost insignificant, most of the British rarities being common in continental Europe, where a much higher percentage of natural vegetation remains. Nonetheless, there is no cause for complacency. Lowland raised bog, an important but increasingly uncommon wildlife habitat, provides an example of the threat to certain plant and animal communities. Since 1850 the extent of this habitat in Britain has declined by 90 per cent and in Lancashire by a staggering 99 per cent.

Botanic Gardens and Conservation

With these grim and impending threats to plant life, gardens like Kew become all the more important as oases of plant diversity and as holding grounds for the future. Plants grown for many years simply for their general interest are suddenly found to be the only remaining individuals of their species, the plant in the wild having become extinct. Kew was one of the first gardens to recognize this and has been host to two international conferences on developing the role of botanic gardens in plant conservation. Out of the second conference developed a small organization, the Botanic Gardens Conservation Co-ordinating Body, an arm of the Threatened Plants Committee of the International Union for Conservation of Nature and Natural Resources (IUCN). The 'Body', as it is usually called, which is based in Kew's Conservation Unit, has the task of tracking down plants on the edge of extinction. Most remarkable of its successes was the rediscovery of Easter Island's only tree, the endemic *Sophora toromiro*. The trees formerly provided local people with their only source of timber for buildings, for canoes and for their famous wood carvings. As with so many islands, introduced sheep devastated the island's flora and by 1917 only one tree remained. A few more were seen in 1955, but by 1962 not one tree could be found. However, since IUCN listed the tree as 'extinct', the Göteborg Botanical Garden, Sweden, has announced that on a trip to Easter Island, the famous explorer Thor Heyerdahl had collected seeds from that last tree and sent them to the garden. On his next visit Heyerdahl found the tree had died. But the seeds germinated in cultivation and the 'toromiro' lives on, saved in a greenhouse on the other side of the world.

The more prosaic work of the 'Body' is to find out which species known to be threatened, rather than extinct, are already in cultivation and where. The aim is to find out which gardens are growing which threatened plants, so that material can be made available for, among other things, research and horticulture without further endangering the remaining plants in the wild.

The plan is to ensure that all threatened species are grown in more than one botanic garden. The tremendous support many gardens have given the 'Body' makes this task not as daunting as it may seem. Already over one hundred botanic gardens around the world are full members of the network and many others provide help and information. Since the living collections at Kew alone contain an estimated 47000 plant species, it should be possible at least to ensure the safe cultivation of the estimated 25000 to 30000 threatened species (excluding some in tropical forests), as a minimum requirement.

Botanists do not have the dilemmas facing zoologists about whether to bring

The attractive 'pico paloma' or dove's beak (*Lotus berthelotii*) is a rare native of the Canary Islands. Until very recently it was believed to be extinct in the wild. It is, however, widely grown in gardens and flourishes as a bedding plant in urns at Kew.
Photo: M. Svanderlik.

175

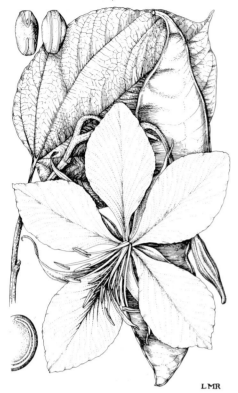

Forest clearing in Kenya and Tanzania threatens *Gigasiphon macrosiphon*, a tree recorded from four localities. The spectacular beauty of its white flowers could make it a good ornamental for the tropics.
From *Flora of Tropical East Africa: Leguminosae–Caesalpinioideae* (1967, fig. 45), drawing by Lura M. Ripley Mason.

an endangered species into captivity for conservation breeding or whether to leave it in the wild. A skilled gardener or botanist can gather a few seeds or cuttings from a wild plant without damage to its population and its breeding success. Most plants produce thousands of times more seeds than will grow into mature individuals.

But growing the plants in the garden is not the answer on its own. First of all there are relatively few botanic gardens in the humid tropics to grow the many rain forest species now in danger. Even if these gardens existed, such a policy would not necessarily allow the species to be reintroduced into their habitats again, because the pollinators may have become extinct. Associated with the trees, their pollinators and their epiphytes, there are innumerable different insects and fungi which break down the dead matter, returning nutrients to the tree roots without allowing them to become dissolved in the soil water and so leached away. A piece of tropical rain forest contains by far the most complex set of interrelationships ever found – on earth or in space – and is far more complicated than any machine made by man. We are only beginning to understand the broad outlines of how the system works, let alone to know each species in the web and the role it plays. We can certainly never put a rain forest back together from its component species, even if we knew what they all were.

There are other snags too in conservation through gardens. In a garden the plants require constant tending by man because their environment is an alien one. Greenhouses require lots of energy, a commodity which will be expensive and in short supply for many years yet. The plants are vulnerable to mechanical breakdown or to human error. A window left open on one frosty night or a single dose of water to a desert plant in its dry season may spell disaster to species carefully treasured for many years.

Another limitation of conservation through gardens is that they can contain only a small proportion of the natural variation within a species. Individuals of all species vary, some imperceptibly, some more obviously. It is important to safeguard this variation as it provides the basis for future evolution and adaptation to changing conditions.

The message is simple: protect endangered habitats now, before they disappear. Here the species can continue to evolve and adapt. Here, too, if the areas are big enough, man only has to protect the vegetation from gross disturbance; the plants do not have to be tended each day.

The plants in a garden may be a useful back-up, but their cultivation cannot be the only long-term policy for conservation. Their importance is not so much as the last resort – though this is important with some species, especially where field conservation is not possible – but in telling people about the need for conservation and in providing material for gardeners and for scientists so that there is no longer any excuse to remove the remaining plants from the wild. Above all we should aim to put the plants back into their habitats – re-introduce them – wherever we can. Gardens like Kew are ideally suited for this kind of work. The horticulturists have unrivalled skills in growing a wide range of difficult and unusual plants. From the experience gained by collecting plants on expeditions, and then in growing them at Kew, these people can best assess how to mimic a plant's environment in cultivation. They tend to know which characteristics of a plant's habitat, such as day-length, temperature or soil acidity, must be provided in the garden and which are not necessary for the plant to thrive.

Kew's experience in cultivating endangered plants could be equally useful when the time comes to reintroduce those plants back into the wild. Here the conservationist must go beyond planting out the individuals he has grown and putting a fence around them. All the needs of the plant must be assessed and then those that are missing made available. Scientists must find out the details of the plant's life history; what are the pollinators, for example, and whether they are present.

The skill of the gardener is just as important in protecting endangered species within their habitats. If a population is reduced to a handful of individuals, often far away from each other, protecting the site may not be enough. Indeed, most experience in the past shows that enclosing the site with a fence may deliver the final *coup de grâce* as it excludes animals which may be essential to keep vigorous plants from swamping the rarity. The 'conservation gardener' may have to pollinate the plants by hand, distribute the seeds and weed around the seedlings, so that the population can rapidly grow beyond the critical stage.

An even more radical idea has taken root. This is that botanic gardens should own and manage nature reserves themselves. Kew has a reserve at Wakehurst Place, which was opened in 1980 and is described in Chapter 13. It is a good sample of Wealden woodland and contains several rare English plants. The Island Council of the Canary Islands have given their botanic garden – the Jardín Botánico 'Viera y Clavijo' – several areas to manage as reserves and these contain some of the islands' endangered plants. Botanist Marius Jacobs from Leiden suggests that gardens in the tropical rain forest zone should go one step further: combine the concept of the botanic garden with that of the reserve by taking an intact piece of tropical forest, making walkways through it – including walkways through the canopy where most of the animals and the flowers can be seen – and labelling the plants for all to see.

Through all these approaches to conservation, directors of gardens realize the importance of convincing people that maintaining the diversity of plant life is important. In times when food comes ready packaged from the supermarket, people need reminding that all our food comes ultimately from plants. The value of fostering diversity and of using it has always been at the heart of Kew's work. In fact the concept goes back a lot further: the early herbalists, who were first to study plants systematically, were looking for drugs to cure disease. In Kew's history there are many examples of opening up new uses for plants. At present, however, most of the world's agriculture depends very heavily, and perhaps precariously, on a handful of crop species. In this century the diversity of these crops has been greatly eroded by breeding programmes that have replaced old and variable forms with new and uniform varieties. The loss of genetic material could prove calamitous as there is always the danger that epidemic disease could take a heavy toll worldwide.

Gathering Information

The many threats to the plant kingdom and the obvious need for conservation have also stimulated another major change of emphasis at Kew. We now need to know urgently which plants grow where and so there is great pressure to speed up taxonomic study and the completion of floras. If the gentlemanly pace of past taxonomy remains, we will not even know which species are being lost in some parts of the world, let alone make plans for their conservation. The United States National Academy of Sciences has called for a crash programme of plant taxonomy and for 1500 taxonomists worldwide. Kew's recent work in

Many palms, some of economic value to man, are rare or threatened with extinction. The wax palm (*Ceroxylon alpinum*) of Colombia is one that is endangered.
Photo: J. Dransfield.

Among the curiosities and mysteries of the living collections at Kew is the sole recorded specimen of *Cestrum psittacinum*, which came to the gardens, from an unknown provenance (possibly Mexico), at the end of the nineteenth century. It is a reminder that, though the chief aim of conservation is the maintenance of natural habitats and their constituent species, one useful role that botanic gardens can play is the cultivation and propagation of very rare plants.

From *Curtis's Botanical Magazine* (1928, pl 9158).

providing a rapid checklist for the Bahia province of Brazil, where the species-rich coastal forests are being decimated, provides an example of the type of work many believe should be the new approach.

It was the pressure from taxonomists, principally at Kew, that stimulated the creation of the Threatened Plants Committee (TPC) of IUCN. In the late 1960s Sir Peter Scott approached Ronald Melville, a retired Kew botanist, and asked him to compile a 'Red Data Book' of endangered plants to complement the animal volumes which were well under way by then. Ronald Melville started work in 1968 and began to uncover the size of the threat to the plant kingdom. It was he who estimated that 20 000 plants were in danger (an estimate now increased to at least 25 000 species and probably many more if rain forest floras are included). Professor Jack Heslop-Harrison, the then newly appointed Director of Kew, was keen to expand the approach. It was felt that a new organization was needed to assess which were the threatened species, where they still grew and how they could be saved. In December 1974 the Threatened Plants Committee was launched with Professor Heslop-Harrison as Chairman and Gren Lucas as Secretary. Its small Secretariat, initially of one Research Assistant, Hugh Synge, was based in the Herbarium at Kew, but the unit was an integral part of IUCN and was funded by IUCN's partner, the World Wildlife Fund. By 1982 the committee had a staff of around six, and is well on the way to producing a world list of threatened plants. Lists of threatened plants have been produced for Europe, for North Africa and the Middle East, as well as from many national programmes such as in Australia and the United States that are in close touch with TPC. Programmes for tropical Africa, the Caribbean Islands and Central America are well underway. A Red Data Book has been published, containing detailed case histories on 250 selected threatened species, chosen to show the differing threats to plants and the kinds of losses that will happen if present trends continue.

But gathering information is only the first step. Even more crucial is mobilizing support and drawing up plans for plant survival. The European list is an example of how the work can proceed: the list, which contains around 2000 threatened species, was submitted to the Council of Europe in August 1975. The environment heads of the countries within the Council signed a strong resolution later that year calling for far more activity to conserve endangered plants. By 1979 the Council had drawn up a legal treaty – the Berne Convention – which incorporated a list from TPC of the European species in most danger. Under the treaty, governments must protect these plants by law and make sure their habitats are safeguarded.

In 1980 TPC also submitted a lengthy report to the European Economic Community (EEC) on the sixty-two plants endangered in the EEC countries and action seems hopeful. So here is a practical example of how gathering information on threatened plants and conservation can lead to legislation for their protection. This legislation will then give those people on the ground the power and resources to ensure that endangered species survive. There is no reason why any more species in Europe should become extinct. Only lack of purpose will thwart this aim.

In the years to come Kew looks to increasing still further its own role in the conservation of nature. The IUCN Threatened Plants Committee is now part of an extensive monitoring network of IUCN and is in touch with many hundred botanists, in virtually every country of the world. Kew also provides a home for IUCN's and WWF's main computer, which contains all their information on threatened species – plant and animal – and on national parks worldwide.

A big and varied institution like Kew is ideally suited to play a crucial role in building up concern for saving plants. Indeed the concept of conservation is deeply embedded in Kew's philosophy of its work around the world. The foundation of Sir William and Sir Joseph Hooker in building Kew as a garden and scientific institution has proved a good basis for developing the science and practice of conserving plant life. Kew itself cannot save plant habitats around the world, but it can – and does – provide the information and the skills for those in a position to do so. Above all it must tell people why conservation is so important to all our futures.

H.S.

The Main Gates, Kew

Postscript
Kew in the Future

Any prediction, no matter how personal or subjective, of the way the Royal Botanic Gardens might develop has to take into account that, to some extent, what Kew is controls what Kew will be. The present and the past are powerful constraints on the future. The gardens are of course much more than a beautiful collection of plants; they have been part of English history for the past two hundred years and more, and the historic buildings they contain, such as the Pagoda, the Orangery and Kew Palace, reflect this. The display of plants is thus only one facet of the many-sided complex that goes to make up the Royal Botanic Gardens, Kew. Nevertheless, the combination of public pleasure and instruction with botanical research is likely to influence Kew's development in the future in the same way that it has done in the past.

That part of Kew that makes the greatest impact on its many visitors is undoubtedly its extraordinarily rich collection of living plants. Nowhere else in Britain can such a diverse assemblage of plants from so many different parts of the world be seen in one place. However, if the collection is to fulfil its scientific purpose, it must be well documented. Already the records of the living collection are mostly computerized and the capacity for selective recall of information, vital for the functions of a large botanic garden, is already there in essence. Nevertheless, this facility has still to be exploited to the full. In the future, it is likely that, with the help of computers, there will be production of specialized lists of and information about plants in cultivation at Kew on a much wider scale and much more economically than is possible by conventional printing, which for long has been prohibitively expensive. There are many other areas where the power and storage of the computer would be beneficial.

The need for rapid and selective retrieval of information is nowhere stronger than when serving the purposes of plant conservation. Such work as Kew is doing, not only in the carrying out of research but also in the assembling and making available of basic information so vital in drawing up conservation policies, is already urgently needed, but with the speed of destruction of plant communities, particularly in the tropics, the urgency is likely to increase. Many species of plants with possible human value have certainly been destroyed for ever already, and others will continue to go, whatever we can do. However, it is a matter for pride and satisfaction that now and in the future Kew is likely to make an increasing contribution towards saving some of the world's vegetation on which we all ultimately and totally depend. Kew's objectives have for many years been farsighted, extending usually beyond the confines of Europe. The task of improving knowledge of the environment and conditions of human life in the developing countries of the world is a daunting but also an immensely stimulating one in which Kew will, I am sure, play a significant future role.

Flowering magnolias and bulbs make the Mound an attractive feature of Kew in spring. The hillock is artificial in origin and is surmounted by the Temple of Aeolus, which was designed by Sir William Chambers in 1760 and rebuilt in 1845 by Decimus Burton. Photo: T. A. Harwood.

Linked with this also is the important aim of informing those who come to Kew to enjoy the Gardens of the importance and significance of plants, not only in giving visual pleasure but in being essential for mankind's existence.

For whatever purpose the living collections may be used it is important that they are correctly named. In recent years a vigorous campaign for verification of the names of plants at Kew has been undertaken and this will actively continue. Too often in the past botanic gardens have been content to display plants, even when adequately verified, often accompanied only by a label bearing a Latin name, a family and a country of origin. At Kew there has been encouraging development of educational labels and leaflets. In the future the importance of conveying to the public such information as the relevance of plants to human welfare, the economic value of individual plants and the conservational significance of endangered species will be increasingly important tasks.

Though Wakehurst Place did not become Kew's annexe in the country until the 1960s, the gardens already contained a superb collection of choice trees and shrubs. The 400-year-old Mansion, seen here in autumn across the Mansion Pond, provides a splendid focal point.
Photo: F. N. Hepper.

Effective instruction through a botanic garden such as Kew depends greatly on plants being displayed in attractive surroundings. Already the Temperate House, which has recently emerged from a long period behind screens and scaffolding, can be seen for the important and handsome building that it is. The Ferneries and T-Range have developed over the years in a haphazard and uncoordinated way so that they now present problems in maintenance and cultivation which will be greatly lessened when these old complexes are replaced as an architectural unit on a single site.

The museum buildings at Kew contain, among many other things, one of the finest collections in the world of economic plant products, amounting to something near a million items in all and covering a very wide range of products and uses from all over the world. This collection has for long not received the public or scientific attention that it deserves mainly because of its archaic and unsatisfactory accommodation and of the consequential difficulties in consulting and studying it. Furthermore it is not adequately catalogued. Plans have been made, and in the near future a fine new building to house not only these collections but other aspects of the museum and public education work at Kew may be confidently expected to have been added to the landscape. The prospect of new accommodation will add impetus to cataloguing.

A by-product of the verification programme has been to show how much unintentional duplication in the collections there has been. Often this may be no bad thing, especially where plants are grown for ornament or beauty. For example, no one would complain of the multitude of bluebells in the Queen's Cottage woods but, where reference collections are concerned and where space is limited, unnecessary duplication can mean the exclusion of important plants.

One's assessment must probably be that, in common with those of many other botanic gardens, the living collections are still under-utilized for research purposes. In the future the research usage of the collections is likely to increase, given the remarkable opportunities offered by Kew in bringing together in one place such a diverse representation of the flora of the world. The more comprehensive the living collections are the more potentially valuable in general they are for research purposes. However, it is impossible even for Kew to grow everything, so inevitably specialization takes place, and already selected parts of the collections are of special value on account of the wealth of different plants contained. The orchids and Bromeliaceae are two examples; and, in recent years, in response to research needs, an exceptional wealth of New World Commelinaceae has been built up. It can be expected that other specialized collections will be developed and that there will be a continuing increase in size and richness of some of those Kew already possesses.

Kew's research work on plants is centred principally in the Herbarium and the Jodrell Laboratory. The reference collections of plants in the Herbarium, unrivalled in their wealth and comprehensiveness, are nevertheless in a state of growth–growth which now and in the future more than in the past is likely to be selective and carefully controlled. This constant growth is both healthy and necessary, but it poses almost perpetual problems of accommodation. The new wing of the Herbarium and Library, opened as recently as 1969, is already proving insufficient, and consideration has to be given to utilizing the present space to the maximum efficiency as well as to providing new accommodation.

The world's need for the research work of the Herbarium is increasing. Against the speed of destruction by mankind of his natural environment, the need to fill the gaps in our knowledge of plant life, especially in the tropics, and of its potential use to mankind becomes a task of daunting urgency to be performed with resources inadequate both in money and staff. A firm basis of order and classification by which people, in whatever country, may refer to the plants they wish to know and use by an internationally agreed nomenclature–a nomenclature that is also, particularly in these days of computerization, a vital key to unlocking existing sources of accumulated knowledge–is a continuing necessity, but still far from reality. Uncertainties and disagreements abound, and can only be resolved by careful study of plants often on a world basis and through the exercise of wise judgment. Monographic and co-operative taxonomic projects such as those on *Crocus*, *Senecio* and *Aloe* will probably be undertaken with greater frequency in the future. The demand for floras is as great today as in the past.

The Jodrell Laboratory has a long and distinguished tradition of research into several branches of plant science, particularly cytology, anatomy,

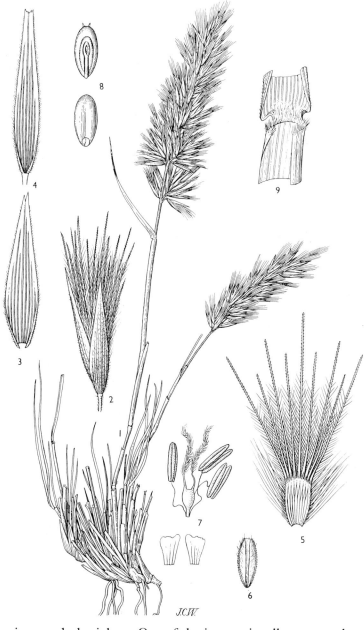

J.C.W.

The worldwide Herbarium collections place Kew in a favoured position for major taxonomic research. The grass family has been studied since the time of George Bentham, whose work was published in the 1880s. Otto Stapf and Charles Hubbard continued the research and at present a major comprehensive work on the genera of the world's grasses is being undertaken. Many accounts of grasses have been prepared for regional floras, including the *Flora of Iraq* (1968) by the late N. L. Bor, illustrated by line drawings such as this of *Enneapogon persicus.*

biochemistry and physiology. One of the internationally renowned works of reference prepared at Kew was the systematic *Anatomy of the Dicotyledons* by Metcalfe and Chalk. This work sought to analyse a daunting mass of anatomical information in relation to the families of plants concerned. The first volume of a new and completely revised edition has just been published and more will emerge during the years to come. Concurrently a similar systematic survey of the monocotyledons is under way with some half a dozen volumes published. Major works of this sort are so large that they may take many years to complete. These disciplines are not only valuable in their own right but as adjuncts to the wider-based plant classification than that derived solely from the traditional analysis of external form. Such classifications are the more reliable and certain if they are supported by evidence from as many different disciplines as possible. One area of study at the Jodrell Laboratory likely to grow in importance is the chemical analysis of plants, which may yield significant practical results.

Kew is an historic garden, the principal features of whose design have been so wisely and desirably established that it would be difficult to better them. Wakehurst Place, Kew's other garden, is in contrast a comparatively young garden where many major alterations and developments have taken place during the last decade or so and are likely to continue in the future, to enhance the existing combination of plants and scenery. Natural vegetation, particularly woodland, is a more important element at Wakehurst than it is at Kew and is likely to remain so, in order to display and explain the natural vegetation of the area, particularly in relation to the conservation of the plant life of that part of southern England. Although the Loder Valley Reserve, adjacent to an arm of the Ardingly Reservoir, has recently been opened, its development and exploitation as an area for conservation has really only just started. Much will happen in the future. This is, however, not to imply that the horticultural features of Wakehurst are not highly important and likely to increase. The Himalayan Glade, for example, has surely much of its development yet to come; other such features appropriate to the sorts of plant that grow well at Wakehurst are likely to be developed, particularly for example round parts of Westwood Lake. The plant collections at Wakehurst are in many ways complementary to those at Kew. Unnecessary duplication of reference collections is to be avoided, and for that reason the decision has been taken to concentrate certain species collections at Wakehurst rather than at Kew. This applies for example to the genera *Betula* and *Rhododendron*. Probably, other genera, especially suited to Wakehurst's soil and climate, will in the future be concentrated there.

Although Wakehurst Place is primarily a garden, the Elizabethan mansion at the heart of the estate is, as all those who have seen it agree, an outstandingly attractive feature. Most people want to see more of the interior and before long more rooms will become accessible to the public, with some of the furnishings actually used in the mansion during its last private occupation by Sir Henry and Lady Price. Better restaurant and exhibition facilities should follow.

The Seed Bank at Wakehurst Place is likely to have a greater future involvement with tropical plants than in the past and with a special emphasis on plants of economic importance. It is in the tropics that the greatest threat to many species of plant occurs and against that background the relevance of the Seed Bank to plant conservation is obvious. There are still many problems to be solved but this is a part of Kew where work is likely to be of increasing significance. Its efficiency depends on basic knowledge about seed behaviour and for that reason research on seed physiology and germination associated with the Bank is likely to play an important role.

As we look into a future in which one of the few certainties is the continued threat to plant and animal life and natural environments, the existence of the Seed Bank is reassuring evidence of Kew's valuable scientific work. Twenty-five years ago seed-banking, as well as conservation work, cytology and biochemistry, did not exist as established disciplines at Kew; they are now integral parts of the work undertaken there. The Royal Botanic Gardens will continue to respond in an energetic and measured way to needs perhaps now unknown or only dimly seen. The tradition that has earned for Kew national and international affection and respect will maintain it as an unusual if not unique combination of a garden designed for public pleasure and instruction with an institution engaged in scientific research.

J.P.M.B.

186

Directors of the Royal Botanic Gardens, Kew
Since 1841

1841–1865 Sir William Jackson Hooker 1785–1865

1865–1885 Sir Joseph Dalton Hooker 1817–1911

1885–1905 Sir William Turner Thiselton-Dyer 1843–1928

1905–1922 Sir David Prain 1857–1944

1922–1941 Sir Arthur William Hill 1875–1941

1941–1943 Acting Director Sir Geoffrey Evans 1883–1963

1943–1956 Sir Edward James Salisbury 1886–1978

1956–1971 Sir George Taylor 1904–

1971–1976 Professor John Heslop-Harrison 1920–

1976–1981 Professor John Patrick Micklethwait Brenan 1917–

1981– Professor Ernest Arthur Bell 1926–

Select Bibliography

AITON, William. *Hortus Kewensis; or A Catalogue of the Plants Cultivated in the Royal Botanic Garden at Kew.* London, 1789. Second edition by W. T. Aiton, 1811.

ALLAN, Mea. *The Hookers of Kew 1785–1911.* London, Michael Joseph, 1967.

BEAN, William J. *The Royal Botanic Gardens, Kew: Historical and Descriptive.* London, Cassell, 1908.

BLUNT, Wilfrid. *In for a Penny; A Prospect of Kew Gardens: Their Flora, Fauna and Falballas.* London, Hamish Hamilton, 1978.

BROCKWAY, Lucile H. *Science and Colonial Expansion; The Role of the British Royal Botanic Gardens.* New York, Academic Press, 1979.

CHAMBERS, Sir William. *Plans, Elevations, Sections and Perspective Views of the Gardens and Buildings at Kew in Surry.* London, 1763. Re-published Farnborough, Gregg Press, 1966.

COATS, Alice M. *Quest for Plants; A History of Horticultural Explorers.* London, Studio Vista, 1969; New York, McGraw Hill, 1970.

Curtis's Botanical Magazine. London, 1787–. Founded by William Curtis, now published by Bentham-Moxon Trust, Kew.

GOSSE, P. H. *Wanderings Through the Conservatories at Kew.* London, 1856.

GREGORY, Mary. *Jodrell Laboratory.* Publications, 1877–1975. *Notes from the Jodrell Laboratory No. 8,* 1976.

HEDLEY, O. *Queen Charlotte.* London, Murray, 1975.

Hooker's Icones Plantarum. Kew, 1837 onwards.

Index Kewensis. London, Oxford University Press, 1896 onwards (5-yearly supplements).

G. B. PARLIAMENT, HOUSE OF COMMONS. *Copy of the report made to the Committee appointed by the Lords of the Treasury in January 1838 to inquire into the management, etc. of the Royal Gardens, by Dr. Lindley . . . who . . . made an actual survey of the botanical garden at Kew, in conjunction with Messrs Paxton and Wilson, two practical gardeners, in the month of February 1838.* London, 1840. (H. of C. Paper 292.) 6pp.

Index Londinensis. London, 1929, Supplement 1941.

Kew Bulletin. Formerly *Bulletin of Miscellaneous Information, Kew.* London, Her Majesty's Stationery Office, 1887 onwards.

Kew Guild Journal. Kew, Kew Guild, 1893 onwards.

Kew Record of Taxonomic Literature. London, Her Majesty's Stationery Office, 1971 onwards.

KEW, ROYAL BOTANIC GARDENS. *The wild Fauna and Flora of the Royal Botanic Gardens, Kew. Bulletin of Miscellaneous Information, Kew,* Additional Series 5. 1906. Supplements published in *Kew Bulletin.*

KING, Ronald. *The World of Kew.* London, Macmillan, 1976.

LYTE, C. *Sir Joseph Banks; Eighteenth-Century Explorer, Botanist and Entrepreneur.* Newton Abbot, David & Charles, 1980.

METCALFE, C. R. and CHALK, L. *Anatomy of the Dicotyledons.* Oxford, Clarendon Press, 1950. 2nd ed. 1979–.

METCALFE, C. R. (ed.). *Anatomy of the Monocotyledons.* Oxford, Clarendon Press, 1960–.

NORTH, Marianne. *Recollections of a Happy Life.* London and New York, Macmillan, 1892.
Some Further Recollections of a Happy Life. London and New York, Macmillan, 1893.
A Vision of Eden; the life and work of Marianne North. Kew, R.B.G. and Exeter, Webb & Bower, 1980. (Selections from the 'Recollections' and the paintings.)

RUTTON, W. L. 'The Royal Residences of Kew'. *Home Counties Magazine* 1950, pp. 1–13, 85–98, 157–170, 229–243.

SMITH, John. *Records of the Royal Botanic Gardens, Kew.* [1822–1864]. London, 1880.

TURRILL, W. B. *The Royal Botanic Gardens, Kew, Past and Present.* London, Herbert Jenkins, 1959.

TURRILL, W. B. *Joseph Dalton Hooker: Botanist, Explorer and Administrator.* London, Nelson, 1963.

Index

Page numbers in **bold** refer to illustrations; those in *italic* refer to information in captions. Garden features listed are at Kew unless specified as belonging to Wakehurst (Wkst).

191